Knowledge Matters

Also by Elias G. Carayannis

THE STRATEGIC MANAGEMENT OF TECHNOLOGICAL LEARNING: Learning to learn-how-to-learn in High Tech Firms and its Impact on the Strategic Management of Knowledge, Innovation and Creativity Within and Across Firms

IDEA MAKERS AND IDEA BROKERS IN HIGH TECHNOLOGY ENTREPRENEURSHIP: Fee vs. Equity Compensation for Intellectual Venture Capitalists
(with Todd Juneau)

THE STORY OF MANAGING PROJECTS: A Global, Cross-Disciplinary Collection of Perspectives
(with Young Kwak and Frank Anbari)

MODE 3: KNOWLEDGE CREATION, DIFFUSION AND USE IN INNOVATION NETWORKS AND KNOWLEDGE CLUSTERS: A Comparative Systems Approach Across the US, Europe and Asia
(with David Campbell)

e-DEVELOPMENT TOWARD THE KNOWLEDGE ECONOMY: Leveraging Technology, Innovation and Entrepreneurship for "Smart Development"
(with Caroline Sipp)

GLOBAL AND LOCAL KNOWLEDGE: Transatlantic Public-Private Partnerships for Research and Technology Development
(with Jeffrey Alexander)

RE-DISCOVERING SCHUMPETER: Creative Destruction Perspectives on Creativity, Invention and Innovation Diffusion and Impact
(with Chris Ziemnowiscz)

LEADING AND MANAGING CREATORS, INVENTORS AND INNOVATORS: The Art, Science and Craft of Fostering Creativity, Triggering Invention, and Catalyzing Innovation
(with Jean-Jacques Chanaron)

Knowledge Matters

Technology, Innovation and Entrepreneurship in Innovation Networks and Knowledge Clusters

Edited by

Elias G. Carayannis

and

Piero Formica

First published in 2008 by
PALGRAVE MACMILLAN
Houndmills, Basingstoke, Hampshire RG21 6XS and
175 Fifth Avenue, New York, N.Y. 10010
Companies and representatives throughout the world.

PALGRAVE MACMILLAN is the global academic imprint of the Palgrave
Macmillan division of St. Martin's Press, LLC and of Palgrave Macmillan Ltd.
Macmillan® is a registered trademark in the United States, United Kingdom
and other countries. Palgrave is a registered trademark in the European
Union and other countries.

ISBN-13: 978–1–4039–9872–9 hardback
ISBN-10: 1–4039–9872–8 hardback

This book is printed on paper suitable for recycling and made from fully
managed and sustained forest sources. Logging, pulping and manufacturing
processes are expected to conform to the environmental regulations of
the country of origin.

A catalogue record for this book is available from the British Library.

A catalog record for this book is available from the Library of Congress.

10 9 8 7 6 5 4 3 2 1
17 16 15 14 13 12 11 10 09 08

Printed and bound in Great Britain by
Antony Rowe Ltd, Chippenham and Eastbourne

Contents

List of Figures

List of Tables

List of Boxes

Notes on the Contributors

Elias G. Carayannis is Full Professor of Science, Technology, Innovation and Entrepreneurship, as well as Co-founder and Co-director of Global and Entrepreneurial Finance Research Institute, and Director of Research on Science, Technology, Innovation and Entrepreneurship, European Union Research Centre at the School of Business of the George Washington University, in Washington, DC. He received his PhD in Technology Management and his MBA in Finance from the Rensselaer Polytechnic Institute in Troy, NY, and his BS in Electrical Engineering from the National Technical University of Athens, Greece. He has published more than 50 refereed journal articles and several other papers in innovation and technology management journals (*IEEE TEM, Research Policy, R&D Management, Journal of Technology Transfer, Technovation, IJTM, JETM*) as well as ten book chapters on technology, innovation and knowledge management, creativity and entrepreneurship. He has eight published and another eight books under contract on science, technology, innovation and entrepreneurship on Science, Technology, Innovation and Entrepreneurship.

George Chorafakis is a qualified Engineer with specialization in Regional and Urban Planning from the National Technical University of Athens. He has also studied Regional and Urban Planning and Development Studies at postgraduate level at the LSE and Economics at Birkbeck College, University of London. He is a researcher in the 'European Research Area Watch' (ERA-Watch) project for the European Commission, Institute for Prospective Technological Studies, working on the regional dimension of the ERA structure, and in particular on the evolutionary dynamics of industrial clusters and of entrepreneurial 'ecologies' at regional level. This project runs in parallel to his PhD research at the University of Cambridge. His ongoing doctoral research involves the study of the technological dynamics of mesoeconomic systems – such as industrial clusters and spatially non-embedded inter-firm networks – that behave as complex adaptive systems.

Piero Formica is Professor for Knowledge Economy, Innovation and Entrepreneurship at Jönköping International Business School and Dean of the International Entrepreneurship Academy, Sweden. He has over 30 years of experience in the fields of international economics and economics of innovation, working with the OECD Economic Prospects Division in Paris, large corporations and small companies, governmental bodies and the European Union. His special interests include industrial clusters, knowledge clusters, knowledge-based economic policy, digital economy, regional technology transfer strategies and infrastructures, regional innovation strategies, and models of public–private partnerships for innovation policy. Professor Formica is a member of IKED (International Organisation for Knowledge Economy and Enterprise Development, in Malmo, Sweden), founding member of the Global Trust Centre Association, Sweden, and member of the Board of Advisors of the Competitiveness Institute – the cluster practitioner's network, Barcelona, Spain.

Holger Graf is Assistant at the Chair of Professor Dr Uwe Cantner, Department of Economics, Friedrich-Schiller-University Jena, Germany. His research interests include systems of innovation, economics of technological change, social network analysis and market evolution industrial economics.

Seppo Hänninen is Researcher at Helsinki University of Technology, Lahti Centre, Finland. He received his MSc degree in management and strategy from the Helsinki School of Economics, Finland, in 1984 and the MBA degree from Helsinki University of Technology in 2000. He is completing his doctoral dissertation on innovation-based diversification. His research interests are in innovation management, marketing of technology-intensive products, developing technology programmes, commercializing technological inventions, and technology-based companies.

Tomas Hellström is acting centre leader for the Centre of Entrepreneurship at the University of Oslo, Norway. His research interest concerns innovation and social action and university-industry partnerships. He has a PhD in Theory of Science and Research from Göteborg University, Sweden.

Merle Jacob is center leader at the Center for Technology, Innovation and Culture at the University of Oslo, Norway. Her main academic interests concern knowledge and commodification and policy transformations in the research system.

Wu Jisong is Advisor to the Beijing 2008 Olympic Games Organizing Committee, President of Beijing Recycle Economy Association and the Asian member of the Advisor Committee of International Association of Science Parks. He serves as Director-General of Recycle Economy Research Centre, is Dean of the Economic and Management School, Beijing University of Aeronautics and Astronautics, and Professor of postdoctoral researcher of water resource, Environment School of Hehai University, China. Dr Wu has published over one hundred articles in resources management, environment, high technology, knowledge economy and recycle economy.

Mattias Johansson is a research fellow at the department of Technology Management and Economics at Chalmers University of Technology, Sweden. His main interest lies with resource acquisition in start-ups. Presently, his focus is on knowledge-based entrepreneurship and the networks that surround such firms. Apart from research, Mattias has also been involved in educational programmes on entrepreneurship and innovation; for example, in Chalmers School of Entrepreneurship.

Ilka Kauranen is Visiting Professor at the School of Management, Asia Institute of Technology, Thailand. He serves as a referee for the Finnish *Journal of Business Economics*, is Editor-in-Chief of the Publication Series and the Research Series of the Institute for Regional Economics and Business Strategy, and Editor of the Publication Series of the Institute of Industrial Management at Helsinki University of Technology, Finland.

Patrice Laget returned to the Institute for Prospective Technological Studies (DG JRC) in May 2004, where he is responsible for support to the implementation of the European Research Area. He has long experience in Scientific International Relations and in Research and Innovation policies, first with the French government and then with the European Commission. He has occupied various positions within the Ministry of Foreign Affairs, the French Embassy in the United States, DG Research, the JRC and the Delegation of the EC to the United States in Washington. He received his PhD (biochemistry) in 1972 from the University of Paris and his MD from the University of Angers in 1973. One of his main achievements was to chair DG RTD Task Force on Universities and to organize the Liège Conference on the future of university-based research which was held in April 2004.

Mathew J. Manimala is Professor of Organization Behaviour, Jamuna Raghavan Chair Professor of Entrepreneurship, and Chairperson of the N S Raghavan Centre for Entrepreneurial Learning at the Indian Institute of Management, Bangalore. Prior to this he served as Senior Member of Faculty and Chairman, Human Resources Area at the Administrative Staff College of India and as lecturer at the University of Cochin and the University of Bhopal. He obtained an MBA degree from the University of Cochin, an MBSc degree from the University of Manchester and a Doctoral degree from the Indian Institute of Management, Ahmedabad.

Randolf Margull is Managing Director of Jena Technology and Innovation Park, Germany.

Tõnis Mets is a Professor of Entrepreneurship and Head of the Centre for Entrepreneurship at the University of Tartu, Estonia since 2003. He has worked as a management consultant in his own company ALO OÜ, and as an entrepreneur, engineer and manager in various high-tech companies in Estonia. He holds degrees from the Tallinn Technical University (Electronics Engineering) and a PhD (Technical Sciences, Diagnostics of Mechanisms) from the St. Petersburg Agricultural University, awarded in 1987. His main research interests are entrepreneurship, technology and knowledge management, organisational learning, and innovation.

Andreas Panagopoulos is Lecturer in Economics at Lancaster University Management School. Andreas completed his postgraduate studies at UCL, and did a post doc at Toulouse. Andreas's research focuses on intellectual property protection and innovation. His work has appeared (or is to appear) in the *American Academy of Management Best Papers and Proceedings*, the *International Journal of Industrial Organisation*, the *Journal of Technology Transfer*, the *International Journal of Technology Management*, the *European Political Economy Review*, the *Journal of Interdisciplinary Economics*, as well as *Technology Innovation and Intellectual Property*, and the Oxford e-*Journal of Intellectual Property Rights*.

Michael Provance is a Visiting Professor of Entrepreneurship at the University of Richmond while completing his dissertation at the George Washington University, and an advisor on organizational innovation to corporations and emerging ventures. His research focuses on the evolution of young firms within markets and regions. Research includes the roles of knowledge, institutions, market structure and competitive dynamics in the formation, operation and trajectories of entrepreneurial ventures.

Birgitta Sandberg is an Associate Professor in international business at the Turku School of Economics and Business Administration, Finland. She is the co-ordinator of Global Innovation Management Master's Programme and teaches on various master's level courses related to international business, innovation management and qualitative research methods. She also supervises Bachelor's and Master's theses and Doctoral studies. Her main research interests include the development and marketing of radical innovations, proximity in strategic alliances and management of stakeholder relations during the international relocation of business operations. She has several publications in both academic journals and conferences.

Urmas Varblane (born 1961) is a Professor of International Business in the University of Tartu, Estonia. His main research interests include the role of foreign direct investments in the technology transfer in transition economies, internationalization of Estonian economy and systems of innovation. He has written chapters in books published by Routledge, Ashgate, Kogan Page, Haworth Press, Nova Science and in journals such as *Transnational Corporations, Acta Oeconomica, Journal of East West Business, Post Communist Economies*, etc. Prof. Varblane has worked as the guest researcher in the Augsburg University, Kiel Institute of World Economy, School of Slavonic and East European Studies in London University. He has been involved in many research programmes e.g. EU-Integration and Prospects for Catch-Up Development in CEECs – The Influence of Structural and Technological Transformation on the closure of the Productivity Gap, Knowledge-Based Entrepreneurship: Innovation, Networks and Systems, Knowledge and Competitiveness in the Enlarged EU.

Preface

The focus of this manuscript book is on profiling, analysing, benchmarking, and modelling in socio-technical terms, ways and means that creativity, invention and innovation are manifested and flourish in select American, European and Asian knowledge-based *innovation networks*[1] and *knowledge clusters*[2] (see definitions below) and may also serve as catalysts and accelerators of new and sustainable technological venture formation and growth.

In this context, innovation-triggering *technological entrepreneurship* is viewed as a core element of local, regional and national innovation systems, as well as *'glocal'* knowledge production and innovation-triggering networks.[3]

Moreover, the focus of this book is on highlighting *critical success and failure factors*, and *lessons learned* about entrepreneurial *initiatives, outcomes, outputs* and *impacts* in America, Europe and Asia and in the context of knowledge creation, diffusion and use in innovation networks and knowledge clusters.

The book will present a number of conceptual and empirical studies from the United States, Europe and Asia that contribute to a better understanding of the role of knowledge in the theory and practice of technological entrepreneurship in *the context of socio-technical networks architecture design, form* and *function* and from diverse theoretical perspectives, including, regional development economics and the sociology of innovation, as well as regional science and technology and knowledge management:

- Selected industries of focus will be biotechnology, advanced materials and ICT, and in each region or country innovation networks and clusters will be identified and studied.
- Public-private partnerships for research and technology development, transfer, deployment and commercialization will also be studied, and, in particular, their relationships and roles in catalysing and accelerating the formation and growth of new ventures.
- Top-down policies and bottom-up initiatives will be documented and reviewed to identify what works, how and why in each region, country and industry.

In conclusion, the purpose of this book is the identification and articulation of insights that could inform *both public sector policies and private sector practices* to render them more effective and efficient. A series of recommendations for policy makers and practitioners will conclude this comparative, conceptual and empirical research, contributing to the growing literature on the role of knowledge on *technology, innovation and entrepreneurship* and, in particular, with regard to the role of knowledge creation, diffusion and use in *local, national, regional* and *global* innovation networks and knowledge clusters.

Notes

1 Carayannis, Elias G. and Jeffrey Alexander, 'Strategy, structure and performance issues of pre-competitive R&D consortia: Insights and lessons learned, *IEEE Transactions of Engineering Management*, May 2004, Vol. 52, No. 2.
2 Excerpts from '"Mode 3" knowledge creation, diffusion and use in innovation networks and knowledge clusters: A comparative systems approach across the United States, Europe and Asia', Technology, Innovation and Knowledge Management (TIK-M) Series, Ed.Elias G. Carayannis and David Campbell, Greenwood Press/Praeger Books, Oxford, 2005.
3 Carayannis, Elias G. and von Zedtwitz, Maximilian, 'Architecting gloCal (global-local), real-virtual incubator networks (G-RVINs) as catalysts and accelerators of entrepreneurship in transitioning and developing economies: Lessons learned and best practices from current development and business incubation practice, *International Journal of Technovation*, Vol. 25, No. 2, February 2005.

Key Working Concepts Defined[1]

We provide here a set of working definitions developed in the context of this and prior related research projects that are meant to inform the author contributions:

- **'Mode 3'.** 'Mode 3' for Knowledge Creation, Diffusion and Use: 'Mode 3' is a multi-lateral, multi-nodal, multi-modal, and multi-level systems approach to the conceptualization, design, and management of real and virtual, 'knowledge-stock' and 'knowledge-flow', modalities that catalyse, accelerate and support the creation, diffusion, sharing, absorption and use of co-specialized knowledge assets. 'Mode 3' is based on a system-theoretic perspective of socio-economic, political, technological and cultural trends and conditions that shape the co-evolution of knowledge with the 'knowledge-based and knowledge-driven, gloCal economy and society'.[2]
- **Innovation networks.** Innovation Networks[3] are real and virtual infrastructures and infra-technologies that serve to nurture creativity, trigger invention and catalyse innovation in a public and/or private domain context (for instance, Government–University–Industry; Public–Private Research and Technology Development; Co-opetitive Partnerships[4,5]).
- **Knowledge clusters.** Knowledge Clusters are agglomerations of co-specialized, mutually complementary and reinforcing knowledge assets in the form of 'knowledge stocks' and 'knowledge flows' that exhibit self-organizing, learning-driven, dynamically adaptive competences and trends in the context of an open systems perspective.

Notes

1 Excerpts from '"Mode 3" knowledge creation, diffusion and use in innovation networks and knowledge clusters: A comparative systems approach across the United States, Europe and Asia', Technology, Innovation and Knowledge Management (TIK-M) Series, Ed.Elias G. Carayannis and David Campbell, Greenwood Press/Praeger Books, Oxford, 2005.
2 Carayannis, Elias G. and von Zedtwitz, Maximilian, 'Architecting gloCal (global-local), real-virtual incubator networks (G-RVINs) as catalysts and accelerators of entrepreneurship in transitioning and developing economies: Lessons learned and best practices from current development and business incubation practice, *International Journal of Technovation*, Vol. 25, No. 2, February 2005.
3 Networking is important for understanding the dynamics of advanced and knowledge-based societies. Networking links together different modes of knowledge production and knowledge use, and also connects different sectors or systems of society

(sub-nationally, nationally, trans-nationally). Systems theory, as presented here, is flexible enough for integrating and reconciling systems and networks, thus creating conceptual synergies.

4   *Inter alia* see: Carayannis, Elias G. and Alexander, Strategy, Jeffrey, 'Structure and performance issues of pre-competitive R&D consortia: Insights and lessons learned', *IEEE: Transactions of Engineering Management*, May 2004, Vol. 52, No. 2.

5   *Inter alia* see: Carayannis, Elias and Alexander, Jeffrey, 'Winning by co-opeting in strategic government-university-industry (GUI) partnerships: The power of complex, dynamic knowledge networks, *Journal of Technology Transfer*, Vol. 24, No. 2/3, pp. 197–210, August 1999. Note: Awarded 1999 Lang-Rosen Award for Best Paper by the Technology Transfer Society.

Acknowledgements

The editors and publishers are grateful to the following for permission to reproduce copyright material:

Chapter 8, 'Product Innovation as Micro-Strategy: The "Innovation-Based Diversification" View', by Seppo Hänninen and Ilkka Kauranen. A previous version of this chapter was published by Inderscience Publishing Ltd (UK) in the *International Journal of Innovation and Learning*, Vol. 4, No. 4, 2007, pp. 425–43.

Chapter 9, '"The Strength of Strong Ties": University Spin-Offs and the Significance of Historical Relations', by Mattias Johansson, Merle Jacob and Tomas Hellstrom. Originally published by Springer in The Journal of Technology Transfer, Springer US, Vol. 30, No. 3, pp. 271–86, reproduced with kind permission from Springer Science and Business Media.

Chapter 11, 'Consumer Learning Roadmap: New Buzzword or Necessary Tool?', by Seppo Hänninen and Birgitta Sandberg. A previous version of this chapter was published by Inderscience Publishing Ltd (UK) in the *International Journal of Knowledge and Learning*, Vol. 2, Nos 3/4, 2006, pp. 298–307.

1
Introduction

Elias G. Carayannis and Piero Formica

1.1 The concentration of resources and academic performance: reinventing learning and research in the twenty-first century

The more money governments put into elite universities, the better those institutions will perform, with the associated benefits for the national R&D system, and the more likely it is that their academics' work will be published in highly reputed journals. This is a cherished tenet of most European public educational and research policies, which are currently under attack.

Yet, the strategy of concentrating public money on the 'citadel' of a few select academic institutions for the dual purpose of education and research (as is done, for example, in Germany, Sweden and the UK) is highly questionable. What matters far more is the creation of a free and 'co-opetitive' environment which, through the interrelated forces of competition and cooperation, will spur all universities – not just the most prestigious – to innovative excellence across all aspects of their activities. In Europe, this is the much-needed environment – not one that complies with the standards of the US-style elite universities.

There are various reasons for this proposition. Size is not always an advantage: this is now clearly understood in the private sector. Nimble and more flexible structures, less subject to the pressures of well-established incumbent interests, carry great advantages. Moreover, in the 'gloCalizing' (globalizing and localizing) knowledge economy and society, the ideas and knowledge marketplace is not divided into towns and regions but into affinity groups that derive from a high propensity to sociability and are structured by knowledge creation, diffusion and use modalities (in other words, 'knowledge-ducts' along which flow 'knowledge nuggets' such as innovation networks and knowledge clusters – see Carayannis and Gonzalez, 2003).

Box 1.1   Knowledge nuggets, innovation networks and knowledge clusters

We consider the following quotation useful in elucidating the meaning and role of a 'knowledge nugget':

> People, culture, and technology serve as the institutional, market, and socio-economic 'glue' that binds, catalyzes, and accelerates interactions and manifestations between creativity and innovation as shown in Figure 1.1, along with public–private partnerships, international Research & Development (R&D) consortia, technical/business/legal standards such as intellectual property rights as well as human nature and the 'creative demon'.

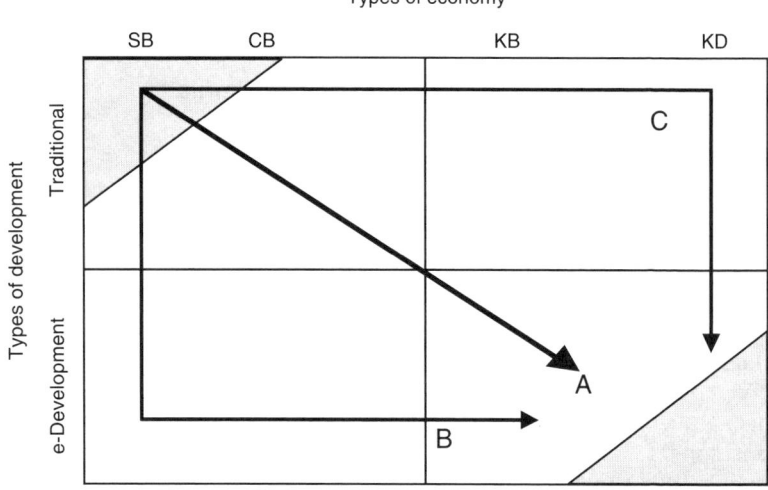

Types of economy

Spectrum of stages of economic development

Subsistence ⟶ Emerging ⟶ Developing ⟶ Transitioning ⟶ Developed
- SF: Subsistence-focused economy • KB: Knowledge-based economy
- CB: Commodity-based economy   • KD: Knowledge-driven economy

Attributes of Pathways A, B, and C:

A) *Faster, easier and better way to move towards knowledge-based economy.*
B) *Costly, slow but more common way in transitioning economies for moving towards the knowledge economy.*
C) *Slowest, costly and more limited way.*

Figure 1.1   Spectrum of the stages of economic development: subsistence® emerging® transitional® developed.

Key: SF – subsistence-focused economy; CB – commodity-based economy; KB – knowledge-based economy; KD – knowledge-driven economy.

Attributes of pathways A, B and C: A – a faster, easier and better way to move towards a knowledge-based economy; B – a costly and slow, but more common way in transitional economies to move towards a knowledge economy; C – the slowest, most costly and most limited way of moving towards a knowledge economy.

Sources: Adapted from Carayannis et al., 2006; Carayannis and Sipp, 2005.

The relationship is highly non-linear, complex and dynamic, evolving over time and driven by both external and internal stimuli and factors such as firm strategy, structure, and performance as well as top-down policies and bottom-up initiatives that act as enablers, catalysts, and accelerators for creativity and innovation that leads to competitiveness.

(Carayannis and Gonzalez, 2003, pp. 587–606, at p. 593.)

'Innovation networks' are real and virtual infrastructures and infratechnologies that serve to nurture creativity, trigger invention and catalyse innovation in a public and/or private domain context: for instance, government–university–industry, public–private research and technology development 'co-opetitive' partnerships (Carayannis and Sipp, 2005; Carayannis and Alexander, 2006; Carayannis and Campbell, 2006; Carayannis and von Zedtwitz, 2006; Carayannis and Ziemnowicz, 2006; Carayannis et al., 2006.)

'Knowledge clusters' are agglomerations of specialized, mutually complementary and reinforcing knowledge assets in the form of 'knowledge stocks' and 'knowledge flows', which exhibit self-organizing, learning-driven, dynamically adaptive competences and trends in the context of an open systems approach (Formica, 2003; Carayannis and Sipp, 2005; Carayannis and Alexander, 2006; Carayannis and Campbell, 2006; Carayannis and von Zedtwitz, 2006; Carayannis and Ziemnowicz, 2006; Carayannis et al., 2006).

From this perspective, as Kim and colleagues (2006) point out, the prestige and authority of the traditional mainstay of academic institutions will be eroded by the reduced importance of physical access to productive research colleagues now that the decline in communication costs has changed the formerly localized nature of research interaction. In Europe, on the other hand, the proliferation of second-rate research universities has raised the lid on the quality of education and the fragmentation of research.

Universities, university-related institutions and firms should join together in innovation networks and knowledge clusters (see Formica, 2003; Carayannis and Campbell, 2006). Even if the division of labour and the functional specialization of organizations persist with regard to the type of R&D activity, universities, university-related institutions and firms can nevertheless carry out basic and applied research and experimental development.

The concept of the 'entrepreneurial university' captures the need to link university research more closely with the R&D market activities of the firm. Just as important as the entrepreneurial university, however, is the concept of the 'academic firm', which represents the complementary business organization and strategy vis-à-vis the entrepreneurial university. The complementary and mutually reinforcing roles of academic firms and entrepreneurial universities are crucial for advanced knowledge-based economies and societies – and they should be at the heart of any strategy to reinvent learning and research in the twenty-first century.

Despite the significant functional differences between universities and firms, there is the potential for productive overlap between entrepreneurial universities and academic firms, thanks to the fact that such organizations can engage more easily in university–business research networks.

We must ensure that the crisis in both US and European higher education institutions is turned into an opportunity. From the European perspective, proper incentives and reward mechanisms conducive to pluralism – an environment that allows for excellence in different ways – are critically needed. Such a policy will liberate universities from their traditional relationships and restrictions and make them more competitive. National governments should deploy public resources in accordance with three key strategies: increasing the independence of universities, introducing more competition between universities, and channelling funds to departments that excel in multiple ways. As for the last criterion, the 'best' should be judged in terms of their capability to master the entire knowledge chain: from creation to the diffusion, conversion and entrepreneurial exploitation of scientific and technological knowledge (Formica, 2006).

The knowledge chain has profound implications for higher education institutions and business schools. Much is lacking with regard to their capabilities to cooperate with companies in creating knowledge and becoming part of knowledge streams, and this is especially the case for the old incumbents. In the knowledge space in which we are embedded, universities that master the knowledge chain will be the cradles of knowledge-intensive entrepreneurship.

To stimulate competition between universities, national governments should liberate them from the rigid regime of tuition fees and student recruitment. Each university should have the right to specialize as it chooses, fix its own fees for tuition and select its own students. Quality control and measurement are needed, but not in ways that stifle differentiation, innovation and renewal. To achieve a state of successful competition, the lifelong tenure of professors must also be ended. This would trigger a healthy process of horizontal and vertical mobility for scientists, researchers and teachers.

No less important is the mobility of scholars and highly educated and talented young students and graduates. 'Brain circulation' (mobility in a physical sense that stimulates face-to-face communication) and 'brain waves' (mobility in a virtual sense that takes advantage of new open-space technologies) are the basic ingredients for combining competition with cooperation. Universities should embrace the creation of a co-opetitive transcultural and transdisciplinary context of mobility and integration, as opposed to a competitive multicultural context of emigration and separation.

Responsibility for all this rests on the shoulders of those responsible for changing the academic foundations on which human capital was built in the age of the machine. New foundations are needed for an innovative learning environment that will epitomize the knowledge city of the twenty-first-century renaissance. Here, academics will indeed become entrepreneurs of the mind, in the business of 'growing' people intellectually, culturally and spiritually. Knowledge and skills will be encouraged, the love of learning and an inquiring mind will be fostered, and creativity and imagination will be emphasized. And a digitally connected collective intelligence will maximize the creative collaboration of 'knowledge nomads', who will come together in dense groups of scientists, researchers, graduates, students and entrepreneurs to address issues that concern them and compel them.

1.2 Intellectual venture capitalists: at the source of the academic firm

It has previously been said that in the knowledge economy the market-place is not divided into towns and regions but into affinity groups that emerge from a high propensity to sociability (also known as 'invisible networks of peers' – see Carayannis and Allbritton, 1997). Goethe, in his novel *Elective Affinities*, adopts a striking scientific metaphor for such creative affinity, drawing parallels between personal and social relation-ships and the chemical process by which two different substances combine to form a third. In a truly open global economy, no one country is able to dominate others in isolation: knowledge-driven economies and knowledge-based societies can materialize only through the 'chemistry' of community.

The transition to such a state of social, political and economic affairs is full of challenges as well as opportunities, and even advanced industrial economies struggle to capture the potential benefits of the modern-day knowledge society, economy and polity. The path from knowledge through business to a new age of prosperity is full of pitfalls that can trigger socio-economically regressive trends and patterns (from *nouveaux pauvres* to fun-damentalists of all hues, including the neo-Luddites – see Carayannis, GWU Lectures, 1996–2005).

Industrial culture focuses mainly on the production of 'things' – of static objects. Knowledge, on the other hand, is constantly in flux, like a flowing stream. Conventional industrial notions lead policy makers to believe that the addition of a knowledge-based industry to an existing industrial base makes a knowledge economy. This is not the case. Pieces of knowledge, purchased like objects, do not make a knowledge economy. What is missed in such perceptions is the importance of managing and synthesizing knowledge and of conducting conventional business in innovative ways. Capitalizing the knowledge economy requires an entirely new way of viewing the economic landscape. An emerging breed of knowledge entrepreneurs – intellectual venture capitalists – is setting the scene for an entrepreneurial revolution that will transform that landscape. For example, in a knowledge economy it is essential to collaborate to compete. This requires a transformation of the tra-ditional notions of competition, market advantage and adversarial market relationships.

The development of an enterprising culture is a primary objective of all progressive nations. Entrepreneurs, and the small and medium-sized businesses they build, are the backbone, and represent as much as 70 per cent of the economic base of first-world countries. Entrepreneurial activity creates business diversity, reduces reliance on a single industry or natural resource and develops an enterprising culture capable of rapid response to emerging economic threats. A robust entrepreneurial climate – such as is often present in 'hotspots' of entrepreneurial activity that appear in the form of real and/ or virtual clusters – is one in which *people, culture and technology* converge to build entrepreneurial activities on firm foundations of *charisma*, *character* and *culture*, the three essential 'C's of entrepreneurial success (Carayannis, GWU Lectures, 1996–2005; Carayannis, ECE Lectures, 2005).

Entrepreneurial activities postulate what we call the 'triadic complex' of entrepreneurial energy, entrepreneurial mass made up of the attributes and motivations necessary for entrepreneurship and creativity in business – see Table 1.1. The entrepreneurial energy performs a function that corresponds to that of the knowledge energy: see the 'First Law of Knowledge Dynamics' in Amidon and colleagues, 2006.

Table 1.1 The 'triadic complex' of entrepreneurial attributes and motivations and creativity in business

---

$E = MC3$

where E = entrepreneurial energy; M = the attributes and motivations necessary for entrepreneurship and $C3$ = creativity in business.

Components of M:

Entrepreneurial attributes
Clarity of leadership
Openness and inquisitiveness, stimulating innovation and learning
Ability to create new value or organizational capability
Flexibility and capacity to change
Relationship-building skills
Ability to convince others (employees, individual investors, suppliers and landlords) to share start-up risks

Entrepreneurial motivations
Capacity to think for oneself
Self-confidence: optimism and personal drive
Sense of autonomy, independence and risk-taking
Intense emotions

Components of C3:

Creativity in business = creativity in technology x creativity in planning x creativity in marketing

---

Note: C is the equivalent of the speed of light. C in Latin is Celeritas, meaning 'velocity'. Creativity in business is like a beam of light that spotlights one or more opportunities to start up a business.

While entrepreneurship may occur regardless of external conditions as a natural result of personal drive, it occurs most often, most robustly and is most sustainable in an environment that is designed to encourage it. Potential entrepreneurs become active entrepreneurs when the conditions are most supportive of their commercial opportunities and their business, thus helping to channel the key qualities they exhibit as individuals – those of the *obsessed maniac* and the *clairvoyant oracle* (Carayannis and Juneau, 2003; Carayannis, GWU Lectures, 2000–2005) – towards the generation of sustainable wealth.

To date, entrepreneurial scholars who turn into intellectual venture capitalists by founding academic firms have remained among the least explored species in the territory of entrepreneurship. *Intellectual venture capitalists* (Carayannis and Juneau, 2003) are in essence *knowledge entrepreneurs* (Formica, 2005) who hold intellectual capital[1] and are willing to undertake risks investing it towards the pursuit of larger pecuniary benefits – that is, they have the ability and the potential to transform knowledge and intangible assets into wealth-creating resources.

They typically do so by leveraging two key qualities they possess via a unique combination of *nature, talent, experience* and *fortune* (Carayannis, GWU Lectures, 2000–05; Carayannis and Juneau, 2003; Carayannis and Sipp, 2005; Carayannis and von Zedtwitz, 2005; Carayannis and Alexander, 2006; Carayannis and Campbell, 2006; Carayannis and Ziemnowicz, 2006; Carayannis et al., 2006):

- **strategic knowledge arbitrage** – the capacity to uniquely create, identify, reallocate and recombine knowledge assets better and/or faster to derive, develop and capture non-appropriable, defensible and sustainable and scalable pecuniary benefits; and
- **strategic knowledge serendipity** – the capacity to uniquely identify, recognize, access and integrate knowledge assets better and/or faster to derive, develop and capture non-appropriable, defensible and sustainable and scalable pecuniary benefits.

Putting knowledge into action requires the development of win–win relationships, which, in turn, are the outcome of a context conducive to negotiated exchanges (Carayannis and Alexander, 1999). Under the perspective of relationship building, intellectual venture capitalists play a double role of content and context creators, leading and engendering a process and dynamic, leading towards artificial abundance while leveraging and replacing conditions of natural scarcity (see Figure 1.2).

Entrepreneurial scholars, such as Marie Curie – an enterprising woman who became personally involved in the industrial application of her scientific results – show preference sets that are affected by the convergence of two character profiles: that of *homo scientificus*, breaking away from convention

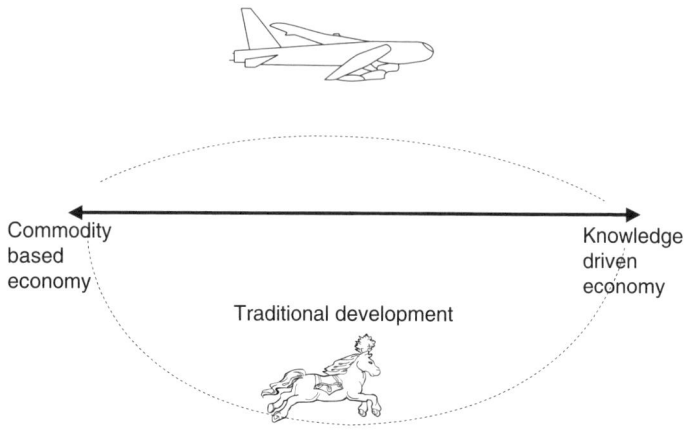

Figure 1.2   A new development path towards a new economy
Sources: Adapted from Carayannis and Sipp, 2005; Carayannis et al., 2006.

to search for ground-breaking discoveries, and that of *homo economicus*, with a special acumen for marketing and sales. In other words, entrepreneurial scholars have a relatively clear sense of the probability of a successful commercial outcome from their curiosity-driven research – and their research evolves into business-driven, goal-oriented work. This evolution results in both a paradigmatic shift achieved by the adoption of a new intellectual model and a phase change necessitated by the transition from research to entrepreneurship.

Entrepreneurial scholars who have turned into intellectual capitalists open up new perspectives for outsourcing innovation. As Figure 1.3 shows, if the supply of intellectual capitalists is low, the outsourcing of innovation is a decision that must be taken within a constrained vision – simply that of a tangible-assets-intensive process controlled by companies making outsourcing decisions. Those companies focus on what they know they do not know. Under these circumstances, outsourcing decisions keep to chartered waters: navigation depends on knowing how to keep innovation-induced pressure on tangible assets under control.

In contrast, an abundant supply of such intellectual capitalists encourages intangible-assets-intensive processes, whereby companies making decisions for outsourcing innovation 'learn' rather than 'control'. In this case the focus is on what companies *do not* know they do not know. To be brave enough to sail in uncharted waters, they have to learn how to govern the impact of leverage on intangible assets. In doing this, they rely on the performance of the intellectual capitalists, acting like the 'merchants of light' of Phoenician (Figure 1.4) and

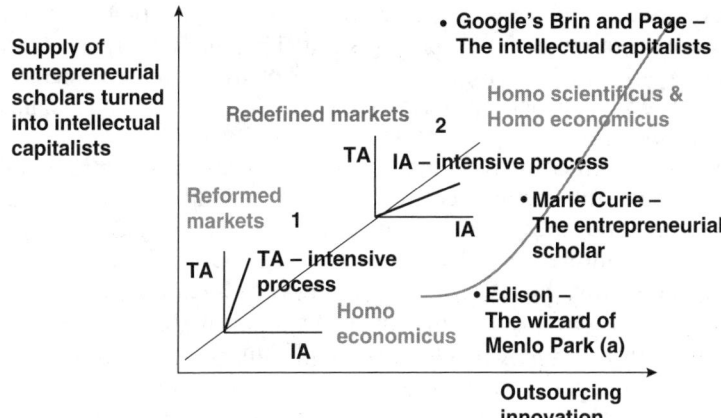

Figure 1.3 Forms of outsourcing innovation

Key: (1) Tangible assets (TA), such as land, labour and capital, are the traditional pillars of value creation. TA-intensive processes are controlled by companies making outsourcing decisions. (2) The value of intangible assets (IA) leads IA-intensive processes, whereby companies making outsourcing decisions 'learn' rather than 'control'.

Note: Edison developed what became known as 'invention factories', the first of which was in Menlo Park. To this day, he is known as the 'Wizard of Menlo Park' and is celebrated for his creation of the world's first full-scale industrial R&D laboratory. It was to transform America's shop-floor tradition of invention.

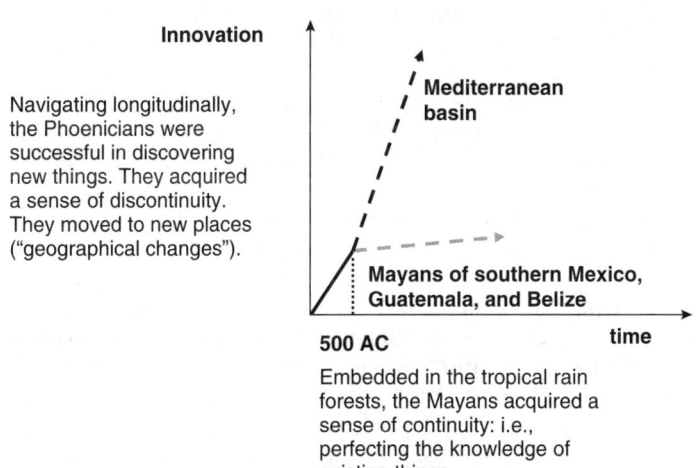

Figure 1.4 The Phoenicians: 'merchants of light' innovation

Note: Intellectual capitalists are the Phoenicians of the twenty-first century, driven by the falling costs of transporting ideas and information. Like the Phoenicians, they make geo-economic changes by navigating longitudinally.

Renaissance times who saw 'into distances most could not' (Rubin, 1998). The behaviour of both parties thus converges in making the outsourcing of innovation an experiment that brings the importance of discovering new markets and of radical organizational transformation to the foreground of the company's business culture.

Whereas reformed markets are a terrain for exploration by incumbent entrepreneurs, intellectual venture capitalists redefine market boundaries and norms, and entirely new markets thus emerge. In doing this, the intellectual venture capitalist endangers the status of the incumbent entrepreneur – for the revolutionary business opportunities envisioned by the intellectual capitalist cannot be encompassed within the incumbent's range of resources, strategies or structures (Figure 1.5).

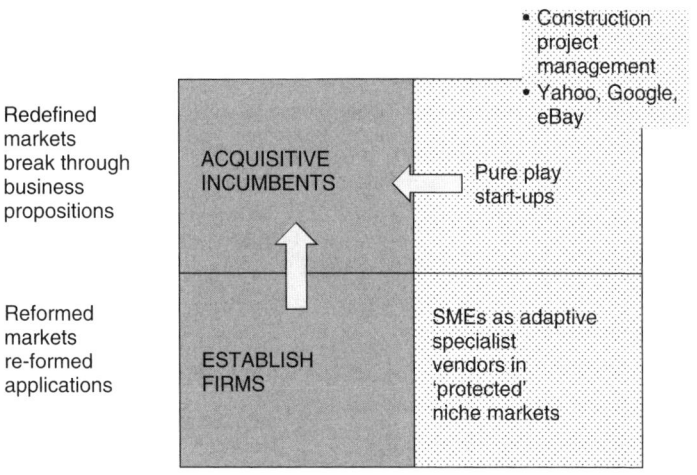

Figure 1.5   Redefined and reformed markets

Notes: Reformed markets are the results of the reformulation of existing ideas. Technologies do not change the basic structure and functioning of the market: they help to squeeze out costs and facilitate interactions. They are improvements rather than a wholesale redefinition of the R&D, marketing and sales processes, supply chains, and so on. Incumbents have built-in advantages: a trusted brand name, an established reputation, established customer relationships, financial depth and a deep pocket. Despite their strengths, they suffer from the disadvantage that their resources, strategies and structures do not allow them to envisage revolutionary possibilities. Adaptive specialist vendors sell in niche markets created by intermediate communities focused on a common interest. Redefined markets are created when market boundaries and norms are redefined and an entirely new market emerges. In the inset example, top right, construction project management is highlighted because it represents an entirely new way, in terms of efficiency and speed, of coordinating the efforts of a chain of firms in different locations.

Source: Adapted from Day, G. S. and Fein, A. J., Shakeouts in Digital Markets: Lessons from B2B Exchanges, California Managementt Review, Winter 2003.

1.3 Academic firms as a category of high-expectation start-ups

Once technology advancements meet intellectual venture capitalists then market novelties are created over time and turned into high-expectation start-ups, launched with the intent of significantly growing their businesses. That encounter is a force that tends to push the economy away from a state of equilibrium. In fact, high-expectation start-ups provoke disequilibrium, which is a state of change-induced imbalance with no tendency to stasis.

High-expectation start-ups exhibit oversized ambitions that mould unpredictable growth patterns: from exponential and oscillating to declining and collapsing trends. Complexity and adaptation emerge as significant characteristics of the economic system insofar as all agents involved in the creative process of high-expectation new ventures interact and adapt to each other and the context in which they are embedded.

High-expectation start-ups explore with new eyes the uncharted territories of unforeseen circumstances and undiscovered opportunities. From scratch, they grow new markets which are evolutionary organisms effective at innovation. Complex problems they track get empirical validation in laboratory experiments where the function and performance of high-expectation start-ups are evaluated. The results of experiments give entrepreneurs, financiers and policy makers a deeper understanding of the actual workings of real-world new markets. Experiments point out how high-expectation entrepreneurs should cultivate market outcomes, which behaviour should guide trust building between the former and their potential financiers, and how policy makers should design and test 'rules of the game'.

The educational context under which high-expectation entrepreneurship could be cultivated would draw benefits from experiences made in the medical schools where different performance learning modes are created whose real impact is part of the educational and research activity. In particular, a business school should go beyond doing detached diagnoses, to really developing experiments, even of a therapeutic kind, and testing them clinically in interaction with private and public organizations.

1.4 Experiments, simulations and clinical treatments

Defined as a 'managerial behaviour which consistently exploits opportunities to deliver results beyond one's own capabilities' (Thompson, 1999, p. 209), entrepreneurship requires enterprising individuals who can identify new opportunities and implement accordingly. Thus, entrepreneurship is a skill, learned through experience and improved with practice.

With experience as the centrepiece for entrepreneurial development, the probability that entrepreneurs will learn from their experiences greatly increases.

Entrepreneurs continuously accumulate experience by conducting and evaluating experiments in the marketplace. Prior to their injection into the market process, inventing and innovating would-be entrepreneurs can find in economic experimenting labs a new *locus* for experimental activity. Experiences made inside the lab give rise to a range of views, which helps the decision maker to limit his exposure to risk and uncertainty in the course of actions once field experiments must be carried out in the marketplace.

Laboratory experiments test propositions derived from new business ideas, which, on the basis of experience, need to be processed by monitoring and revising the assumptions underlying, and performance/reward, predictions ingrained into those propositions.

In labs, participants learn the language of the market through:

- Conducting a test or investigation
- Direct observation of events
- Participation in social interactions with their peers
- Placing the learner under realistic conditions in order to imitate or estimate how events might occur in a real company, in the related industry, in the marketplace, et cetera.

Learning from experience and implementing the experimental results are two essential steps intellectual venture capitalists have to consider for the purpose of reducing the level of risk intrinsic to their high-expectation new ventures.

Experimental results indicate policies to be developed which can significantly reduce the start-up time. Less time needed for completing a start-up launch means that start-up costs are lower, much less up-front capital is required, and the probability is raised that new start-ups are getting started. Moreover, experimental results trace the road conducive to interactions between established firms and experimental ventures. Through interactions, the latter could derive benefits from the accumulated experience of the incumbents in terms of accelerated innovation and growth.

Equally relevant is the re-evaluation effect. On the basis of experience, the conclusion can be reached that experimental businesses have to change direction. Such an experiment-induced behaviour, pursued by high-expectation entrepreneurs who see lab experiments as a potentially stimulating way of evolving their business, is a source of advantage over the established firms, which interpret bad results as a consequence of underperforming managers rather than the outcome of wrong predictions.

Last but not least, since pattern recognition is an inherent feature of our nature as human beings, laboratory experiments must carefully consider the possibility of giving ambitious entrepreneurial individuals seeking fast growing business opportunities a chance to experiment and learn how to become pattern-completers. Those who underperform, having difficulties along the process from pattern recognition to pattern completion, can get help from lab clinics.

If experimental and simulative approaches try to prevent too dangerous and too expensive real errors happening once start-ups are immersed in the actual workings of real-world markets, the clinical approach intends to heal the disorder encountered during experiments in labs or in living, taking on the role of therapeutic counsel that fights its clients' diseases.

1.5   Entrepreneurial experimentation

By entrepreneurial experimentation we mean a method that relates a business concept to an experiment, which stimulates the concept creator to build upon that concept as it has been experimented in lab. Since the opportunity cost of experimentation decreases with the increase in the value of a new business formation, we can expect that high-expectation entrepreneurs whose high-value-added business propositions bear low opportunity costs reveal a higher propensity for conducting experiments than that of entrepreneurs pursuing low-value-added activities.

Would-be entrepreneurs start with beliefs and ideas that they want to turn into a business. By running experiments, business ideas move from an embryonic stance to their full manifestation in the form of new ventures. In particular, conducting experiments gives potential entrepreneurs with high-expectation ambitions the opportunity to get the ability to mobilize their new ideas so as to anticipate changes, take a chance on the future, and organize the context that does let those ideas win access to the marketplace as reasonably successful business propositions.

Quantitative and qualitative data collected during experimental (and clinical) exercises make it easier to ask for support from financiers, evaluate the pros and cons of pure financial backers versus strategic partners, seek industrial allies, and hire employees. Anyone familiar with high-expectation start-ups knows the key to success is having access to the participation of experienced people who bring both talent and funding to the new venture.

1.6   Exposure modes

Would-be entrepreneurs are agents exposed to modes of experimentation which are either analogical or conjectural. The former accomplishes the task of shrinking the entrepreneurial agent's area of known ignorance about her/his business idea. Analogy-based reasoning can be applied to the known unknowns of a new concept whose business domain holds attributes that match with those of another domain. The analogical situation is represented by a typical case-based approach. Past cases from a different domain are used to choose possible solutions for problems incurred with the new idea.

The conjectural mode proceeds by trial (i.e., spontaneous, serendipitous discovery of building blocks of the business idea under experimental scrutiny) and error (i.e., elimination of arrangements whose subsequent result is inappropriate). High-expectation business concepts sail into uncharted waters as they exhibit unfamiliar traits of novelty and complexity. The entrepreneurial agent, who is unaware of her/his ignorance, is exposed to a voyage into the unknown unknowns. Thus, high-expectations propositions cannot be treated by analogical reasoning and, specifically, by case-based reasoning. When no apparent rules or commonalties can be applied, trial and error is the approach that can back the tasks required by an imagination- and conjecture-based process of discovery. The major cost of this approach is the time invested for yielding a solution from the iterative process triggered by selecting what *ex ante* looks like the most suitable choice set. If something does not work, the process has to be iterated until the appropriate answer is founded.

1.7   Concerted entrepreneurship and its governance

Emerging cross-border, transnational communities driven by innovation and entrepreneurship initiatives – in short, international entrepreneurial communities – give impetus to the rise of international public goods. According to the International Task Force on Global Public Goods, 'International public goods, global and regional, address issues that: (i) are deemed to be important to the international community, to both developed and developing countries; (ii) typically cannot, or will not, be adequately addressed by individual countries or entities acting alone, and, in such cases (iii) are best addressed collectively on a multilateral basis.'

With varying intensity, a non-voting, international and mobile public – still a small, but increasing, fraction of the public as a whole – holds strong opinions on and seeks recognition of concerted entrepreneurship (Boettke and Coyne, 2005) as a new type of public good that requires international provision. Prospective and current international business entrepreneurs from various geographical, cultural and racial origins mould this non-voting international public.

Concerted entrepreneurship comes to life via distributed networks formed among colleagues and strategic partners using the technologies of globalization. Their experiences and practices of transnational, cross-border and cross-cultural relationships make possible new venture creation with an international focus from the start – the so-called 'transnational start-ups', 'international start-ups', 'stateless start-ups' and 'global-born start-ups' (Formica, 2004, ch. 3).

Concerted entrepreneurship has significant and positive economic impacts. It serves to reduce the barriers to, and costs of, communication between entrepreneurs of different countries and cultures. By enabling more effective and constructive combinations of complementary skills, concerted entrepreneurship produces positive synergy, or 'strategic complementarities', from the efforts of different actors. Although marked by disparate interests and backgrounds, these entrepreneurs become better able to address shared problems or processes in a consistent manner, to create international firms and to provide spill-over effects by lowering search costs and raising skill levels among other would-be international entrepreneurs, who can benefit from the experiences and practices of previous explorers in this rapidly evolving field of business. The extent to which communities and populations are excluded from the benefits of this international public good will depend on the degree of social trust in the community as well as on its size and the quality of its entrepreneurially oriented labour pools and complementary business activities. The higher the trust level, the lower the search costs and the higher the quality of available pools of complementary activities in a community, the more likely its individual members are to benefit from concerted entrepreneurship. While greater size, in the form of a larger pool of expertise, also has a favourable impact, it may at the same time carry the cost burden of increasing institutional inertia – thus emphasizing the advantages of optimal combinations of critical mass and flexibility.

There is a strong link between governance conditions and non-excludability. Although with a different scale of intensity, excludability principles and practices permeated feudal 'status' societies, later planned economies and the mercantile 'society of contract' of the manufacturing age. In many institutions, frameworks such as guilds or intradisciplinary codes of conduct created new barriers. The 'society of relations' (the prevailing form in the participation age) is better suited to knowledge-driven entrepreneurship and, in particular, to its most advanced form, which relies on the concerting of entrepreneurial developments. In a relations-based form of governance, which we call 'mode 1', the primary role is given to behavioural rules that allow for communication and exchange to take place without rigid, formal contracts. Mode 1 leads to investment in social capital that ends or constrains restrictive practices at many levels, such as those that make the labour market inflexible or protect vested interests. Those restrictive practices lock individuals into particular roles, preventing them from adjusting in accordance with new business ideas brought in by concerted entrepreneurship activity.

Mode 1 allows space for new markets that promote transactions which generate positive externalities. Prediction markets – markets that aim to 'support transactions in claims about unresolved questions of fact' (Bell, 2006) – are a case in point. Prediction markets intervene to support exchanges that spread information about and develop consensus on unsettled questions regarding concerted entrepreneurship.

Just as greater interdependence among different entrepreneurial players acts as a catalyst for a decision-making process that is conducive to the creation of transnational and international start-ups, so are cross-border business opportunities exploited more fully by a larger number of people in a relations-based community.

We call a rule-based governance regime 'Mode 2'. Modes 1 and 2 combined put in motion processes of 'institutional competition' and of mutual influence between policy makers and emerging international entrepreneurial communities. The latter are subject to public regulations while at the same time 'competing' with them by generating the social capital necessary to ensure that trustworthy relations grow. The combination of rule-based and relations-based governance is an indicator of the intensity of 'institutional competition' between rule builders and relationship builders. A trustworthy community constrains the increase in marginal costs of relations-based governance – costs that inevitably occur with the enlargement of the concerted entrepreneurship zone (i.e., with increased numbers of participating entrepreneurs and relationships). The stronger the principle of non-excludability in a community, the more likely it is that 'distant' outsiders will participate. In dealing with each other for the purpose of new venture co-creation, insiders behave much as they as would with close neighbours, and the ability to establish strong trust-based relationships, which do not discriminate against outsiders relative to insiders, limits the increase in the marginal costs of enlarging the area of non-excludability (Dixit, 2006). Mode 1 incurs high marginal costs in a low-trust community, which suffers from free-rider problems and the abuse of loose or non-contractual relationships. In this case it is likely that a rule-based governance regime (Mode 2) will prevail. Unlike Mode 1, Mode 2 bears high fixed costs because it requires a framework of legislation, regulation and formal contracts, and their enforcement by the courts. Once the rules have been fixed and are in place, however, negotiations with outsiders bear a low marginal cost (Dixit, 2006). If a community cannot sustain extensive trust, excludability is the price it has to pay. Communities differ widely in their levels of social capital and entrepreneurial endeavour. A serious focus on how Modes 1 and 2 work, and under what circumstances they are effective, will send a powerful signal that policy makers are engaged in promoting competition between the two modes for the purpose of securing collective advantages from concerted entrepreneurship as an international public good (see Figure 1.6).

What exactly should a government do if it is set on, or forced into, a course of the Mode 2 type? Since over-regulation stifles the development of open economic spaces and is thus an impediment to the full development of concerted entrepreneurship, policy makers must dispense with superfluous regulations and concentrate on striking a balance between the rules they enforce as 'superior' decision makers and spontaneous actions by community members who, as contributors to the development of concerted entrepreneurship, must be taken into account in policy decisions. In order to meet the conditions of non-excludability, policy makers should focus on strategies and policies that favour the spread of concerted entrepreneurially oriented efforts and opportunities. This calls for coherent action across a range of policy domains, spanning from early childhood training that plants the seed of entrepreneurial motivation and encourages

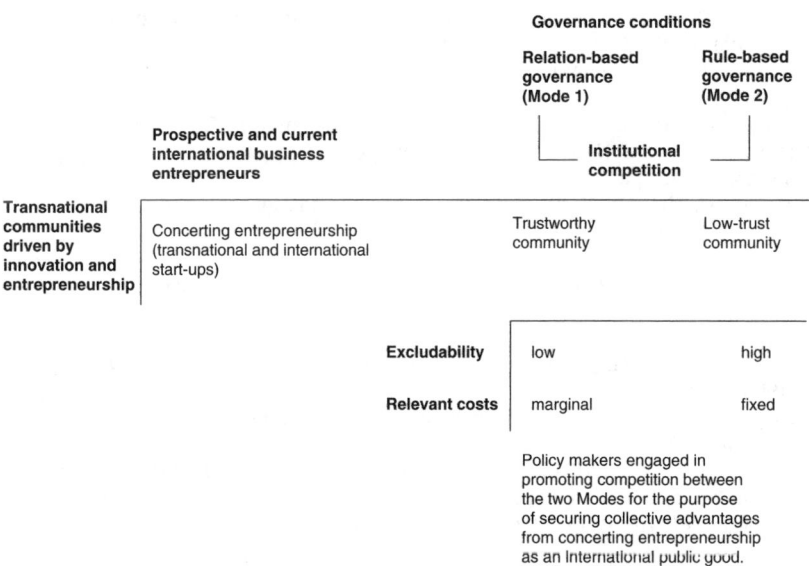

Figure 1.6 The concerted entrepreneurship environment: a theoretical framework of institutional competition

the learning of foreign languages and openness to other cultures, to city planning, regional policies, the science–industry interface and labour market institutions that help to create environments favourable to concerted entrepreneurship. If policy makers are committed and effective in their efforts to reduce exclusion, the vast majority of the community will reap the benefits of concerted entrepreneurship.

Note

1   In a broader sense, 'intellectual capital refers to the total knowledge within an organization that may be converted into value, or used to produce a higher value asset. The term embodies the knowledge and expertise of employees; brands; customer information and relationships; contracts; internal processes, methods, and technologies' (Prior, 2005).

References

Amidon, Debra M., Formica, Piero, and Mercier-Laurent, Eunika, eds (2006), *Knowledge Economics: Emerging Principles, Practices and Policies*, Vol. 1, Tartu University Press, Tartu.

Bell, T. (2006), 'Prediction markets for promoting the progress of science and the useful arts', *George Mason Law Review*, Vol. 14, http://ssrn.com/abstract= 925989.

Boettke, Peter J., and Coyne, Christopher J. (2005), 'Concerting entrepreneurship: an international public good', in Boyd, Gavin, Rugman, Alan M., and Padoan, Pier Carlo, eds, *European–American Trade and Financial Alliances*, Edward Elgar, Oxford, pp. 199–226.

Carayannis, Elias G. (1993), 'Increméntalisme stratégique', *Le Progrès technique*, No. 2.

Carayannis, Elias G. (1994), 'Gestion stratégique de l'apprentissage technologique', Le Progrès technique, No. 2.

Carayannis, Elias G. (2000), 'Investigation and validation of technological learning versus market performance', *Technovation*, Vol. 20, pp. 389–400.

Carayannis, Elias G. (2000a), *The Strategic Management of Technological Learning: Learning to Learn-How-to-Learn in High Tech Firms and its Impact on the Strategic Management of Knowledge, Innovation and Creativity Within and Across Firms*, IEEE/ CRC Press, Boca Raton, FL.

Carayannis, Elias G., GWU School of Business *Lectures on Science and Technology*, 1996–2005.

Carayannis, Elias G., GWU School of Business *Lectures on Entrepreneurship and Innovation*, 2000–05.

Carayannis, Elias G. (2004), 'Measuring intangibles: Managing intangibles for tangible outcomes in research and innovation', *International Journal of Nuclear Knowledge Management*, Vol. 1, pp. 49–67.

Carayannis, Elias G., ECE Programme on Entrepreneurship Lectures, 2005.

Carayannis, Elias, and Alexander, Jeffrey (2006), *Global and Local Knowledge: Glocal Transatlantic Public–Private Partnerships for Research and Technological Development*, Palgrave Macmillan, Basingstoke.

Carayannis, Elias G., and Allbritton, Marcel (1997), 'A case study of computer-mediated communication among 100 scholars in 15 countries', *Online Journal of Internet Banking and Commerce*, http://www.arraydev.com/ commerce/ JIBC/9806=07.htm

Carayannis, Elias G., and Alexander, Jeffrey (1999), 'Winning by co-opeting in strategic government–university–industry (GUI) partnerships: The power of complex, dynamic knowledge networks', *Journal of Technology Transfer*, Vol. 24, pp. 197–210.

Carayannis, Elias G., and Campbell, David F. J., eds, (2006), *Knowledge Creation, Diffusion and Use in Innovation Networks and Knowledge Clusters: A Comparative Systems Approach Across the United States, Europe and Asia*, Praeger, Westport, CT.

Carayannis, Elias G., and Gonzalez, Edgar (2003), 'Creativity and innovation = competitiveness? When, how, and why?', in Shavinina, Larisa V., ed., *The International Handbook on Innovation*, Pergamon, Amsterdam, pp. 587–606.

Carayannis, Elias, and Juneau, Todd (2003), *Idea Makers and Idea Brokers in High-Technology Entrepreneurship: Fee vs Equity Compensation for Intellectual Venture Capitalists*, Praeger Books/Greenwood Press, Westport, CT.

Carayannis, Elias, and Sipp, Caroline (2005), *e-Development Towards the Knowledge Economy*, Palgrave Macmillan, Basingstoke.

Carayannis, Elias G., and von Zedtwitz, Maximilian (2005), 'Architecting GloCal (Global–Local), real-virtual incubator networks (G-RVINs) as catalysts and accelerators of entrepreneurship in transitioning and developing economies', *Technovation*, Vol. 25, pp. 95–110.

Carayannis, Elias G., and Ziemnowicz, Chris, eds (2007), *Re-discovering Schumpeter*, Palgrave Macmillan, Basingstoke.

Carayannis, Elias G., Popescu, Denisa, Sipp, Caroline and Stewart, McDonald (2006), 'Technological learning forentrepreneurial development (TL4ED) in the knowledge economy (KE): Case studies and lessons learned', *Technovation*, Vol. 26, pp. 419–43.

Dixit, A. (2006), 'Evaluating recipes for development success', World Bank Policy Research Working Paper 3859, World Bank, Washington, DC.

Formica, Piero (2003), *Industry and Knowledge Clusters: Principles, Practices, Policy*, Tartu University Press, Tartu.

Formica, P. (2004), *Strengthening the Knowledge Economy*, EffeElle Editori, Ferrara.

Formica, Piero (2005), 'Knowledge entrepreneurs: leveraging knowledge clusters for economic development based on innovative advantages', *IC Mag [Intellectual Capital Magazine]*, No. 1.

Formica, Piero (2006), 'Knowledge-relevant economic policy: Analyzing knowledge policymaking in managed and free-market economies', in Amidon, Debra, Formica, Piero, and Mercier-Laurent, Eunika, eds, *Knowledge Policy: Principles, Practices and Policies*, Tartu University Press, Tartu.

Goethe, Johann Wolfgang von (1809), *Die Wahlverwandtschaften, as Elective Affinities*, trans R. J. Hollingdale, Penguin, London, 2005.

Kim, E. Han, Morse, Adair, and Zingales, Luigi (2006), 'Are elite universities losing their competitive edge?', Working Paper 12245, http://www.nber.org/papers/w12245, National Bureau of Economic Research, Cambridge, MA.

Prior, V. (2005), *The Language of Business Intelligence, Society of Competitive Intelligence Professionals*, Alexandria, VA, http://www.scip.org/ci/languagebi.asp

Rubin, H. (1998), 'The new merchants of light', *Leader to Leader*, No. 10, pp. 34–40.

Thompson, J. (1999), 'The world of the entrepreneur – a new perspective', *Journal of Workplace Learning: Employee Counselling Today*, Vol. 11, No. 6, pp. 209–24.

2

Knowledge Transfer Mechanisms from Universities and Other HEIs to the Sector

Professor Piero Formica
Dean, International Faculty Economics of Entrepreneurship –
Emirates Centre for Entrepreneurship, UAE

With the contribution of Professors
Urmas Varblane and Tõnis Mets
University of Tartu, Faculty of Economics and Business Administration

Introduction

The sustained phase of transition to economies characterized by considerable, and sometimes revolutionary, advances in science, technology and related industries, coupled with subsequent profound changes in economy and society, has increased the importance of the knowledge-intensive phases of production for value-creation. As enterprises, in fact, become more reliant on technology, they will become more dependent on knowledge. Accordingly, policy makers in a growing number of countries have become increasingly concerned with the management of the entire knowledge chain: from creation to the diffusion, conversion and entrepreneurial exploitation of scientific and technological knowledge. The knowledge chain also has profound implications for higher education institutions and business schools, which to be successful need to help companies create knowledge and become part of knowledge streams.

Knowledge transfer (KT) can be seen as a basic process for speeding up the flow of knowledge among all components of the knowledge chain. To the advocates of KT, this process brings about a self-reinforcing circuit between productivity, economic growth and entrepreneurial activity.[1]

KT can push the economic performance of a country, a region or an industry insofar as it provides a competent guide to the innovation process, which relies on a complex web of relationships. A broad range of competences to identify, capture, industrialize and commercialize free-flowing knowledge and technologies intervene to make KT conducive to economic growth. The higher the quality of these competences, the more likely an entire economy is to receive benefits from new venture creations that are superior entrants in the market, as well as from the successful reorganization of existing firms.

While explicit or institutionalized and codified knowledge (i.e., the official rules codified and written down in books and manuals) certainly contributes to the transmission of *information*, it is not a substitute for tacit knowledge (i.e., the informal, occupational wisdom and experience generated by people grappling with everyday problems and passed on in café-type communities of practice and online communities[2]) in the transfer of *knowledge*.

Inventions, products and services, great and small, are created through talking. The best preceptor is a participative engagement in the conversation between knowledge seekers and knowledge users. Conversations are the sense-making conduits through which knowledge flows (Kilpi, 2005). This is where learning dynamics and learning value can be optimized. From this perspective, an effective KT process directs its attention to a 'conscious conversation' (Yin and Lin, 2002[3]) as the central activity that involves the deployment of a wide range of 'soft skills'.[4]

Interactions between academic research and industry are a cornerstone of KT. From the perspective of economic performance it is vital that knowledge flows from academia into business and society at large.

Box 2.1   Knowledge flow: the Latvian case

The lack of knowledge flow between universities (public research institutions) and enterprises is one of the major problems. On the one hand, there is the low innovation literacy level of business, which cannot formulate its own ideas and find sophisticated partners and is not open to cooperation. On the other hand, one has to recognize the unsatisfactory business literacy level of academic society, with its accompanying inability and unwillingness to offer co-operation. The result is not only small industry investment in R&D, but also the far more destructive lack of outcome with an extremely low contribution to knowledge, technology intensive industries and products, the GDP and national budget. The necessary positive economic feedback does not exist (Karnitis, 2005).

If University-Industry (U-I) linkages are to have and to develop excellence, a number of mechanisms need to be in place. Traditionally, mechanisms that lead to advances in U-I relationships include training activities that a university provides to industrial personnel, student placements in companies, university faculty members employed as consultants in industry, industry researchers and business experts as visiting professors, or members of advisory boards to universities, research projects co-funded by industry, licensing of university intellectual property, and university spin-offs.

This chapter considers the existing and potential channels for KT from Higher Education Institutions (HEIs) in Central, Eastern and South Eastern European (CESE) countries. A preliminary field survey examines how appropriate the existing links between HEIs and regional small and medium-sized enterprises (SMEs) are in those countries, and what the role of university spin-offs is. Since a supportive environment is needed to improve the current interaction between academia and business, the chapter sets out proposals to give policy makers a proper role in their attempt, together with university and industry, to establish new avenues for KT and to innovate the existing channels for the purpose of pursuing a process of knowledge interchange conducive to higher productivity, economic growth and entrepreneurial activity from the exploitation of scientific and technological knowledge.

Closer co-operation between academia and business underpins growth in a knowledge economy. First and foremost in the United States – as an OECD report submits – 'stronger interactions between science and industry have characterized the innovation-led economic growth of the past decade and are currently helping the country to secure a lead in science-based industries ranging from IT and biotechnology to the new field of nanotechnologies' (OECD, 2002). Other large advanced economies, such as Japan, Germany and France, are responding – the same report highlights – with reforms 'aimed at removing regulatory barriers to closer industry-science relations, while creating incentives for public research to join forces with business' (OECD, 2002).

When compared to the most advanced economies and the core EU 15 countries, the recently admitted new EU 8 countries (Czech Republic, Estonia, Latvia, Lithuania, Hungary, Poland, Slovakia and Slovenia) and other emerging market economies in Central and South Eastern Europe are lagging behind in bringing academia and business close together. Paradoxically, the ability to harness the right conditions for mutually reinforcing research and commercialization goals that can feed cutting-edge entrepreneurial opportunities is one among few available alternatives for the emerging market economies to boost their economic activity.

When aiming to learn the lessons of U-I interactions from the last two decades, CESE countries should enact a KT strategy that embraces:

A symbiotic relationship between research and commercialization. U-I interactions are not mere adaptations of technology in tandem with the university, but they involve significant development activities undertaken by the industrial partner (Motohashi, 2004). Which means working in a collaborative way among knowledge creators and knowledge users at the intersections of different fields of academic disciplines and industrial activities.

An increasing interdependence with a large number of smaller firms. Traditional and family-run, middle-size and smaller enterprises have relatively low levels of employment, technical specialists and research expertise, and therefore encounter more difficulties in establishing communication with external sources of knowledge and scientific and technological expertise. This results in higher opportunity costs and transactions costs relative to large companies (Harvie and Lee, 2003). However, when compared to larger business organizations, innovative small enterprises are more closely linked to scientific research (US Council of Competitiveness, 2004). In addition, service firms show lower levels of R&D activity and a higher demand for education and training (OECD, 2004). Overall, smaller manufacturing companies and service firms are more dependent on the acquisition of knowledge from external sources. In this respect, closer links between academia and small businesses are justified and must be addressed in order to lower the costs of access to complementary, external sources of cognition for traditional small companies. This strategy would also deal with the need for research expressed by the innovation-driven, small-scale enterprises, and deliver the education and training required by service firms.

The acquisition and improvement of soft skills. It is argued that from 'the importance of not only knowing a great deal but also [of appreciating] the value of being able to effectively use that knowledge', it follows that higher education institutions of CESE countries should attempt 'to improve the tacit knowledge related to soft skills'. The same authors note that the lack of soft skills has been exacerbated by overrating the value of providing 'a critical mass of explicit knowledge' embedded in 'traditional academic disciplines – especially economics' (Volkova and Schmit, 2005).

There are a variety of definitions of KT and differing viewpoints as to the extent to which it is possible to establish a difference between KT and technology transfer (TT). By tapping into the positions taken by parties to the KT debate, in Section 1 we examine the main characteristics of these two different, albeit related, concepts. Section 2 proposes a theoretical model in conjunction with the results of a preliminary field survey (expounded on in Section 3), which is a contribution to an extensive empirical work that has to be undertaken in order to attempt to assess the impact of U-I interactions, especially in the CESE countries. Policy recommendations aimed at forging even-closer ties between HEIs and regional SMEs in CESE countries are discussed in Section 4.

2.1 Defining knowledge and technology transfer

KT is the process that puts knowledge in action. It relies upon the action and flow by which largely tacit knowledge, not technology per se, is transmitted among people: from one unit (the source: a single person, group or organization) to another (the recipient), with all kinds of feedback loops. The process is in fact complex and non-linear with a large number of interactions, not simply a matter of knowledge that passes down a production line linking academic researchers upstream and their business counterparts downstream.

KT is concerned with the subsequent absorption through which the recipient is affected by the experience of the source. How to transfer knowledge that exists in a given unit into another is more than a communication problem that information technology (IT) tools can fully accomplish.

First and foremost, KT is an evolutionary process of communicative interaction. It involves human action to construct and transform a mental content, and then human interaction ('action of social relating') for an effective sharing of knowledge, ideas and experiences – whereby mental tools akin to knowledge resource maps that 'show who has what knowledge and what sources are used' (Stanford, 2005) should be designed.[5]

Moreover, since human interaction happens in a community and needs behavioural rules that allow relationships to take place without the rigidity of formal contracts, critical to a viable KT process is the amount of social capital available in a given community. A vibrant social capital infrastructure founded on the intelligence and interactions of people with shared visions and common purpose invigorates the KT performance.[6]

Knowledge in action that secures availability of pertinent knowledge at the point-of-action, and just in time, has the power to produce innovation as its desired result (Wiig, 2005). KT gives attention to innovation not only in the sense of significant identifiable technological advances, but also from the perspective of the discovery process and its imaginative exploitation (Kirzner, 1985). Hence, KT is about the effectiveness of the knowledge value chain, which allows for unrecognized means and ends to be discovered.

Technology transfer (TT) is a related but different subject. TT places importance on information and efficiency rather than on knowledge and effectiveness. A TT programme is a search/respondence mechanism that uses technical concepts to transfer technical information and data from the results of scientific research. If implemented with efficiency and speed, an information- and data-oriented approach helps develop practical applications that solve practical problems in products and processes of an individuated industry.

In the academic context, KT covers the processes of transferring knowledge, research, skills, experience, and ideas within the universities, and from universities to the greater community of users (the business sector and the wider community), for the purpose of increasing economic returns from this investment and achieving cultural, educational and social benefits for society (see Exhibit 1) (HMSO, 2003, p. 39). This definition embraces both the form of KT and that of TT. These two forms sit side by side under the organizational umbrella of a multidisciplinary entity (known as 'Office of Technology Transfer', which often includes scientists, engineers, economists, and marketers) dedicated to identifying research results of potential commercial interests, and to developing strategies for how to exploit them.

Exhibit 1   KT activities from an academic perspective

- Creation of new knowledge through research, often collaborative in nature. From the standpoint of knowledge produced by the scientific community, this includes knowledge presented in scientific papers, pieces of scientific knowledge not yet formalized in a scientific paper and that type of tacit knowledge concerned with the methodology used in scientific processes and experiments.
- Exchange of knowledge through teaching, training, research or industrial partnerships involving faculty members and students.
- Application of knowledge to social and political issues of the day through participation in advisory boards, government consultations, advice to interest groups, public commentary and other forms of community service.
- Codification of knowledge through written articles, conference presentations or patent applications.
- Commercialization of knowledge through the development, exploitation and marketing of products for the domestic and international marketplace.
  (*Trends in Higher Education*, 2002; Natural Environment Research Council (NERC): http://www.nerc.ac.uk/using/ktcall.shtml)

Collected experience shows that transfer processes are, in general, affected to a considerable degree by a number of impediments. Factors that hinder the desired course of those processes include:

- Inability to bring together the right competencies
- Inability to detect those competencies that are highly intuitive rather than consciously perceived
- Internal conflicts stemming from 'professional territoriality' in a given area of expertise
- Generational gaps
- Inappropriate identification of the key holders of a specific knowledge or content
- Problems with sharing beliefs, assumptions, heuristics and cultural norms
- Lack of or not well-defined motivations and incentives aiming for significantly greater interaction among the parties involved in the transfer process
- Inadequate mentoring or guided experience

Much research effort has to go into examining the impeding factors that stand in the way of what would otherwise be a satisfactory transfer process.

2.2 Theoretical foundations of the field survey

The KT process from CESE universities and other HEIs to the SME sector, particularly with firms in the same region or locality as the HEI, is the subject of the field survey.

KT can occur by various routes. Processes of integration, collaboration, communication and commercialization of knowledge are associated either with the softer side of the transfer process, such as sponsored students, contract and collaborative research, or with the harder side of it, such as intellectual property, licensing and spin-off companies (HMSO, 2003, p. 39).

2.2.1 Knowledge integration process

The rationale that sustains this process is that we are no longer in the age of information. Economies are shifting from information to knowledge integration economies. Hence, the view that the economy is poised to bounce forward has to be built on its knowledge bases. This requires an integrated approach to respond to the new economic and social needs.

The field survey examines the knowledge integration process from two angles:

- One perspective looks at the interdependency between academic institutions and SMEs, taking into account the number of research partnerships between the HEI surveyed with SMEs embedded in its environment (from now on, Local Business Enterprises (LBEs)).
- The second perspective reveals two basic types of relationship for KT:

  > *Type A: Transfer of inputs ('supply push').* A type of relationship that concerns contract research, consultancy and other university outreach initiatives to business, such as transfer of research, skills, management strategies and knowledge capital in general. This relationship emphasizes the supply of input (of a 'knowledge package'), lending relatively little weight to the interaction with the end users. The crucial consequence of a linear approach to KT is that organizational and behavioural characteristics of LBEs, as well as their capacity to absorb the input transferred, are neglected.
  > *Type B: Knowledge transfer designed in a demand-led way ('demand pull').* This is a coupling type of relationship that holds two properties. One property makes the relationship dependent on the needs of business and, therefore, its primarily objective is that of fitting the cognitive characteristics of the recipient actors (Garavelli,

Gorgoglione and Albino, Part 1, 2001). A second property is that the relationship is driven by the interplay between the supplier and the receiver of knowledge. The better the interchange, the higher the value of KT, and the more intense the iterative process that by trial and error produces new knowledge at every stage.

It has been found that knowledge transfer, designed in a demand-led way and capable of fostering ties with knowledge providers outside the region, is to a significant degree important in those regions or countries with a low density of knowledge services (which reflects an inadequate knowledge base) and where local firms are learners whose very limited capacity of absorbing new knowledge fields requires a language of communication that reflects the learners preferred ways of being instructed about that new knowledge (Powell, 1987; Tödtling and Trippl, 2004).

In these problematic regions, a critical role could be played by a relationship promoter who would be responsible for gathering subject-specific knowledge that backs local firms thus improving the effectiveness of the knowledge exchange (Gissing, 2005). Relationship management would contribute to raising the meagre demand for the knowledge and skills available at university sites, redirecting a share of university research to be driven by the needs of the LBEs.

2.2.2   Knowledge collaboration

Collaboration, together with social cohesion and connectivity, is crucial for knowledge sharing and value creation. The value of leveraging knowledge between partners creates a greater wealth and sustainability for us all (see the 'Third Law of Knowledge Dynamics' in Amidon, Formica and Laurent-Mercier, 2005, Introduction).

Knowledge collaboration describes an open process of value creation in which contributing members make every effort to capture all the relevant pieces of knowledge across functions, businesses and even across nations. Different tools are used to create meaningful venues for collaboration. The tools described below are those moulded over many years of collaborative experience between academia and business. They show two facets: one is that of a controlled situation (closer to the concept of a contrived consultation) in which each party involved solicits a demand or a response from the other component(s), and the other is that of an unstructured, unpredictable and spontaneous interaction which promotes cross-fertilization of ideas for prosperous innovation.

2.2.2.1   *Traineeships/Internships*

In this organizational form, knowledge transfer occurs by means of interaction between the knowledge provider ('teacher') and the recipient individual ('learner'). The training process enables the learner to use, in a well-defined context, the knowledge transferred by the source. The provider knows a priori the solution to a specific problem that the recipient has to solve (Garavelli, Gorgoglione and Albino).

Knowledge practice includes both project-based placements of students in a company[7] and company employees in an academic lab for the realization of a specific project, which is the mission of the partnership between the university and that company.

2.2.2.2   Continuing professional development

The *Lambert Review* acknowledges that continuing professional development (CPD) is an important form of knowledge transfer, which an increasing number of universities are providing to business employees. The Review comes to the conclusion that through CDP 'Businesses can raise the skill levels of their workforce and learn about the latest academic ideas, while universities gain access to the latest developments in professional practice' (HMSO, 2003, p. 122).

2.2.3   Collaborative research

The collaborative research form of knowledge transfer aims at promoting a context where academic researchers work alongside company employees for the purpose of creating, developing and testing a prototype based on their reciprocal ideas, and which could be the platform for the development of a new product or service possibly leading to a new venture creation that is focused on application fields far from the original application of the knowledge transferred.

Along with staff, the data and equipment necessary for the successful testing and development of the prototype, the company can provide the partnership with funds that secure the sustainability of the project. The academic partner can tilt the university action in the direction of offering access to both in-house expertise and its international network of scientists and researchers.

Collaborative research can be carried out in a 'collaboratory' – an appropriate lab-type infrastructure that link up teams of people from university and companies with disparate cultures, different cognitive systems and skills. In a collaboratory, research focused on specific company problems and scientific research is carried out through the interactions between academic trained corporate researchers and university researchers willing to put their scientific results to practical use.

By providing access to the use of this infrastructure to groups of talented students or postgraduate students who can benefit from the knowledge exchange among the participants, spending more time working alongside academic researchers and company employees on shared problems and projects, new business formation becomes more likely to happen through spin-offs and start-ups that lead to new knowledge-based enterprises founded by students and graduates, and supported by in-collaboratory companies.

Box 2.2 'Collaboratories': the programme to establish Co-operative Research Centres in Hungary

One of the objectives of the Hungarian R&D and innovation policy is the promotion of R&D in enterprises and their collaboration with universities. This aims to promote joint R&D actions undertaken by universities and enterprises and the appropriate transfer, which may lead to new processes or products in the productive sectors.

Objectives. To create, or to strengthen the operation of, research centres allowing the formation of integral ties between the institutions of Hungarian college and university (higher) education, other non-profit research institutions and the enterprise-business innovation sector, and wherein the strategic integration of education, research and development, knowledge and technological transfer can be realized.

Hungarian universities and colleges can submit bids, individually or jointly, or in a consortium form with enterprises in the capacity of Co-operative Research Centre (CRC) recipients. The leading institution of the consortium may only be an establishment accredited by the Hungarian Accreditation Committee for PhD training. CRC proposals shall be submitted exclusively with the participation of business partners. The centre to be established can be an independent legal entity or a separately financed, economically independent unit – within the organization of an institution of university or college education.

The proposal shall detail a strategy for long term (minimum three, but preferably six–nine years) research, training, plus knowledge and technological transfer, developed jointly by the participating partners, supplemented by the business plan required for the operation of the centre.

(http://europa.eu.int/comm/enterprise/enterprise_policy/
enlargement/cc-best)

2.2.4 Knowledge communication

Tacit knowledge is not transferable without communication between individuals. In order to share knowledge, trust and understanding are important factors. Each participant in the transfer process needs to develop autonomous critical capabilities and practices for the purpose of making an effective use of the knowledge transferred.

The extent to which knowledge communication is built on the principle of participation, by being evocative and not only informative, is a sign of how powerful it could be in shifting the current emphasis on information in favour of imaginative ideas to be converted into sound commercial ventures.

At the present time, most universities are still organized to inform faculty and students about the process of commercial development from academic research. Workshops and seminars help to communicate an understanding of this process, but their informative content is too limited in its scope – it does not address the recipient's need to acquire that autonomous practice which would allow the recipient to play in the realm of imagination where the information is interpreted and turned into knowledge in action.

The much-vaunted university channel of knowledge communication is at the intersection between disciplines, both technical and business, and capable of melding the worlds of science and industry. Funding interdisciplinary chairs that focus on both technical and business topics is a first step toward that, and would give fresh weight to the question of how universities can contribute to effective knowledge communication.

2.2.5 Knowledge commercialization

The conversion of knowledge creation into economic knowledge that can constitute a business opportunity is the aim of an increasing number of academic institutions.

2.2.5.1 One-stop centres

In this respect, there are universities that have set up one-stop centres to guide faculty inventions and scientific research through the commercialization process. These centres are focused on:

- How to assess the commercial applications of the results of a research project
- How to effectively formalize them into a business plan
- How to identify the best way (product, service, technology) to employ to the commercialization of the results of a research project

UK universities, for instance, have established science enterprise centres whose aims are 'to foster the commercialization of research and new ideas; to stimulate scientific entrepreneurialism; to incorporate the teaching of enterprise into the science and engineering curricula; to act as centres of excellence for the transfer and exploitation of scientific knowledge and expertise' (European Commission, 2004).

2.2.5.2 Incubation of research-based start-ups

Knowledge transfer involves new business launches or identification of new business opportunities within existing organizations.

Universities and other higher education institutions that put in motion processes of knowledge transfer are often also interested in embarking upon a process of incubation ventures through which knowledge-based opportunities flow across conventional intellectual and business borders. By doing so, they support ventures that originate from scientific research.

The incubation process, in general, is embedded in a physical and organizational infrastructure called an 'incubator', which measures the success of higher education not only in graduates but also in faculty-student promoted real business start-ups. Scientists, academic researchers and talented students, who perceive practical implications from their findings, often lack the strategic vision and profit-seeking approach that a would-be entrepreneur should have. The incubation process brings together, in a single organization, these entrepreneurial scientists, researchers and students, and enhances their ability to interface knowledge and innovation. Research findings and novel technologies, which are the result of their curiosity-driven research projects, are redirected toward business concepts that can be converted into viable commercial products and services.[8]

2.2.5.3   Spin-in

Developing spin-off firms based on sharing university potential is not the sole role of the incubation process. The same process can also spin in creative ideas from local businesses and help to form partnerships for new venture creation with the pool of knowledge-rich scientific and technical personnel, and talented students, backed by the incubator infrastructure and its support staff (Powell, Harloe and Goldsmith, 2000, p. 11).

2.2.5.4   Licensing

A good number of university spin-offs that have the status of a joint closed stock partially or fully owned by both an academic institute, which is committed to the exploitation of its research results, and one or more scientific entrepreneurs (entrepreneurial scientists included) may not prove to be sustainable. Rather, this increases the likelihood that something negative will occur, and therefore the propensity of universities to shift the emphasis from developing commercially viable academic spin-offs to being much more focused on licensing.

MIT, a leading institution in the transfer process, has been a pioneer of policy efforts designed to tackle the issue of licensing. As observed by the *Lambert Review*:

> Unlike many UK universities, MIT has no business incubation activities at all. The strategy of the technology licensing office (TLO) is to encourage as many invention disclosures as possible from faculty members by minimizing the barriers to disclosure – currently MIT discloses about 450 inventions per year. MIT's TLO then licenses these inventions as nonexclusive or exclusive licences to industry and local venture capital firms. Rather than getting involved in the complexities of spin-out formation, the TLO provides a shop window for industry to view its IP and agrees as many licence deals as possible.
>
> (HMSO, 2003, p. 67)

A licensing policy opens up opportunities for incentives that motivate inventor academics to patent as a means of maintaining control over future research (Strandburg, 2005).

2.3   Results of a preliminary field survey

In this section, we present the results of a preliminary field survey (see Exhibit 1) concerning knowledge transfer mechanisms from universities and other HEIs to the SME sector. This survey is part of a broader research targeted to identify the main features of entrepreneurship teaching and links between entrepreneurship-oriented academia and the business community in the new EU member states, South European transition countries and Russia.

The research method, which was a convenient and non-probability sampling approach, is illustrated in Formica and Varblane (2005). A special section of a questionnaire (Formica and Varblane. 2005), which was sent to 35 schools selected in the first stage of the research, covered university–industry relationships for knowledge transfer. In total, 15 answers were received, which makes the return rate of surveys 43 per cent. In addition, phone interviews were held with specialists.

Overall, universities of the Central, Eastern and South European Countries appear to be connected with a variety of KT processes. However, two points are worth noting: first, additional efforts are to be made to capture all the relevant processes of knowledge transfer, embracing those related to KT designed in a demand-led way ('demand pull') (see Section 2.1), continuing professional development (Section 2.2.2), spin-in (Section 2.4.3), and licensing (Section 2.4.4), which are not fully ingrained in the practices of the institutions surveyed. Second, the incubation process of academic, research-based start-ups is at a very early stage of development. Making those actions develop further will be to provoke universities in the CESE countries to put into effect research-based start-ups as a key step in their KT strategies for the years to come.

2.3.1   Kaunas University of Technology

Respondent: Pranas B. Milius, Lecturer, Director of
KTU Regional Business Incubator

Kaunas University of Technology (KTU), Lithuania, established in 1922, 13 faculties, 17,000 students, has been teaching entrepreneurship as a special component (module) in Bachelors and Masters programmes since 2000.

Entrepreneurship teaching modules emphasize SME management, new venturing, and technological and international entrepreneurship. The titles of courses are Innovation Management, Engineering Economy, SME's Policy in Lithuania and the EU, and Innovation Problems of Telecommunication Technologies. The courses were initiated by KTU itself. Teaching staff consists of 20 local academics (Formica and Varblane, 2005).

2.3.1.1   *Links with the business community*

To transfer knowledge, KTU has university–industry joint teams and ten joint laboratories for special purposes in the following fields: commercialization of research results, solving technology problems raised by industry, organizational and business development. The KTU also has its own structural unit to commercialize faculty inventions.

Regular workshops and seminars, multidisciplinary chairs that focus on both technical and business topics and other regular events to synchronize educational resources with the requirements of local business help to develop faculty members' and students' awareness about university–industry (academic) knowledge transfer.

Students and academics have created approximately 20 spin-off companies. The role of students is very important in founding spin-offs: they act as catalysts of new cluster formations and agents of innovation within the value chain of local businesses.

Kaunas University of Technology has one incubator, established in 1998, with 64 tenants, in its infrastructure.

2.3.2   University of Tartu

Respondent: Tõnis Mets, Associate Professor, Head of Centre for Entrepreneurship

University of Tartu (UT), Estonia, established in 1632, 11 faculties, 17,500 students, started teaching *Basics of enterprise creation and activities* as the special course in their BBA programme in 1997. Now there are courses for *Small business, International entrepreneurship* and *Entrepreneurship & business planning* for students of the Faculty of Economics and Business Administration, as well as elective courses for other faculties.

Entrepreneurship and Technology Management (ETM) as a new Masters curriculum was started in 2002 in collaboration with Tallinn University of Technology and Zernike Group (Holland). Nearly 60 part-time Masters students are studying in the ETM programme. The Masters is focused on new venturing, intrapreneurship, SME management, innovation and technological entrepreneurship (Formica and Varblane. 2005).

2.3.2.1   *Links with the business community*

Three members of the Faculty of Economics and Business Administration have proven experience in entrepreneurship and business. The University established the Institute of Technology (TUIT) in 2002 for the purposes of applying results of scientific research into practice and commercializing faculty inventions.

A Centre for Entrepreneurship (CFE), where three faculty members are permanently involved, was launched in 2003 as the faculty unit. Since April 2005, the CFE has transferred into the UT interdisciplinary centre, which is committed to developing international co-operation for KT, creating new practices, fostering entrepreneurship research and training, advising university members and founders of new ventures nurtured in the incubators, and participating in a regional development network. The CFE is financed partly by faculty and approximately 80 per cent of funding comes from the EU and the Estonian government innovation and entrepreneurship development projects.

Knowledge Transfer is led by TUIT and CFE through local, regional and international knowledge transfer projects (Marie Curie programme of EU), consulting services and international knowledge transfer and development projects. Internship is an elective component of full-time Bachelors and Masters studies. Faculties, institutes and research centres of UT have joint teams with companies in order to implement new technologies and address issues arising from research results.

The events arranged by the TUIT license office include regular workshops and seminars. They also provide leaflets, a web-page and E-Journal *Novaator* to help entrepreneurs, faculty members and students to develop an awareness about university–industry (academic) knowledge transfer.

Since 1990, approximately 15 spin-off companies have been created by students and academics, mainly in the field of biotechnology and IT.

In 2004, students and graduates of ETM Masters courses established their own association *House of Ideas* (Chamber for Entrepreneurship and Technology Development).

2.3.3 Jagiellonian University in Krakow

Respondent: Jacek Klich, Assistant Professor

Jagiellonian University in Krakow (JUK), Poland, established in 1364, 16 faculties, 41,086 students. JUK is teaching *Entrepreneurship and Innovation* courses to business students at Bachelors level (45 students/year) as well as at Masters level (60) (Formica and Varblane, 2005).

2.3.3.1 *Links with the business community*

A Centre of Innovation, Technology Transfer and University Development (CITTRU) was created as a unit of the Jagiellonian University aimed at promoting entrepreneurship among the scientific staff and encouraging academic researchers to create businesses within the University. CITTRU provides active support to technology transfer, contacting the business environment and promoting scientific projects eligible for commercialization. At present CITTRU is working on the commercialization of scientific projects, mainly in the field of biotechnology, to which it offers business support during the commercialization of projects. In practice, CITTRU evaluates every project presented by the potential academic entrepreneur and eventually selects the one which stands the best chance of commercial success. CITTRU prepares a business plan for the project and takes care of all formalities related to the creation and operation of the company. If needed, CITTRU will search for an investor – a partner who will co-finance the project.

A second centre owned by the University is the Jagiellonian Innovation Centre. The aim of this company is the creation of a technology incubator to assist the development of entrepreneurship based on the scientific potential of the University. Modern technical infrastructure, low operating costs and professional services (e.g., legal and economic consultancy, access to laboratories and contact with scientific experts) should give the academic entrepreneurs from the incubator the possibility to successfully compete on the market of advanced technologies. Students and academics have created one spin-off company.

A third centre, the Academic Science and Technology Centre (AKCENT) is committed to fostering interdisciplinary research and training programmes lasting several years, as well as to effectively transferring and commercializing new technologies developed by Krakow universities: the Krakow Technical University, the Krakow Agricultural University, the Academy of Metallurgy and Mining and the Jagiellonian University. The Centre has been legally formed as a consortium coordinated by the Jagiellonian University and represented by the CITTRU. The research programme of AKCENT includes the following priorities: (1) Biotechnology; (2) Informatics; (3 Product quality and competitiveness; (4) Shaping and protection of the environment in the context of sustainable growth; (5) Nanotechnologies, new construction and functional materials; (6) New technologies in medicine; and (7) Renewable energy sources (http://www.uj.edu.pl/cittru/ang/o-nas.html). Regular workshops and seminars, leaflets and web-pages help to develop faculty members' and students' awareness about university–industry knowledge transfer.

2.3.4   University of Miskolc

Respondent: Andrea Gubik, Assistant Lecturer (http://www.uni-miskolc.hu/)

University of Miskolc (UM), Hungary, established in 1735, 7 faculties, 15,000 students, started teaching *entrepreneurship* as independent Bachelors and Masters programmes in 1990. Entrepreneurship curricula have been established in collaboration with local and foreign business partners (Formica and Varblane, 2005).

2.3.4.1   Links with the business community

Three centres lead knowledge transfer. Namely:

1   The Innovation and Technology Transfer Centre, whose main activities are: technology transfer, promotion of innovation, PR activities and services,

expert and consultancy service, patenting, and services for innovative entrepreneurs (www.uni-miskolc.hu/ittc).

2　The Cooperation Research Centre in Mechatronics and Material Science (established in 2001) (www.meakkk.uni-miskolc.hu).

3　The Innovation Management Co-operation Research Centre (established in 2005), which conducts research in the field of innovation strategy, innovative organization and marketing innovation.

A university-industry joint team with the Borsodi Brewery Corporation provides organizational and business development.

In the UM there are approx. 35 joint university-industry laboratories. Regular workshops and seminars, leaflets, in addition to web-pages help to develop entrepreneurs', faculty members' and students' awareness about university-industry knowledge transfer.

Academics and students have created five spin-off companies.

Main partners in KT are the Regional Office of the International Technology Institute, North-Hungarian Regional Office of the Hungarian Innovation Association, North-Hungarian University Association, Chamber of Trade and Industry of Borsod-Abaúj-Zemplén, Heves and Nógrád Counties.

2.3.5　Budapest Corvinus University

Respondent: Dr Peter Szrimai, Director of Small Business Development Centre (http://www.uni-corvinus.hu/index_angol.php?org=2&LNG=eng)

Budapest Corvinus University (BCU) is an internationally recognized institution for both education and research. Entrepreneurship is currently presented as a major in the Faculties of Business Administration and Social Sciences. Therefore, the coverage of students with fundamental entrepreneurship knowledge is rather widespread (Formica and Varblane, 2005).

The Small Business Research Centre founded in 1990 has played a key role. In 2000, the Centre, which employs many PhD students and 40 faculty members, was reorganized into the Small Business Development Centre (SBDC), responsible for teaching activities in the field of SME specialization (Major) at Corvinus University. During the academic year 2004/05, more than 550 students (of whom 300 come from majors other than economics and business) have been enrolled in special courses on entrepreneurship. The Centre is organizing an international network with the participation of other Universities in Eastern Europe. About 70 per cent of SBDC funding comes from local public sources, 10 per cent from the private sector and 20 per cent from other sources.

2.3.5.1　*Links with the business community*

A strong link with the business community is the Chair *System of Corporate Professorships*, under which the companies sponsor particular research areas and the professors represent them for a period of five years. This system of sponsorship is the first of its kind in Hungary and unique in the region. It enables stable, long-term, mutually beneficial co-operation between the sponsors and the University.

The University has set up three university-industry joint laboratories.

Another interesting institution is the IKU – *Innovation Research Centre*, established in May 1991 in the Postgraduate School of the Budapest University of Economics. The aim of the Centre is to shape innovation policy through research and education and, within this, to improve international competitiveness. Research in science and technology policies, measurement of R&D and innovation and scrutiny of the strengths and weaknesses of the national/local innovation system are the main activities carried out in the Innovation Research Centre. The Centre also plays a vital part in education.

IKU attaches great importance to the dissemination of scientific research findings between academic, business-economic and government decision makers in Hungary and abroad.

2.3.6   Matej Bel University

Respondent: doc.Ing. Jaroslav Ďad'o, PhD

Matej Bel University (MBU), Slovakia, established in 1992 (Faculty of Economics in 1977), eight faculties, 15,260 (2489) students, started teaching entrepreneurship as independent curriculum at Bachelors level with an emphasis on SME management. Effective from 1993, a Masters curriculum in entrepreneurship has been in place (Formica and Varblane, 2005).

2.3.6.1   *Links with the business community*

Over the past five years or so, 14 faculty members have developed best practices in entrepreneurship and business. A Centre for Research and Development (CRD) has been established at the Faculty of Economics for the purpose of applying and developing faculty competencies in education, consultancy and research into practice. Nine of the faculty members are involved in the Centre. Thirty per cent of the CRD budget is financed by local public funding, 20 per cent comes from international public funding, 5 per cent from local private funding, and 45 per cent from other sources. About 200 students participate in internship programmes as a component of their studies, over a period of six weeks per year. 60 employees of local business enterprises (LBEs) take part in exchange programmes with academic labs, totalling 70 months per year. Faculties, institutes and research centres of the University have joined forces with companies with the aim of the commercialization of university research results, and in addition to develop solutions concerning organizational and business development.

Regular workshops and seminars help to develop faculty members' and students' awareness about university–industry knowledge transfer. Students and academics in partnership with LBEs have created five spin-off companies.

2.3.7 The University of West Bohemi

http://www.zcu.cz/

The University of West Bohemi (UWB), Pilsen, Czech Republic, seven faculties, 15,200 students, was established by the decree of the Czech National Council in 1991 when the Institute of Technology in Pilsen and the College of Education were merged (Formica and Varblane, 2005).

Interdepartmental and interfaculty teams work on projects closely related to the fields offered in the PhD study programmes in the Faculties of Applied Sciences, Electrical and Mechanical Engineering.

Students of the technical faculties are invited to apply for the Annual Emil Skoda Award in various categories by submitting a Diploma or PhD dissertation. This award is part of a contractual collaboration between the University of West Bohemia and the SKODA HOLDING, AS.

In order to facilitate co-operation for international projects in science and research, the University, the Plzen (Pilsen) Business Innovation Centre in Plezen (Pilsen) and SKODA RESEARCH LTD founded the Regional Contact Organization in West Bohemia. The EUPRO Programme of the MSMT supports the activities of this organization.

2.3.7.1 *Links with the business community*

Instrumental in forging links with the business community are the New Technologies Research Centre (NTC) in West Bohemian Region, the Plzen (Pilsen) Business Innovation Centre and the Science and Technology Park, which is a joint project of BIC Plzen, University of West Bohemia and the City of Plzen.

The Business Innovation Centre is focused primarily on the development of small- and medium-sized enterprises. It has been providing its services since 1992.

In order to facilitate and speed up technology transfer processes, a Science Park was established in Pilsen in 1996 as a result of an agreement on co-operation between the University and the Business Innovation Centre.

The Science and Technology Park provides support to the:

• Formation of new innovative businesses
• Creation of new (skilled labour) jobs
• Transfer of R & D to innovative firms
• Growth of innovative companies

The first phase of the STP Plzen project was the Business Incubator for innovative start-ups. The BIC Plzen, together with the University of West

Bohemia, has managed this incubator since 1997. The second phase was setting the stage for the creation of the Technology Centre for the purpose of addressing the needs of well-established high-tech and R&D companies.

The Business Incubator offers to technology-driven SMEs:

- Spaces for light-industry production and services
- Secretarial services
- Technical facilities – copy-machine, fax, computers, telephone exchange
- Conference and meeting rooms
- Electronic security system
- Parking space
- Consultancy and advisory services
- Access to information and databases
- Contact with the University of West Bohemia for technical facilities (laboratories and campus infrastructure)

Among the 18 firms located in the Science and Technology Park there are: Automatizace stroju a procesu, s.r.o. – automation processes, controlling and monitoring systems; ATG s.r.o. – non-destructive testing, materials testing and quality management; and BEST Group Software s.r.o. – software solutions for logistics and design optimization.

2.3.8   The University of National and World Economy – Sofia

Respondent: Matilda I. Alexandrova, PhD, Lecturer, Department of Management

The University of National and World Economy – Sofia (UNWE), Bulgaria, established in 1920, five faculties, 22,000 students, offers special courses as Fundamentals of Entrepreneurship, Small Business Management and Industrial Entrepreneurship. About 2000 students (80 foreigners) in all fields are enrolled in entrepreneurship courses (Formica and Varblane, 2005).

2.3.8.1   *Links with the business community*

The University has established an Entrepreneurship Development Centre (EDC) where ten academics are employed. The main activities at the Centre are: (1) Training – designing and organizing specialized courses; (2) Consulting – in business plan development, enterprises privatization, restructuring and recovering, establishment and development of joint-ventures and other kinds of strategic alliances; (3) Research – local and international research projects in the field of entrepreneurship, small- and medium-sized businesses, and large-scale enterprises; (4) Publishing – books and teaching materials in the area of Entrepreneurship and Management, giving prominence to the distinctive traits of Bulgarian and Eastern European economies. The Centre is financed 30 per cent by local public funding, 50 per cent by international public funding and 20 per cent by international private funding. Three researchers, for a total amount of 12 man-months per year, are exchanged with local business enterprises.

Knowledge transfer processes have as constituent elements the transfer of research results, training in the field of SME strategic management, export management, growth management, and the creation of East-West joint ventures. Approximately 200 students take part in internship programmes as a component of their studies, with a duration of one month per year.

UNWE has university-industry joint teams for the purpose of improving processes of organization and business development – for example, in the area of Business Evaluation and Appraisal, and Privatization and Restructuring Strategies. Regular workshops and seminars help to develop faculty members' and students' awareness about university–industry knowledge transfer.

2.4 Policy implications

Knowledge transfer is an increasingly important area of public policy that poses a challenge to the role of policy makers in the process of enhancing the economic potential of a country or region through developing stronger mutual interaction between higher education and business.

CESE countries must shape a comprehensive system for increasing the flow of new ideas into and out of both academia and business. In this section we suggest measures to influence existing patterns in knowledge transfer. Our programme for action encompasses:

- *Mobility.* Human interaction through the movement of people from the camp that sets the stage for knowledge creation to the camp that sets in motion a process of business creation, and vice versa.
- *Knowledge Transfer Partnerships (KTPs).* Project-oriented collaboration between a source of knowledge and its business user.
- *Incentives to entrepreneurial scientists.* Awards and other forms of incentives that can encourage academic investigators to change their current status as potential science-based entrepreneurs either into active founders of start-up ventures emerging from their research activity or into employees who perform an entrepreneurial function ('sub-entrepreneur') inside existing firms.
- *Relationship promoters.* Persons or ad hoc organizations that facilitate the communication between academia and business by lowering the barriers between the research and the business communities.
- *Knowledge Transfer Funds (KTFs).* Supporting different forms of KT.
- *'Start on Campus' and 'Incubators of Entrepreneurial Ideas'.* Pilot actions for the promotion of university-based start-ups and university-embedded incubators that host academic spin-off firms.

- *A code of governance for universities.* Improving the KT relevance of research undertakings.

2.4.1 Mobility

Geographical mobility between EU countries – in particular, making KT successful between the Eastern European countries and Western Europe has become a crucial point – and intersectoral mobility between academic and business is necessary to achieve the transfer of scientific tacit knowledge. Cross-border KT initiatives such as the 'Mobility Strategy for the European Research Area' (ERA), which has given rise to the European Network of Mobility Centres (ERA-MORE) and the European Researcher's Mobility Portal (European RMP) are measures that should allow CESE countries to set up their own national Mobility Centres and Researcher's Mobility Portals. Latvia has already achieved this by the creation of the Latvian Researcher's Mobility Centre (Latvian RMC) and the Latvian Researcher's Mobility Portal (Latvian RMP – http://www.eracareers.lv/) as a part of the ERA-MORE network and its Internet portal (Kokorevics, 2005).

2.4.2 Knowledge Transfer Partnership (KTP)

If experience is any guide, CESE countries can formulate a good transfer policy by looking to learn the lessons of the Knowledge Transfer Partnerships (KTPs), formerly known as the Teaching Company Scheme (TCS), in the UK. It is argued in the *Lambert Review* that:

> [this mode of transfer] is one example of a successful scheme that has promoted knowledge transfer between universities and business. A KTP brings together business in collaboration with universities, colleges and other research organizations. At the heart of each partnership is one or more KTP associates, a high-calibre graduate who is recruited to work in a business on a project that is central to its strategic development. A project may last from 12 to 36 months. The university partner provides its expertise and jointly supervises the project together with a representative from the company. The costs are part funded by Government with the balance being borne by the participating business. The total investment by Government in the TCS was £25m in 2002–03.
>
> (HMSO, 2003, p. 35)

Not least because KT is essentially an entrepreneurial process, KTP is a mode of transfer that requires the ability of scientifically trained personnel to channel towards, and deploy in commercial activities, both tacit and encoded knowledge. In turn, this process entails the migration of scientists, researchers and engineers from academic research to the private sector. As to how it actually occurs, setting up a new entrepreneurial venture by those individuals, or becoming employees or guest employees in someone else's entrepreneurial business, are the possible organizational models (Witt and Zellner, 2005).

Insofar as scientists and researchers who are about to emigrate from academia to the commercial sphere cannot sign on with existing firms either because they are too alien to join them, or for the lack of profitable employment opportunities (Witt and Zellner, 2005), which are unlikely to come from local small businesses whose in-house research activities are not significant or from large companies as a consequence of the restructuring that the transition to the market economy in CESE countries leaves in its wake, a successful KT process depends largely on whether, and to what extent, academic scientists and researchers are willing to migrate from science to business for the purpose of pursuing an entrepreneurial career path by founding technology-driven start-up firms. CESE countries still fail most strikingly in this respect. Their policy makers must do more to put academic spin-off programmes at the heart of their KT policy.

2.4.3 Incentives to entrepreneurial scientists

The role of government-sponsored programmes in encouraging professors to found companies based on their research appears to be growing in importance. The US experience shows that the availability of awards and direct grants to university researchers encourages applications from academics, who would not otherwise be likely to directly commercialize their own technologies, and urges those researchers who do not actually have a firm allowing work with entrepreneurs to see common business opportunities in new scientific knowledge (Wessner, 2005; Lupke, 2005).

Incentives must also serve the purpose of facilitating professional career options inside the small business typology for academic scientists and researchers, so they can contribute to creating a cognitive absorptive capacity[9] in middle-size and smaller local enterprises.

Thus, CESE policy makers should anticipate actions that favour incentives whereby entrepreneurial scientists can compete in some sort of 'market contest' for entrepreneurial business conceptions.

2.4.4 Relationship promoters

The transfer process is hindered by a combination of factors in which the lack of communicative ability, weak level of motivation and scarce resources sit side by side in both the academic and the business spheres of the relationship. Relationship promoters, be they professionals imbued with talent for communication or ad hoc organizations, can help both parties surmount these barriers, making them permeable in both directions.[10] Their challenging task consists in defining a common knowledge context by revealing the real needs of the migrating scientists and their entrepreneurial counterparts as well.

Relationship promoters would have to be given the power to organize 'a gathering place' where knowledge could be shared, imparted and disseminated by means of their skills as facilitators. From this standpoint, relationship promoters have to rely upon policy-triggered regional and national initiatives by which they can draw on a sound pattern of university and private sector involvement and commitment.

2.4.5 Knowledge Transfer Funds (KTFs)

With a view toward improving the quality of the knowledge flow, a knowledge-based funding policy in CESE countries should be structured by which more stress would be laid on the creation of Knowledge Transfer Funds reliant on competitively awarded collaborative projects between academia and business. These funds will support the forms of knowledge transfer we have described. For the specific purpose of improving the performance of the university transfer offices, a special fund should channel resources, on the one hand, into the knowledge transfer training of academics and university administrators involved in the delivery mechanism and, on the other hand, into the recruitment process of people with substantial industry experience and proven skills in negotiation and deal making.

2.4.6 'Start on Campus' and 'incubators of entrepreneurial ideas'

CESE universities should develop models that permit university-based new business ventures to start and remain on university campus, and to receive support during their initial phase.

An approach that should greatly interest both CESE policy makers and universities is the Baden-Württemberg State Government's 'Start-up Initiative', which has put the 'Start on Campus' model project into action. In the frame of the 'Start-up Initiative', more stress is laid on a greater role for the array of pilot actions that Universities could put in practice in order to support innovative start-ups among their researchers and graduates. Universities could apply for funding of those pilot actions.

Box 2.3   Baden-Württemberg: State Government's 'Start-up Initiative'

The aim of the 'Start on Campus' project is:

- To create a positive entrepreneurial spirit at the university
- To select the business starters to be supported
- To offer and arrange consulting and training of business starters
- To arrange access to resources and experts
- To establish a network of entrepreneurs, researchers and support organizations
- To develop pilot action for the promotion of university based start-ups that can be the base for further support schemes

(Diegelmann, 2005)

In light of evidence that the spontaneous phenomenon of new venture creation does not appear adequate to configure a dense fabric of knowledge-based spin-offs ensuing from universities in the CESE countries, a second approach to be adopted is the establishment of incubators of entrepreneurial ideas. In some respects, a situation not unlike those countries may be found in the *Mezzogiorno* of Italy. In the case of the University of Sannio in Benevento (Campania region), a tool for the purpose of sustaining the growth of entrepreneurial ideas and thereby incrementing the number of academic spin-offs has been identified in an 'incubator of entrepreneurial ideas' (Corti and Bianca, 2004).

It is argued in a paper written by two academics of that University that such an incubator:

> should be organized in two phases. In the first phase it operates to promote the birth of a suitable number of entrepreneurial ideas in every [university] department by means of several initiatives, such as institutional education on innovation management, including also how to evaluate the technical and economical feasibility of each idea by learning how to realize a suitable Business Plan, to organize seminars with successful entrepreneurs, and to promote visits to successful small companies. In the second phase the incubator of entrepreneurial ideas must take care of each entrepreneurial idea from its birth towards a more mature stage, by sustaining the editing of the reports of the Business Plans, by helping to identify the most suitable financial sources for each Business Plan, and then to evaluate and to select the most promising entrepreneurial ideas. Besides the incubator of entrepreneurial ideas in this phase there must develop a suitable policy of protection and exploitation of the intellectual property rights , and it must facilitate the acquisition of some selected business ideas by already operating companies through effective technology transfer process.
>
> (Corti and Bianca, 2004)

2.4.7 A code of governance for universities

In transitioning countries nascent entrepreneurs are negatively affected by a higher uncertainty and ambiguity of the external regulatory environment. In the case of universities as part of that environment, broad calls to 'reform the university' must aim to improve the relevance of research for knowledge transfer. In this respect, the CESE university sector should develop a code of governance adept at:

• Modifying the institutional culture and career incentives for researchers
• Encouraging researchers to bring their research to the market
• Identifying the market signals between employers and students
• Stimulating industry interaction through contract research and mobility of students and researchers

- Designing, implementing and communicating a policy that clearly establishes the ownership of intellectual property (IP) in research collaborations[11]

What lies inside the policy makers' scope is the introduction of a range of reforms that have much to do with:

- Greater autonomy for universities
- A risk-based approach to the regulation of universities
- New legislation that makes KT an explicit mission of universities
- The removal of obstacles to co-operation between universities and industry (e.g., the Slovak Republic has taken steps aimed at smoothing the path between the country's science base and the business community).

2.5   Conclusion: what does the future hold?

The economic potential that SMEs in the CESE countries can harness through developing collaboration with universities is worthy of consideration. By this measure, in the CESE region there is a need to increase the flow of knowledge between higher education institutions and firms.

It is policy focus and execution that makes or breaks technology transfer operations. The fragile environment of countries in transition calls for some action to take place in order to consolidate university–industry links. University and industry working hand-in-hand is a result of targeted and controlled governmental strategy that supports university departments which are undertaking work that industry values. Interested universities and firms all over the country must implement this strategy.

In this chapter we have described KT modes and policy instruments that will be required to initiate and sustain effectively concerted and persistent interactions between the intellectual resources of universities and the SME sector. In particular, because human interaction is the most effective form of knowledge transfer, we have placed importance on university staff skilled in KT and staff transfer between universities and firms as a gateway for businesses wanting to access expertise and facilities available at the university.

To secure a better future for knowledge flow between universities and firms, knowledge transfer needs trustful and outward-looking knowledge brokers with excellent interpersonal skills, commercial awareness and contractual experience. Trust is a critical component of the business formula for those who would build bridges in a field so subtle and ambiguous as that of transferring know how, know what, know why, know whom, know when.

For the foreseeable future, KT advancements would not be imperilled inasmuch as arrangements for KT are likely to be made within a frame of reference that fits with the enterprising role of knowledge intermediaries organized in trust-promoting groups. These groups could play a greater role in building sustainable relationships between the academic community and the business sector, with an emphasis on SMEs.

Notes

1 According to van Stel, Carree and Thurik (2005), '... entrepreneurial activity affects economic growth, but ... this effect depends upon the level of per capita income. This suggests that entrepreneurship plays a different role in countries in different stages of economic development.'

2 Café-type communities of practice are life forms whose behaviour is organized from the bottom up. Café-type face-to-face based communities are suitable for enabling participants to exchange and transfer 'skills' or 'technical elements of tacit knowledge'. The odd point is that face-to-face interaction induces 'conformity effects' and 'group thinking', which gets participants to think inwards. Online knowledge communities generate ideas to be turned into new ventures for the knowledge economy. One feature of these communities is the sense of individualism felt by their participants who 'behave as self-contained decision-makers', instead of going along the 'group-type behaviour' path seen in face-to-face based communities. Another feature is that most knowledge community-participants tend to use nicknames. The use of nicknames makes interactions easier, for knowledge exchange happens in an equal-footing context – i.e., irrespective of status considerations. Insofar as these features prevent 'conformity effects' from occurring, online knowledge-community participants would settle for being schooled in the art of outward looking. As a result, new companies would be established that look forward rather than backward. In other words, there would be more start-ups whose scope extends well beyond the horizon of the traditional industrial basis to envisage the needs of the knowledge economy (Formica, 2004).

3 Yin and Lin define conscious conversation as 'a transformational change technique that incorporates deep dialogue skills of reflecting, deep listening, interacting and connecting. It intends to foster common sense, build trust and understanding, and create positive and harmonious relationships among community members. It is familiar to communities of practice in Asia.'

4 Soft skills are behavioural and social components of 'emotional intelligence' as opposed to 'technical intelligence' (Leonard, 1997). They encompass values, motivations, attitudes, and emotions. Namely:
   • Skill in self-awareness (recognizing your own strengths and weaknesses)
   • Skill in self-regulation (keeping emotions under control)
   • Skill in motivation (having optimism and personal drive)
   • Skill in reading emotions and motivation of other people (empathy)
   • Ability to build and manage relationships (negotiation skills)

5 See the seminal works on knowledge mapping by Xenia Stanford (2005), Editor-in-Chief, KnowMap: The Knowledge Management, Auditing and Mapping Magazine (http://www.knowmap.com). As Stanford puts it:
   A knowledge map differs from an information or data map by its function or purpose. Generally the purpose of an information map is to show us what we have and where to find it. A knowledge map is intended to help us learn, build, elicit, share, create and regenerate knowledge. It is one of the tools used to make implicit knowledge explicit so it can be made implicit again.

A knowledge map includes a text connected to symbols, directions, routes and other key map elements. The text should be concepts, questions or ideas – not paragraphs of information or simply objects.
A knowledge map shows relationships between or among the concepts.
The value of the true knowledge map can be broken as follows:
What you have that you need – so you can leverage it.
What you have that you do not need – so you can eliminate the 'fat' and concentrate on more important elements (the 80/20 rule).
What you do not have that you need – so you can obtain it.

(Stanford, 2005)

6   The OECD definition of social capital 'includes such structural and psychological elements as the networks of personal relationships and sense of mutual understanding that enable people to live and work together effectively. Social capital is associated with greater trust, co-operation, reciprocal engagement and social cohesion. Furthermore, social capital can enhance the rapid diffusion of knowledge between individuals, communities as well as within and between firms' (OECD/ONS, 2002; OECD/Government of Canada, 2003). The PRISM REPORT 2003 by the European Commission Information Society Technologies Programme defines social capital as 'the set of collective (in the sense of shared) intangible assets available in a territory' (a city, a region, a country, a set of countries). Collective intangible assets allow communication and exchange to take place without rigid, formal contracts because they provide behavioural rules (formal or informal) that avoid free-rider problems or other abuses of loose contractual relationships (Eustace, 2003).

7   The Shell Technology Enterprise Programme (STEP) is a nationwide scheme which provides placements for undergraduates, mostly during their summer vacations, to work on a project in an SME that meets a specific business need. All students receive a skills assessment package and three days' training from their local provider (usually a business support agency or university), to enable them to record the transferable skills learnt during their placement. Many businesses receive contributions towards the cost of the placement from local business support agencies, which play an active role in helping them define the project, and in quality assuring it (HMSO, 2003, p. 120).

8   The overriding concern is the conflict of interest that develops as research teams give birth to spin-off phenomena. As Strandburg has observed:

Commercialization of spin-offs of curiosity-driven university research may involve the active participation of the scientist inventor. It is not clear what impact the involvement of scientists in such entrepreneurship is likely to have on the market for curiosity-driven research. One salient concern is that an entrepreneur-scientist might seek to suppress the work of another scientist if that work had the potential to threaten the commercial success of his entrepreneurial project. The usual personal preferences and social norms that mitigate such a scientist's desire to suppress competing work in the basic research community are still operative, of course, but they may be less effective against the entrepreneurial scientist because of the added personal incentives to suppress that the commercial enterprise provides. The basic research community might effectively avoid this potential distortion of the curiosity-driven demand function by using more stringent conflict of interest screening of peer reviewers. Scientists with commercial stakes in enterprises related to particular areas of curiosity-driven research could be precluded from reviewing proposals and publications in those areas.

(2005, p. 64)

9 Witt and Zellner (2005, p. 5) defines a firm's cognitive absorptive capacity as its 'own knowledge to understand context and meaning of the information transmitted'.

10 Walter (1999) describes a relationship promoter as a person who actively facilitates inter-organizational exchange processes based on a network of good personal relationships to important actors of (potential) partner organizations and relevant third parties as well as on abilities to develop and use new network relationships (quoted from Gissing, 2005).

11 The *Lambert Review* argues that 'the rewards from research collaboration should reflect the relative contributions of the parties to the partnership. Companies should have secure rights to the IP they want to commercialise, but it is also important that any deal on IP should not unreasonably constrain the university from publishing the results in a timely fashion, from doing further research in the same area, or from developing other applications of the same IP in different fields of use. It follows from both these points that there should be as much flexibility as possible in the distribution of IP rights between universities and business (HMSO, 2003, p. 13).

References

Amidon, D., Formica, P., and Mercier-Laurent, E. (2005), *Knowledge Economics: Emerging Principles, Practices and Policies*, Vol. 1, Tartu University Press.

Andre van Stel, A., Carree, M., and Thurik, R. (2005), 'The effect of entrepreneurial activity on national economic growth', *Discussion Papers on Entrepreneurship, Growth and Public Policy, Group Entrepreneurship, Growth and Public Policy*, Max Planck Institute for Research into Economic Systems, Jena, Germany.
URL: http://d.repec.org/n?u=RePEc:esi:egpdis:2005–04&r=ent

Corti, E. and Bianca, M (2004), 'The incubator of entrepreneurial ideas for knowledge-based spin-offs: The case of the Regional Centres of Competences in Campania region', revised version of the paper presented to the International Entrepreneurship School 'Entrepreneurship in Europe: Best Practices and Regional Development', Paris, 27 June – 2 July, 2003.

Diegelmann, C, (2005), 'Start on Campus – support for university-based start-ups', in Formica, P. and Stabulnieks, J., eds, *Knowledge Based Entrepreneurship*, EffeElle Editori, Cento-Ferrara.

European Commission (2004*), Helping to Create an Entrepreneurial Culture: A guide on good practices in promoting entrepreneurial attitude and skills through education*, Directorate-General for Enterprise, Brussels.

Eustace, C., ed., (2003) *THE PRISM REPORT 2003: Research findings and policy recommendations*, European Commission Information Society Technologies Programme, Report Series No. 2, October, Brussels.

Formica, P. (2004), *Strengthening the Knowledge Economy: Essays on Knowledge Policy and International Entrepreneurship*, EffeElle Editori, Cento-Ferrara.

Formica, P. and Varblane, U. (2005), 'Report About the Current Developments in the Teaching of Entrepreneurship in the European Transition Economies', OECD, LEED Programme International Conference on LOCAL DEVELOPMENT AND GOVERNANCE IN CENTRAL, EAST AND SOUTH-EAST EUROPE, OECD LEED Trento Center for Local Development, Trento, Italy, 23–4 June.

Garavelli, A. C., Gorgoglione, M., and Albino, V. (2001), *Strategies for Knowledge Transfer: Transmission and Acquisition*, Politecnico di Bari, mimeo.

Gissing B. (2005), 'Improving science-industry-regional authority collaboration', in Formica, P. and Stabulnieks, J., eds, *Knowledge Based Entrepreneurship*, EffeElle Editori, Cento-Ferrara.

Harvie, C. and Lee, Boon-Chye (2003), *Public Policy and SME Development*, Economics Working Paper Series, WP 03–18, University of Wollongon.

HMSO (2003), *Lambert Review of Business-University Collaboration: Final Report*, London.

Karnitis. E. (2005), 'A small country's innovative economy: Latvia's case', in Formica, P. and Stabulnieks, J., eds, (2005), *Knowledge Based Entrepreneurship*, EffeElle Editori, Cento-Ferrara.

Kilpi, E. (2005), *Why We Simply Need to Get Better at Working Together: Theoretical considerations behind management challenges today*, mimeo, Helsinki.

Kirzner, Israel M. (1985), *Discovery and the Capitalist Process*, University of Chicago Press, Chicago.

Kokorevics, A. (2005), 'Researchers mobility within the European Research Area – new facilities for innovations and RTD: Mobility support and promoting', in Formica, P. and Stabulnieks, J., eds, *Knowledge Based Entrepreneurship*, EffeElle Editori, Cento-Ferrara.

Leonard, Dorothy A., 'Mining knowledge assets for innovation', *Knowledge Management*, Vol. 1., No. 1, August–September.

Lupke, D. (2005), 'Financing entrepreneurship in the United States', in Formica, P. and Stabulnieks, J., eds, *Knowledge Based Entrepreneurship*, EffeElle Editori, Cento-Ferrara.

Motohashi, K. (2004), 'Economic analysis of university–industry collaborations: The role of new Technology based firms in Japanese national innovation reform', *NEP – New Economics Papers*, Issue nep-ent-2004–01-25 .

OECD (2002), *Benchmarking Industry-Science Relationships*, Directorate for Science, Technology and Industry, OECD, Paris .

OECD/ONS (2002), *Conference on the Measurement of Social Capital. Rapporteur's Summary*, London, 25–7 September .

OECD/Government of Canada (2003), *The Opportunity and Challenge of Diversity: A Role for Social Capital? Synthesis Report*, International Conference, Montreal, Québec, November 23–25.

OECD (2004), *OECD Science, Technology and Industry Outlook*, Directorate for Science, Technology and Industry, OECD, Paris .

Powell, J. A. (1987), 'Is design a trivial pursuit?' *Design Studies* , Vol. 8, No. 4.

Powell, J, Harloe, M., and Mike Goldsmith M. (2000), 'Achieving cultural change: Embedding academic enterprise', Paper presented to the IMHE Conference, *Beyond the Entrepreneurial University? Global Challenges and Institutional Responses*, OECD, Paris, 11–13 September.

Stanford, X. (2005), 'The knowledge management strategy Vee: A framework for creating a new strategic direction, in Amidon, D., Formica, P., and Mercier-Laurent, E., eds, *Knowledge Economics: Emerging Principles, Practices and Policies*, Vol. 2, Tartu University Press.

Strandburg, K. J. (2005), 'Curiosity-driven research and university technology transfer', Paper presented to the Colloquium on Entrepreneurship Education and Technology Transfer, 13 January.

Tödtling, F. and Trippl, M. (2004), 'One size fits all? Towards a differentiated policy approach with respect to regional innovation systems', Vienna University of Economics and Business Administration, Department of City and Regional

Development, Paper prepared for the conference *Regionalization of Innovation Policy – Options and Experiences*, German Institute of Economic Research (DIW Berlin), 4–5 June .

US Council of Competitiveness (2004), *Innovate America*, National Innovation Initiative Report, December.

Volkova T. and Schmit, Thomas J. (2005), 'Multiple routes to improving tacit knowledge for knowledge based environment: The role of higher education', in Formica, P. and Stabulnieks, J., eds, *Knowledge Based Entrepreneurship*, EffeElle Editori, Cento-Ferrara.

Walter, A. (1999), 'Relationship promoters: Driving forces for successful relationship management', in *Industrial Marketing Management* 28, pp. 537–51, Elsevier Science, New York.

Wessner, C. W. (2005), 'The US small business innovation research program: A model for Europe? ', in Formica, P. and Stabulnieks, J., eds, *Knowledge Based Entrepreneurship*, EffeElle Editori, Cento-Ferrara.

Wiig, Karl M. (2005), 'Stories, mental models and situation-handling', in Amidon, D., Formica, P., and Mercier-Laurent, E., eds, *Knowledge Economics: Emerging Principles, Practices and Policies*, Vol. 1, Tartu University Press.

Witt, U. and Zellner, C. (2005), *Knowledge-based Entrepreneurship: The Organizational Side of Technology Commercialization*, Max Planck Institute for Research into Economic Systems – Evolutionary Economics Group, Jena, Germany.

Yin, D. and Lin, J. (2002), 'Sharing tacit knowledge in Asia', *KM Review*, Vol. 5, No. 3, July–August .

3
Mesoeconomic Structure, Innovation and Complexity: The Concept of Mesoeconomic Plexus

George Chorafakis[a,b] *and Patrice Laget*[b]
[a] *University of Cambridge, Department of Geography, Cambridge, UK*
[b] *European Commission, DG-JRC, Institute for*
Prospective Technological Studies, Seville, Spain

Introduction

The transition to the knowledge economy is the most salient element of the recent transformations of the world economy. The predominant feature of this transition is the intensified use of technological and scientific knowledge in the production process. This transition is also related to a seemingly paradoxical phenomenon, the emergence of localities as focal points of economic activity in a globalizing world economy. Many see this phenomenon as an indication that the world economy is gradually shifting from a polycentric economic geography of almost self-sufficient, highly diversified, state-protected and inward-looking national production systems to one of interconnected, globally positioned and regionally embedded concentrations of specialized economic activity.

In order to understand the connection between the intensification of knowledge creation and utilization in the production process on the one hand, and the emergence of localities as nodal points of global economic activity on the other, we need to examine the process of innovation beyond the national and regional levels, down to the locus where productive relationships are articulated and where technological knowledge emerges: We refer to this level as the **mesoeconomic level**. In this chapter we employ the term **mesoeconomic plexus** to refer to the constituent unit of this level. This will be defined as a quasi-integrated system of interconnected microeconomic agents that exhibits a relatively stable external division of labour. This generic term includes territorially embedded formations, such as regional clusters, as well as territorially non-embedded, inter-firm networks. In the new economy, the plexus is the par excellence locus where competitive advantage is built and where the techno-economic paradigm shift that instigates the transition to the knowledge economy occurs.

The focus on the innovation process at this analytical level raises a number of fundamental epistemological and methodological issues with regard to the adequacy of our traditional analytical tools. On the one hand, 'orthodox' economic theory has failed to incorporate into its epistemic core a comprehensive theory of innovation. Mainstream economic models seem to be unable to explain the processes of knowledge creation and innovation per se. The reason is that most modern economic theory is rooted on the neoclassical paradigm. As we show in the next section, this paradigm is founded on a metatheory that is inherently antagonistic to the conceptualization of the complex, out-of-equilibrium dynamics of technological change and innovation. The attempts to endogenize technological change in formal growth models have partially tackled the shortcomings of the neoclassical growth model. However, being themselves subject to the fundamental limitations of the neoclassical paradigm, these approaches are still far from producing a comprehensive theory of the way knowledge creation and innovation emerge in economic life. On the one hand, systemic approaches to knowledge creation and innovation do emerge in economic life. On the other hand, systemic approaches to knowledge creation and innovation lack the epistemic coherence, robustness and formalism of the mature neoclassical models. Moreover, despite their contextual relationship with interdisciplinary scientific fields like cybernetics, general systems theory and the science of complexity, the links between the former and the latter have not been sufficiently explored and developed.[1]

This chapter aims to contribute to the development of a theoretical framework for the study of the mesoeconomic locus, where innovation and technological change emerge, from a systemic point of view that accommodates out-of-equilibrium dynamics and incorporates evolutionary notions; in our view, the theory of **complex adaptive systems** (CAS) offers an appropriate epistemic context for this purpose. It also aims to point to a potential way of integrating into this epistemic context various theories of industrial organization and social networks. A general underlying assumption of this chapter is that mesoeconomic plexuses exhibit the characteristics of complex adaptive systems and, as such, are endogenously innovative.

The chapter is organized in three parts: the first section examines the limitations of orthodox approaches to innovation and technological change as a result of the epistemic and metatheoretical shortcomings of the neoclassical paradigm. It then analyses the paradigm shift instigated by evolutionary and complexity approaches to socio-economic phenomena and presents some of their fundamental concepts. The second section examines the relational structure of mesoeconomic plexuses as a source of their competitive advantage and in comparison to other micro- and mesoeco-nomic formations with a focus on their industrial organization. The third section formulates the hypothesis that mesoeconomic plexuses can be treated as complex adaptive systems and examines the indications that support this hypothesis.

3.1   The paradigm shift from equilibrium to complex adaptive systems

3.1.1   Shortcomings of the neoclassical paradigm

3.1.1.1   *Core assumptions*

Standard microeconomic theory involves the study of 'the behaviour of individual economic actors and the aggregation of their actions in different institutional frameworks'.[2] The universal behavioural rule for all actors is the optimization principle, and more specifically, utility maximization for households and profit maximization for firms. Optimizing behaviour is based on the implicit assumptions that actors are unboundedly rational and that they possess perfect information on prices and market structure. The institutional structure that governs the interaction of agents is the market mechanism, normally under conditions of perfect competition. The aggregate outcome of agents' interaction is deduced by equilibrium analysis.

The optimization principle is the first pillar of the neoclassical paradigm;[3] the fundamental concept of equilibrium is its second and most indispensa-ble one.[4] The neoclassical equilibrium is static and *ex ante*: The plans of all economic agents are immediately compatible without the mediation of mar-ketplace interaction. More specifically, prices are determined in all markets by a fictional 'Walrasian auctioneer' and price adjustment is achieved through an a-temporal '*tâtonnement* process' before any real exchange takes place. The set of equilibrium prices exists and is unique, stable and Pareto optimal only under a set of restrictive conditions regarding the shape of utility and production functions.[5] The behavioural adjustment of economic agents to exogenous shocks is assumed to be instantaneous and completely frictionless, and, under the assumption of perfect foresight, shocks are fully anticipated. The adjustment process, which is essentially a dynamic phe-nomenon, occurs in the transitional phase between equilibria and is not considered as analytically relevant. These two 'pillars' constitute the axio-matic core of the neoclassical paradigm.

3.1.1.2   *Limitations*

A general and frequently evoked shortcoming of the neoclassical paradigm is its unrealistic and often counterfactual underlying assumptions. The plausibility of these assumptions has been exhaustively questioned and there is an extensive body of literature on this topic.[6] This metatheory, among other things, has been accused of being tautological, of suffering normative bias and of achieving internal consistency at the expense of empirical verifiability by logically deducing its axioms rather than by referring to observable economic reality. In this section we examine some of the limitations of this metatheory in the specific context of our topic.

With regard to the cognitive attributes of economic agents, a direct corollary of the assumed hyperrationality and perfect information of economic agents is that learning and hence adaptation are excluded. These are fundamental dynamic processes in real socio-economic systems. Hodgson (1993) observes with regard to the neoclassical assumption of unbounded rationality: 'How can agents be said to be rational at a given point in time when they are in the process of learning and acquiring relevant information? The very act of learning means that not all information is possessed and global rationality is ruled out.'[7]

From a systemic point of view, the economic systems envisaged by the metatheoretical approach of neoclassical economics are **conservative** – as opposed to **dissipative**,[8] and thus ignore the very typical in socio-economic systems phenomena of path dependence, complexity and emergence. These systems are governed by linear interactions among individual agents and are modelled as aggregations of homogeneous agents, by assuming the existence of a representative agent with axiomatically determined behavioural rules. This is a direct corollary of the Weberian doctrine of **methodological individualism**, on which the neoclassical paradigm is founded. According to this philosophical precept, all social phenomena can be ultimately explained as aggregations of individual actions; the whole is treated as a mere 'sum of its parts'.[9] These limitations also reflect the influence of **positivism** on economic theory: More than any other social science, modern economics adheres to the positivist quest for universal behavioural laws, which are supposed to govern the life of *homo œconomicus* similarly to the way Newtonian laws govern celestial mechanics. These fundamental laws are assumed to fully explain the observed reality, even in systems as complex as human societies. Equilibrium analysis introduces Newtonian determinism in economic phenomena. Newtonian mechanical systems are structurally invariable and symmetry preserving, in that their dynamic evolution over time does not alter their qualitative characteristics and their internal structure and symmetry. As a result of this, they are time-symmetric, they exhibit deterministic, path-independent dynamics, and novelties are completely exogenous to them. Such systems possess no endogenous ability to generate innovations and their attained equilibrium depends exclusively on their initial conditions, their laws of motion and the region of their parameter space.[10] All these attributes of mechanical dynamical systems are also present in the perceived dynamics of equilibrium models in orthodox economics.

As a result of all the above, the neoclassical paradigm is inherently incapable of providing an epistemological basis for explaining and modelling economic phenomena that exhibit out-of-equilibrium dynamics and structural change. Processes like innovation and technological change belong by definition to this class of phenomena. With regard to innovation, standard neoclassical growth models, by construction, deal with shifts along the production function that correspond to factor substitution, while, as Schumpeter remarks, innovations correspond to changes in the form of the production function itself.[11] Related to this is the problem of the exogeneity of technological change in neoclassical growth theory: In the Solow-Swan model technological change is the only determinant of the long-run (steady-state) growth rate. However, the rate of technological progress is exogenously determined and thus out of the scope of this model.[12] More recent developments led to models that endogenize technological change by incorporating in the production function important determinants of economic growth, such as human capital, R&D investment, and so on, and that take into account increasing returns and the production externalities related to technological diffusion and knowledge spill-overs.[13] Such models, however, still fail to explain why and how innovation and technological change emerge in economic dynamics. This limitation results from the fact that endogenous growth theories are founded on the same equilibrium-centred epistemic paradigm.

3.1.2 Evolutionary concepts and analogies in economics

Even though the neoclassical paradigm still remains dominant in mainstream economic theory, its theoretical impasse is gradually leading to a Kuhnian paradigm shift as a result of which its fundamental metatheoretical assumptions are being challenged. The potential successor to the neoclassical paradigm is inspired by the analogies between biological and socio-economic systems and makes extensive use of concepts drawn from evolutionary theory. The flirtation between economics and biology – and in particular the Darwinian and Spencerian evolutionary theory – is not something new though: It goes as far back as Alfred Marshall and Karl Marx. The first explicit and mature transfer of ideas between these two disciplines, however, took place in the writings of economists like Thornstein Veblen, Joseph Schumpeter, Friedrich Hayek – who are often seen as precursors to this paradigm shift in economics – and in more recent times, Alchian, Nelson and Winter, and many others who followed them. In this section we briefly examine some fundamental characteristics and assumptions of this emerging paradigm.

3.1.2.1 *Analogies between biological and socio-economic systems*

The underlying driving forces of evolutionary dynamics are the processes of **selection**, **mutation** and **inheritance**. According to Vega-Redondo (1996), a dynamical model will be considered to be evolutionary as long as its laws of motion reflect these three processes.[14]

Evolutionary economics focuses on the adjustment process instead of the equilibrium outcome of agents' economic interaction. In a socio-economic context macroscopic adjustment is a selection process and, similarly to biological selection, a systemic principle applying to whole populations of economic agents rather than individuals. Selection in socio-economic environments is the driving force of Schumpeterian **creative destruction** that leads uncompetitive firms to extinction, while competitiveness corresponds to the Darwinian concept of **individual fitness**.

Box 3.1 The driving forces of evolutionary dynamics

Selection. A concept introduced by Darwin in his *Origin of the Species*. It refers to the biological process that favours some phenotypes over others, that is, explicit behavioural patterns, which can also be thought of as survival strategies. Selection determines the chances of survival and reproductive success of an individual endowed with a particular phenotype, but it is a system-wide principle that refers to whole populations rather than individuals.

Mutation. The genetic process of creating new phenotypes. It is the force that infuses the evolutionary process with new behavioural patterns and enables *adaptation* to changing exogenous conditions. Mutation, however, is neither the only nor the most frequent source of phenotypic variation in biological systems.

Crossover. The reciprocal exchange of genetic material between chromosomes that occurs during the process of meiosis. It is the standard biochemical way of rearranging chromosomal material and generating genotypic variation, which leads to phenotypic variation through *inheritance*.

Inheritance. The process of transmission of genotypes from individuals to their offspring. Through this process *mutations* occurring in individuals can accumulate and cause the intergenerational evolution of species.

Selection dynamics. A dynamic system of differential equations that describes the underlying model of the selection process. *Deterministic models of selection dynamics* lay particular emphasis on the continuity and the reproduction of existing strategies. The process of mutation is introduced indirectly, through the notion of *robustness against mutations*, and it is studied by means of stability analysis. Mutations in such models are assumed to be isolated, infrequent and small perturbations of the population state. A simple deterministic model of selection dynamics is the *replicator dynamics*. Weibull (1998) observes, however, that stability analysis has little to say about robustness against sequential or simultaneous cascades of shocks that cause big perturbations of the population state. Vega-Redondo (1996) observes that mutation is an intrinsically stochastic phenomenon whose appropriate formulation requires a fully stochastic model.[15] *Stochastic models of selection dynamics* focus on the role of mutations in evolutionary dynamics, and for this reason they are more pertinent analytical tools than deterministic models.

Individual fitness. The measure of the outcome in terms of survival and reproductive success of adopting (or of being endowed with) a particular behavioural pattern that undergoes the *selection process*.

Fitness function. A function assigning fitness values to different evolutionary strategies.

Fitness landscape. The visual representation or graph of a *fitness function*. Flake (2000) defines fitness landscapes as 'a representation of how mutations can change the fitness of one or more organisms. If high fitness corresponds to high locations in the landscapes, and if changes in genetic material are mapped to movements in the landscape, then evolution will tend to make populations move in a uphill directions on the fitness landscape.'

In evolutionary economics both individual and systemic adjustment is neither instantaneous nor cost-free, and additionally, it is a **path-dependent** process. Agents are assumed to exhibit only bounded rationality and to possess imperfect information about market conditions, and therefore no perfect foresight. As a result, their response to changes in market conditions, which are often unanticipated, are at best locally optimal and usually suboptimal – even more so since behavioural adjustments are time consuming and incur transaction costs. In evolutionary models adaptive behaviour is recognized as more realistic than optimizing behaviour given the agents' mental, cognitive and informational limitations, and therefore, adaptive procedural routines become the basic behavioural patterns that replace the global optimization principle. These routines should be seen as the socio-economic equivalent of phenotypes.

An underlying assumption in evolutionary models is that agents are usually heterogeneous. As a matter of fact, as Nelson and Winter (1982) argue, heterogeneity in firms in terms of strategy, structure and core competences is the necessary microfoundation for understanding macro-economic change as an evolutionary process and vice versa. This heterogeneity introduces non-linearities in the economic systems, and, as we see in following sections, it can be the source of systemic innovation. Innovation in socio-economic environments can be seen as the equivalent of genetic mutation in biological environments: innovation introduces new procedural routines in analogy to the way mutation causes the appearance of new phenotypes in biological populations. Innovation comes about as a result of either search by incumbent firms or entry of new firms with novel procedural routines; in that respect it is often an intentional or even 'designed' variation consciously introduced in the selection dynamics in order to increase individual fitness, that is, competitiveness. By contrast, biological mutation is not considered to involve intentionality or determinism: it is usually stochastic.

Simple models of selection dynamics show how **individual fitness** is determined by selection in static **fitness landscapes**, but not how inter- and intra-specific (i.e., among- and within-species) interactions generate dynamic fitness landscapes, in which individual fitness is jointly determined with that of other individuals and systemic fitness becomes endogenous: This latter is related to the concept of **co-evolution**. The study of the modes of co-evolutionary and co-adaptive interactions, as we show in a following section, may find interesting applications in the analysis of the forms of industrial organization in mesoeconomic systems. In line with the co-evolution hypothesis, Lewontin (1983) criticizes the metaphor of unidirectional adaptation of organisms to their environment and proposes instead the alternative metaphor of **niche construction** [see Table 3.1].

Box 3.2   Co-evolution and niche construction

Co-evolution.   The process of reciprocal evolution that occurs to interacting species as a result of their ecological interaction. Maynard Smith (1989) distinguishes three types of co-evolutionary interactions in biological systems: *Competitive* (or *antagonistic*), *mutualistic*, and *exploitative*. Competitive co-evolution occurs between different species competing for the same resource. *Mutualism* is a reciprocally beneficial form of *symbiosis*. Exploitative co-evolution occurs when a species itself is the resource of another, and ranges from *predation*, in which individuals from the exploited species are totally annihilated, to *parasitism*.

Symbiosis.   The close and prolonged ecological association of two or more different species. *Mutualism* is a common form of symbiosis. Other forms of symbiosis are *parasitism* (beneficial to one agent and detrimental to the other), *commensalism* (beneficial to one agent and neutral to the other), and *amensalism* (detrimental to one agent and neutral to the other).

Niche construction.   A concept introduced by Lewontin (1983) that refers to the process by which biological systems in the evolutionary process affect and shape their microenvironment by creating their own niches of existence; this concept is also known as *ecosystem engineering*.

The biological concepts of co-evolution and niche construction can find interesting analogies in economics: Niche construction resembles the way oligopolists create market niches for their products, thus shaping consumer preferences instead of adapting their products to existing preferences. Similarly, new technologies open up new market niches instead of merely improving market efficiency and adapting to existing market demand. An example of this process is the way personal computers created a market that did not exist before and became a necessity by shaping demand. When the personal computer market matured, demand and consumer preferences shaped it further. In this case, as in many others, consumer preferences and oligopolistic production trends seem to co-evolve. Further along this line of thinking, competitive firms are not necessarily those that adapt better to existing market demand but those that are able to shape new market trends. Another pertinent analogy can be drawn from mesoeconomic plexuses: These formations can be seen as niches shaped by the co-evolution of particular types of firms with own behavioural rules and local operational regimes. These niches, depending on their size and importance in the global economy, affect the macroscopic dynamics of capitalist growth. A similar approach can be applied to the study of the way multinational corporations have been shaped by capitalist competition and in turn shape the global economy. Finally, the concept of co-evolution can be applied in the study of social institutions: These institutions not only determine the framework of agents' interactions in a top-down fashion, but also emerge in a bottom-up way as a result of these interactions, which clearly implies that social institutions co-evolve with individual behavioural patterns.

3.1.2.2   *Disanalogies between biological and socio-economic systems*

At this point we need to restate some of the fundamental distinctions between biological and socio-economic systems: In biological systems, the adaptation of an agent increases its survival prospects and its fitness, that is, its probability of creating a higher number of offspring. These offspring inherit the parents' genetic material recombined through *crossover* and, less frequently, modified through **mutation**. In terms of time-scale, individual adaptation is a process distinct from evolution: The former involves the intra- or inter-generational, short-run process of behavioural adjustment of individuals to environmental stimuli through learning; the latter, on the other hand, concerns the adaptation of whole populations of individuals and it involves the inter-generational, long-run adjustment of agents' phenotypes through selection, mutation and inheritance. In this process, evolutionary robust genetic building blocks are passed over from one generation to another.[16] Thus evolution, as opposed to adaptation, in biological systems assumes no intentionality or consciousness.

In socio-economic systems, the limits between adaptation and evolution are blurred: individual agents, such as firms or mesoeconomic plexuses, adjust not only their behavioural patterns but also their internal organizational schemes and technology without the mediation of inter-generational inheritance. The transmission of behavioural patterns among individuals, and thus also of 'acquired traits', usually occurs through imitation or learning and 'evolution' may take place within the lifespan of the individual. Not only adaptation but also evolution in socio-economic systems is often intentional: Agents are considered to be conscious and intelligent and mutations in the form of innovations are introduced intentionally. These attributes make the selection process in economics Lamarckian rather than Weismannian. Intentionality is, therefore, one of the main factors that differentiate socio-economic from biological systems.

3.1.3   Fundamental concepts of complexity theory
3.1.3.1   *The emerging complexity theory paradigm*

Complexity is a multidisciplinary field whose aim is the investigation of complex dynamical systems. Its epistemic **corpus** is a not yet entirely cohesive, and it is founded on an emerging paradigm closely associated to that of cybernetics and systems theory. A precursor of this new scientific approach is arguably von Neumann, who laid the foundations of artificial intelligence in the 1940s in his work on **cellular automata**. Even though the initial applications of complexity theory have been in the fields of natural and life sciences, it increasingly finds a range of applications in the social sciences and in particular in economics.

The central concept of complexity theory is that interactions between parts of a complex dynamical system generate aggregate properties of the system that cannot be analytically deduced from the properties of its generative elements; these properties are called **emergent**. As a result of *emergence*, the examination of individual parts of the system in isolation does not reveal its aggregate dynamics, despite the fact that its initial conditions and its evolutionary trajectory (its 'history') are still relevant in understanding its present condition. Applied in the social sciences, the concept of emergence directly challenges the doctrine of **methodological individualism**.

From the methodological point of view, complexity theory introduces a new approach to scientific method which challenges the adequacy of the Hempelian **deductive-nomological** paradigm. This new approach has been termed **constructive** or **generative**:[17] It examines how individual agents' microbehaviour generates aggregate phenomena in a bottom-up, sequential fashion, and it consists in simulating their interactions in an artificial environment. This replaces the top-down approach of deducing general laws governing individual behaviour or of inferring individual behaviour by observing aggregate evidence.

Box 3.3 Dissipative systems and self-organization

The discovery of the second law of thermodynamics introduced the notion of time-irreversibility in the natural sciences, which clearly challenges the implicit time-symmetry of Newtonian mechanics. A corollary of this universal law is that at (thermodynamic) equilibrium,[18] and under the condition that the system is closed, the optimization principle leads to entropy maximization in the system: As a general rule, closed dynamical systems move irreversibly towards a state of increased entropy, the thermodynamic equilibrium, at which the internal structure of the system is eroded.[19] The attainment of a steady state becomes thus equivalent to entropy maximization.[20]

Some types of open dynamical systems under certain conditions may exhibit a local decrease in their entropy related to the emergence of new structure and qualitative characteristics in the system. These systems receive energy from and dissipate entropy to their environment, that is, they locally decrease their internal thermodynamic entropy. This class of dynamical systems is called *dissipative*. By contrast, *conservative systems*, by receiving energy, increase their internal entropy until they reach thermodynamic equilibrium.

The emergence of new structure is a phenomenon related to *self-organization*. It has been observed and theoretically modelled that this phenomenon appears when the open dynamical system is in a *far-from-equilibrium* state.

3.1.3.2 Properties of complex adaptive systems

Complex systems are multiagent dynamical systems. Complex adaptive systems are a particular class of multiagent systems, whose constituent elements are **adaptive agents**. These systems exhibit the following aggregate properties:[21]

1   *Emergence.*   The spontaneous generation of new higher-order properties that are not present at the level of the constituent lower-order elements of a system.

2   *Nonergodicity.*   In non-ergodic systems exogenous shocks have permanent effects on the long-run state of the system. This property is closely related to *path dependence*, the property by which the steady state of a dynamical system depends not only on the initial conditions but also on the adjustment path.

3   *Phase transition.*   A phenomenon that occurs when small changes in the parameters of the system cause a qualitative change in its aggregate properties.

4   *Universality.*   The robustness of the aggregate behaviour of the system to alternative specifications of its microstructure.

5   *Symmetry-breaking and time-irreversibility.*   In fully deterministic systems the steady state exhibits the same structural properties and symmetry as the initial state and, therefore, its qualitative characteristics remain time-invariable. As Allen (1997) observes, 'such models do not anticipate structural change or symmetry braking, and even when their stationary solution is not unique, as in the case of multiple equilibria, the analysis will be biased towards selecting equilibria with the same symmetry as in the initial conditions.'[22] By contrast, complex adaptive systems follow an evolutionary trajectory that is time-irreversible and symmetry-breaking. Time-irreversibility is related to *nonergodicity*, while symmetry-breaking is related to pattern formation and to the concept of *negentropy*.

6   *Dissipation and negentropy.*   The established near-equivalence of thermodynamic and informational entropy means that, in information-theoretic terms, dissipative systems can be considered as systems that absorb information to increase their internal structure or 'negentropy', or equivalently, to decrease their informational (Shannon's) entropy.[23] This phenomenon is an indication of emerging *self-organization*. Negentropy is a concept related to that of 'negative entropy' proposed by Erwin Schrödinger; it is a near-equivalent to information and is often seen as a measure of *systemic complexity*.

7 *Self-organization.* The spontaneous process by which the internal structure of a system increases in complexity without this increase being controlled by another external system. Two necessary, but not sufficient, conditions for self-organization are first, that the system is *far- from-equilibrium*, and second, that nonlinearities in the interactions between the lower-order elements of the system are in place. Nonlinearities, under certain conditions, generate bifurcations leading to chaotic behaviour, but also to *life at the edge of chaos*, which is a form of self-organization. Self-organizing systems are usually complex *dissipative* structures capable of reducing their internal entropy.

8 *Endogenous novelty.* The ability of some dynamical systems, according to Markose (2005), to generate 'irregular innovation-based structure-changing dynamics associated with evolutionary biology and capitalist growth'.[24] Systematic study of the co-evolutionary dynamics of *cellular automata* by Wolfram (1984) has shown that – despite their simple structure and their disordered initial states – some cellular automata exhibit emergent complex behavioural patterns along their evolutionary trajectories that are considered as indications of spontaneous emergence of novelty. Endogenous novelty is the result of *complex* or *undecidable dynamics*.

9 *Complex dynamics and Turing-incomputability.* Complex or 'undecidable' dynamics is the fourth universal class of dynamics in Wolfram's classification scheme (see Box 3.4). This type of dynamics is capable of generating endogenous novelties and is characterized by algorithmic or *Turing incomputability*.[25] Rosen (1999) considers *Turing-incomputability* as a definition of *systemic complexity*. According to Rosen (1999), 'A system is simple if all its models are simulable. A system that is not simple, and that accordingly must have a non-simulable model, is complex.'[26]

10 *Self-organized criticality.* The property of a dynamical system to have a *critical point* as its *attractor* (see Box 3.4). It is similar to the notion of *life at the edge of chaos*.

11 *Adaptation. The ability of a system to detect environmental variation and to adjust* without losing its cohesion and its systemic properties. By doing so the system increases its fitness and its survival probability.

12 *Resilience.* The ability of an open system to restore internal stability – or more precisely to remain within its current *attractor basin* – after an exogenous perturbation. The *resilience* of a system vis-à-vis dynamic exchanges of matter and energy between the system and its environment, achieved by means of internal self-regulatory apparatuses is more specifically called **homeostasis**.

Box 3.4 Universal classes of dynamics, attractors and criticalities

Attractor or attracting set. An invariant subset of the phase space of a dynamical system, towards which the trajectories of the system within a given *attraction basin* converge in the course of time, irrespective of the initial conditions. A system may have multiple attractors. Unlike *dissipative systems, conservative systems* do not have attractors, as they settle in a stable state determined by their initial conditions. An attractor can be a fixed point corresponding to a steady state in the simplest of the cases (*point attractor*), a limit cycle that corresponds to stable oscillations (*periodic attractor*), a n-dimensional manifold, such as a hypertorus, that corresponds to compound oscillations (*quasi-periodic attractor*) or to be of fractal dimension corresponding to deterministic chaos (*strange attractor*). As Wolfram (1984) observes, 'evolution to attractors from arbitrary initial states allows for "self-organizing" behaviour, in which structure may evolve at large times from structureless initial states.'[27]

Cellular automaton. A simple mathematical model for the simulation of the dynamics of complex natural systems. The cellular automaton is a discrete dynamical system consisting of a large number of identical agents with a finite number of states arranged on a lattice. The state of an agent at time *t* is a function of the states of a finite number of neighbouring agents at time *t-1*.

Universal classes of dynamics. Wolfram (1984) has demonstrated that the evolutionary dynamics of *cellular automata* generally fall under four universal classes according to the qualitative nature of the *attractors* of the dynamical systems in which they emerge; these classes are believed to characterize the behaviour of a much broader range of complex physical, biological and even socio-economic systems beyond the basic one-dimensional automaton model. The first class includes *finite automata* with *point attractors*; the second class, *push-down automata* with *periodical* or *quasi-periodical attractors*; the third class, *linear-bounded automata* with *strange attractors* and chaotic behaviour. The fourth class consists of automata described as *Turing machines* exhibiting *undecidable* or *complex dynamics*, whose particularity is that they are algorithmically incomputable despite the fact that they are generated by algorithmic agents, often as simple as one-dimensional *cellular automata*. As Markose (2005) observes, 'dynamic system outcomes produced by algorithmic agents need not be computable and fail to be systematically identified by codifiable meta-models.'[28]

Critical point. The point at which a dynamical system undergoes a *phase transition*. An ordinary criticality, such as the point of phase transition from water to ice, is obtained by exogenously varying a control parameter – in this case temperature. A *self-organized criticality* results from endogenous dynamics of certain classes of systems independently of the value of any control parameter.

Life at the edge of chaos. A term coined by Langton (1992) to refer to the *phase transition* between order and chaos, in which novelties emerge. This phenomenon occurs in the domain of *complex dynamics* (Class 4) between computable order (Classes 1 and 2) and chaos (Class 3).

Table 3.1 Neoclassical versus evolutionary epistemological paradigms

Epistemological paradigm	Neoclassical	Evolutionary
Philosophical influence	Positivism	Realism
Source of metaphors	Newtonian	Darwinian
Approach to scientific method	Deductive-nomological	Constructive-generative
Part-whole construal	Methodological individualism	Emergence, holism
System dynamics	Linear	Nonlinear, complex
Stability domain	Steady-state equilibrium	Resilience in attractor basins
Systemic adjustment	Instantaneous, costless, ergodic	Path dependent, nonergodic
Temporal evolution	Structurally invariable	Symmetry-breaking
Entropic behaviour	Conservative	Dissipative
Novelty generation	Exogenous	Endogenous
Agent's rationality	Unbounded	Bounded
Behavioural assumptions	Global optimization	Adaptation, local optimization
Information	Perfect, symmetric	Imperfect, asymmetric
Aggregation rule	Representative agent	Heterogeneous agents

3.2   The relational structure of plexuses

3.2.1   The plexus as a fundamental mesoeconomic unit

3.2.1.1   The concept of mesoeconomic plexus

We have seen that agency in orthodox microeconomic theory involves individual firms and households interacting under the optimization principle
in an equilibrium framework. This interaction is inherently a-temporal and
a-spatial and only its equilibrium outcome is in analytical focus. In this
type of theory, any aggregation of economic units is based on the assumption of a representative agent and the doctrine of methodological individualism. The only higher level of aggregation is the macroeconomic level,
whose operational entities are the national economies.

In more realistic economic models with heterogeneous, boundedly
rational agents with interdependent, locally optimal and adaptive responses
to limited informational stimuli, complex adjustment dynamics and long
out-of-equilibrium transitions, a new level of aggregate economic activity
comes into existence: it is the one that lies between the microeconomic
level of individual units of production and consumption, that is, firms and

households, and the macro-economic level of national and regional economies – the **mesoeconomic level**. This separate analytical level is the non-isotropic space of economic interactions among individual agents and the *locus* where productive relationships are articulated, where social capital is accumulated and where technological knowledge creation takes place. This space is spanned by local concentrations of interacting microeconomic units, which have their own internal structure, properties and 'laws of motion'.

The **mesoeconomic plexus** is defined as the minimum irreducible network of microeconomic agents connected by a relatively stable division of labour. This formation is a complex system in itself and also the fundamental operational unit of this analytical level. According to this definition, a mesoeconomic plexus belongs to a level of industrial organization, which is ontologically different from that of microeconomic units and their ordinary aggregations. Its structure and properties are also qualitatively different from those of an ordinary agglomeration of firms or any other spatial concentration of economic activity. Next we examine this particularity of plexuses in comparison to other economic entities, such as the region, the corporation and the ordinary agglomeration.

3.2.1.2   Regions and regional innovation systems

In this study we argue, contrary to the dominant belief, that the region is generally not a fundamental unit of spatial economic analysis, and in particular of the mesoeconomic level. The term **region** commonly refers to geographical entities whose boundaries are determined by administrative, political, and in certain cases historical, rather than systemic criteria. Such entities usually are, therefore, arbitrary subnational aggregations of mesoeconomic plexuses without any particular systemic characteristics other than those that accrue from their constituent units. Consequently, the region cannot be considered as an indivisible unit of economic activity but rather as an analysable sum of more fundamental entities.[29]

In certain strands of literature some theorists propose the term **regional innovation system** as the regional analogue of the older concept of national system of innovation.[30] Given the idiosyncratic character of the latter related to the particularities of the national production systems and the limited tractability of their systemic dimension, especially in the case of larger countries, the concept of a regional innovation system has been considered to be a more pragmatic approach to the systemic and geographically specific nature of innovation.[31] The regional innovation system is supposed to represent a particular type of geographical formation possessing a territorially specific institutional structure that supports innovation at the regional level. A functioning innovation system of this type consists of two subsystems: A 'knowledge application and exploitation subsystem', principally occupied by firms organized in vertical supply-chain networks; and a 'knowledge generation and diffusion subsystem', consisting mainly of public organizations.[32] Across the same lines, some studies distinguish between **regional clusters**, regional innovation networks and regional innovation systems: The former are supposed to be spontaneously emerging 'geographical concentrations of firms often developed through local spin-offs and entrepreneurial activity', while the latter are regional clusters enhanced with 'knowledge creating and diffusing organizations, such as universities, colleges, training organizations, R&D institutes, technology transfer agencies, business associations, and finance institutions', which allow firms to engage in innovative activity.[33] In our study, the latter are simply considered as a particular type of spatially embedded mesoeconomic plexuses: To the extent these plexuses engage in R&D-intensive activity they are classified as science-based.[34] The 'knowledge generation and diffusion subsystem', in which we need to include, apart from the knowledge creating and diffusing organizations, the institutional structure that supports innovative activity, is a type of public good, and thus it is a component of the total infrastructure of a territory. Whether regional clusters are 'spontaneous phenomena' in contrast to regional innovation systems, which are supposed to be of a 'planned and systemic character' is a debatable issue, and anyway not essential in our approach: The provision of all public goods – even of the physical infrastructure found in common regional clusters – is undeniably of a 'planned and systemic character', whereas the existence of many knowledge-creating institutions, such as most historical universities, is unrelated to state intervention and planning. Moreover, the presence of a university or of a public research institute in a locality does not guarantee the existence of endogenous innovative activity, since these public institutions may well be disconnected from the local economies. The embeddedness of these public institutions in a plexus is not a matter of planning but it greatly depends on the type of knowledge the plexus generates, which in turn depend on its structural characteristics.

3.2.2 The competitive advantage of mesoeconomic plexuses

3.2.2.1 *Externalities versus external division of labour*

Both ordinary agglomerations and spatially embedded mesoeconomic plexuses are territorial concentrations of economic activity. In the former case, the territorial concentration is generated by agglomeration economies that accrue from exogenous to the firms determinants, such as the existence of physical infrastructure, favourable spatial planning provisions and locally specific public policies (such as tax exemptions), low land rents, and most importantly, proximity to existing labour pools and consumer markets. A distinction must be made here between *localization* and *urbanization* economies: the former are agglomeration economies accruing from the spatial concentration of firms in similar industries, while the latter are agglomeration economies accruing from proximity to urban areas. In general, the agglomerating factors that 'glue' individual firms together in an ordinary agglomeration are either locally-specific public goods (shared physical infrastructure, enabling institutional framework, etc.) or localized positive externalities.[35] The former is usually the result of state intervention, while the latter is an involuntary and incidental effect of individual economic activity, which in neoclassical economics is treated as a 'market failure', that is as a type of inefficiency of the market mechanism. An ordinary agglomeration is, therefore, a local aggregation of microeconomic units bound together by economic factors not necessarily accruing from deliberate action.

Mesoeconomic plexuses have all the above characteristics of an agglomeration, and additionally exhibit efficiency gains to a scale that cannot be explained either by the mere existence of agglomeration externalities or by the individual properties of their constituent microeconomic units, which very often are small and medium enterprises (SMEs). The *differentia specifica* of such formations and the true source of their competitive advantage is the existence of a dense nexus of interdependencies that generates an inter-firm, 'external' division of labour.[36] This division of labour generates a more flexible form of industrial organization, which in certain economic environments, for certain market niches and under certain operational conditions can be more efficient and competitive than other forms of industrial organization, such as the large corporation. In this context, the mesoeconomic plexus can be defined as the locus where firms' interdependencies and an external inter-firm division of labour are articulated.

Box 3.5   Externalities

Externalities are economic effects not captured in the prices of goods or of production factors. A textbook definition of externalities is that they occur 'whenever the well-being of a consumer or the production possibilities of a firm are directly affected by the actions of another agent in the economy', where 'directly' means 'in a way not mediated by the price mechanism'.[37] J. Viner distinguishes between *pecuniary* and *technological* externalities, of which the latter corresponds to the modern definition of externalities. The former rather corresponds to scale economies generated by combined – but not necessarily coordinated – action of individual agents.

3.2.2.2   Joint action and the nexus of interdependencies

This nexus of interdependencies is not an unintended by-product of the spatial concentration of microeconomic agents – an externality – but the result of 'consciously pursued joint action', even though joint action itself may benefit from existing agglomeration economies and give rise to new externalities. As Schmitz (1999) observes, many forms of joint action may emerge in such environments: joint action can be horizontal, in the form of co-operation between competitors for the attainment of scale and scope economies, or vertical, in the form of co-ordination between producers of goods and services that are complementary in the production process, that is, that belong to the same value-chain. It can also be bilateral, when individual firms co-operate to achieve a specific goal, such as the development of a new product, or multilateral, when groups of firms join forces to form producer consortia, cooperatives, and the like.[38] We would add that joint action can also be ad hoc, that is, co-operation that takes place for the realization of a specific project, or repeated, that is, a co-operative scheme on a more permanent basis. Generally speaking, co-operation in this context does not exclude competition. Joint action is the basis of different forms of industrial organization at the mesoeconomic level that we examine in the next paragraph.

In certain strands of economic geography literature, the so-called **untraded interdependencies** have been emphatically proclaimed as the major source of competitive advantage of localities, and, as a matter of fact, the very *raison d'être* of regions. According to Storper (1997), this term refers to all the 'conventions, informal rules, and habits that coordinate economic actors under conditions of uncertainty'.[39] Our approach to this issue is different: We consider that the major source of mesoeconomic competitive advantage is the kind of interdependencies that generates a locally stable external division of labour. Such an approach entails that the most important generative factor of mesoeconomic formations are **traded interdependencies**, that is, interdependencies that involve pecuniary transactions. However, the role of untraded interdependencies in the formation of co-operative norms and structures should by no means be underestimated: Untraded interdependencies are a type of informational or 'soft' externality accruing from and contributing to the external division of labour described above.[40] These externalities constitute the basis for the formation of social capital through the establishment of tacit, informal norms, habits and conventions, and mutual trust that govern economic relations at the mesoeconomic level. This normative structure co-evolves with the nexus of traded interdependencies and also with the formal institutional superstructure. The presence of untraded interdependencies is a very important channel for learning and adaptation, and also for the diffusion of innovative practices and new technologies.

3.2.2.3 Specialization under external division of labour

The relational structure that emerges from joint action – the external division of labour – enables even the smallest of the firms to specialize in specific segments of a more complex production process. Such a specialization allows SMEs to product differentiate and to innovate through gradual adaptation and learning. It also facilitates effective investment by SMEs in small steps, since, for example, producers do not have to buy equipment or train labour for the whole production chain but only for the segment in which they specialize. Moreover, clustering is a well-known risk-pooling strategy in economic environments of high uncertainty, as it gives to smaller firms the opportunity to invest in innovative projects and to introduce relatively risky technical and organizational improvements in their field of specialization, with cascading effects on aggregate performance when the innovations in the whole production process become cumulative. Clustering also reduces all types of entry barriers, thus facilitating the entry of newcomers irrespective of their size.[41] This observation shows the important role of spatially embedded plexuses as 'enterprise incubators', and their ability to 'help small firms to overcome well-known growth constraints and to sell to distant markets, nationally and internationally'.[42] With regard to innovation, there is strong empirical evidence supporting the view that innovative activity tends to cluster; as a matter of fact, cluster research indicates that the propensity of innovative activity to cluster is more manifest at the early stages of the business life cycle, while it tends to become more dispersed at the mature stages.[43]

Some theorists of a neoclassical persuasion question the aforementioned advantages of clustering by stressing those aspects of the phenomenon that, in their view, are in conflict with the concept of perfect competition. Such a neoclassical view on clustering would regard the presence of externalities that are so closely related with the phenomenon of agglomeration in general as an indication of an impending market failure, which could result in free-riding and in under-investment, especially in R&D. A related view regards the phenomenon of clustering as a tendency toward collusion and oligopoly practices and therefore, as another market failure and an indication of underlying rent-seeking practices. In the next section we demonstrate the irrelevance of these assertions by looking in detail at the issue of industrial organization at the mesoeconomic level.

3.2.3   Industrial organization of mesoeconomic systems

3.2.3.1   *Transaction regimes and modes of industrial organization*

The nature of the external division of labour in mesoeconomic plexuses can be further elucidated when compared to the internal division of labour of a corporate conglomerate with hierarchical administrative structure. A corporation has a legal personality that secures and a hierarchy that regulates intra-firm transactions among vertically integrated departments. Transactions take place in an extra-market framework. On the other hand, a plexus has no legal personality. It is characterized by a non-hierarchical, administratively decentralized structure, in which the various production units are interdependent but autonomous. Inter-firm transactions are either governed by contractual arrangements, that is, legally binding bilateral agreements, or are simply spot-market transactions directly mediated by the market mechanism and regulated by the normative nexus of untraded interdependencies, depending on the type of dominant **transaction regime** (see Box 3.6). Different mixes of hierarchical, contractual and open-market transaction regimes are one aspect of what generates the variety of mesoeconomic formations, such as the conglomerates, industrial districts and agglomerations [see Table 3.2].

Box 3.6   Transaction regimes

Transaction regime is the *governance mode* that regulates transactions among microeconomic units in a mesoeconomic system permitting economies in *transaction costs*. A transaction regime may be based on **hierarchies**, **markets** or **contracts**, or indeed any mix of these three types.

The contract-based transaction regime is a 'hybrid' between extra-market and open-market transactions. *Hybrid* is a term used by Williamson (1985) for the governance mode based on contractual arrangements. This definition is based on concepts and terms developed by Williamson (1979; 1985; 2005). His approach is known as *transaction costs economics*, and in his more recent work as *economics of governance*. The 'governance mode' according to Williamson depends on the frequency of transactions, uncertainty and the specificity of the assets involved.

With regard to the duration of the contractual relationships, a transaction regime can be permanent, temporary or ad hoc, depending on the types of joint action that it supports. A large complex mesoeconomic system will most likely involve a multiplicity of coexisting transaction regimes.

Another aspect of the variety of mesoeconomic formations is the **mode of industrial organization**. By this term we refer to the way the links between microeconomic units in a mesoeconomic system are articulated. We distinguish three general modes, **integration**, **quasi-integration** and **disintegration**.

Box 3.7   Modes of industrial organization

Vertical integration refers to the expansion of ownership into upstream or downstream activities. More specifically, downstream expansion is known as *forward integration* and upstream expansion as *backward integration*.

Horizontal integration refers to the concentration of units belonging to the same level of the value-chain under a single ownership scheme by internal expansion of the firm or by external expansion through mergers and acquisitions.

Vertical and **horizontal disintegration**. The first term refers to the externalization of upstream or downstream segments of the value-chain. The second term refers to the externalization of activities belonging to the same level of the value-chain of the firm.

Vertical quasi-integration corresponds to a hierarchical star-like network structure resembling to Markusen's (1996) *hub-and-spoke* type of industrial district. This consists of a dominant firm and its (usually upstream) subcontractors. In this mode of industrial organization the dominant firm sets the rules and the specifications of production to its upstream suppliers. The networking scheme is based on, as Aoki calls it, *authority*. *Just-in-time* production methods favour this type of networking.

Horizontal quasi-integration is the case where there is no dominant partner in the network and the *relational quasi-rent* is distributed more-or-less equally among the partners. The network is entirely decentralized and transactions are based on *trust* and *partnership*, rather than on authority as in the former case. Strategic alliances, joint ventures etc. are usual under this mode of industrial organization.

Oblique quasi-integration is an intermediate mode of industrial organization – a network structure in which the suppliers preserve their autonomy vis-à-vis their customers in that they retain full control of their segment of the value-chain. This scheme is based on *incentive contracts* aiming at eliminating the moral hazard problem, which is usual in principal-agent type of interactions with limited monitoring capacities.

Horizontal integration may generate economies of scale and scope, increase market power over suppliers and buyers or facilitate international transactions. Vertical integration may reduce transaction costs, stabilize and co-ordinate the supply chain, increase entry barriers to potential competitors, and internalize the risk of investment in specialized assets and activities, such as capital-intensive R&D activity, which normally would not be taken up by individual upstream or downstream actors. Vertical integration is intensified by adverse factors such as a restrictive tax regime, an unstable macro-economic environment that increases uncertainty and risk, a weak institutional net, inadequate social capital and lack of trust that make difficult the enforcement and monitoring of contracts, or just missing upstream or downstream markets. On the other hand, compared to alternative modes of industrial organization, vertical integration has a number of potential disadvantages: first, the rigidities in the supply chain with regard to adapting to variable exogenous demand, which may cause excess upstream capacity building and bottlenecks; second, the managerial diseconomies and the potentially increased costs due to lack of supplier competition; and third, the inflexibility of the innovation-generating structure, which gives rise to diminishing returns to research capital. This last limitation is examined in more detail in the next section. The process of disintegration leads to the reorganization of the supply-chain of the firm by increasing outsourcing. It also leads to switches from hierarchy- to contract- or market-based transaction regimes. The transition to the knowledge economy and to the so-called 'post-Fordist' or 'flexible' regime of accumulation in the mid-1980s accentuated this tendency.

A conceptually different mode of industrial organization is quasi-integration, which consists in a decentralized but relatively stable inter-firm division of labour that has a network structure. This mode of industrial organization generates relational quasi-rent, whose mode of distribution among the participating economic agents depends on their centrality, that is, their relative weight and position within the network, and determines the particular type of quasi-integration. The term 'relational quasi-rent' was introduced by Aoki (1986) to refer to the quasi-rent that is generated by investment in relational assets.[44] In the case of quasi-integration, this surplus value is produced by investments made by economic agents in order to sustain their relationship with other agents in a particular joint action scheme.

Whereas the vertically integrated mode of industrial organization is considered as a typical illustration of the Fordist firm and of the 'Taylorist' techno-managerial paradigm, the quasi-integrated mode is often seen as a typical example of post-Fordist, 'flexible' organization. Clearly, mesoeconomic plexuses are based on the quasi-integrated mode of industrial organization. This mode permits the mediation – even partially – of the market mechanism and of inter-firm competition. This introduces a local selection process leading to the 'survival of the fittest', most efficient firms and entrepreneurial behaviour, at least within the boundaries of the plexus. At the same time, it reduces the uncertainty and the co-ordination problems of open-market transactions. As a result, plexuses combine flexibility and relative stability of their organizational structures. By contrast, vertically integrated corporations are much less organizationally flexible and are often infected by managerial diseconomies.

3.2.3.2 Local embeddedness and global sourcing

Despite their flexible organization, most plexuses are geographically immobile: they cannot relocate because of lock-ins, path dependencies and the co-ordination problem present in systems with decentralized ownership and management. As a result, plexuses are usually territorially specific. Corporations, on the other hand, have the ability to relocate according to local factor conditions and market opportunities, and in the case of multinationals, they can even separate and relocate the different components of their value-chain across the world according to these criteria.

The development of advanced telecommunication technologies in conjunction with the liberalization of capital movements has given rise to spatially non-embedded inter-firm networks. In the era of globalization, the tendency to vertical disintegration and the expansion of global sourcing, which until the beginning of the era was a usual practice only for multinational corporations, has accelerated the integration of firms in supra-local value-chains. Depending on the stability of the remote inter-firm links this phenomenon may lead to geographically non-embedded clustering, that is, clustering based on remote networking rather than agglomerating. Several theoretical and empirical studies, however, have demonstrated that the

Table 3.2 Comparison of modes of industrial organization

Mode	Ownership structure	Transaction regime	Advantages	Disadvantages
Vertical integration	Upstream or downstream concentration of ownership	Hierarchy-based	• Reduced transaction costs • Stabilization and co-ordination of supply chain • Economies of scale and scope • Increased market power • Protection against macro-economic instability • Counterbalance to inadequate social capital • Counterbalance to missing upstream or downstream markets	• Internalization of risk of investment in specialized assets • Rigidities in supply chain vis-à-vis variable exogenous demand • Managerial diseconomies • Increased costs due to lack of supplier competition • Inflexibility of innovation-generating structure • Technological lock-in • Diminishing returns to research capital
Horizontal integration	Concentration of ownership at the same level of the value-chain	Hierarchy-based	• Economies of scale and scope • Increased market power • Facilitation of international transactions	
Vertical quasiintegration	Integrated network of dominant firm and subcontractors	Contract-based	• Reduced uncertainty and co-ordination problems compared to open-market transactions	• Geographical immobility and local specificity of resources • Co-ordination problems and increased transaction costs

Oblique quasi-integration	Semi-integrated network of customer and supplier firms	Contract- and market-based	• Externalization of risk of investment in specialized assets • Flexible supply chain *vis-à-vis* exogenous demand • Mediation of the market mechanism and inter-firm competition • Specialization and product differentiation • Risk-pooling • Reduced entry barriers • Flexible supply chain *vis-à-vis* exogenous demand
Horizontal quasi-integration	Distributed network of strategic partners	Market-based	• Mediation of the market mechanism and inter-firm competition • Economies of complexity • Risk pooling • No entry barriers • Exploitation of technological spillovers • Incremental, non-radical innovation • Limited economies of scale

cohesiveness and stability of networks with knowledge-intensive input is greatly affected by proximity due to the significance of face-to-face contacts in the diffusion of tacit, non-codifiable knowledge.[45]

3.2.3.3   Network topologies of mesoeconomic systems

A different approach to the fundamental issue of industrial organization in understanding the structure of the mesoeconomic plexuses, and the innovation process in particular, is the concept of network structure. The advantage of the network approach to industrial organization is that networks are quantifiable and entities capable of being modelled, and that there is a large and growing literature on network analysis and modelling with a high degree of mathematical formalism.

According to Powell (1990), the network is a hybrid form of industrial organization between hierarchical and market organization that expands the boundaries of the firm 'to encompass a larger community of actors and interests that would previously have either been fully separate entities or absorbed through merger'.[46] As a form of industrial organization it corresponds, therefore, to the quasi-integrated mode and to the hybrid transaction regime. These two notions are not explicitly related to networking; in reality, however, they generate network-like structures, among which the mesoeconomic plexuses. Carayol and Roux (2003) propose the following set of relevant network characterization criteria: (1) the expected efficiency of the network, according to the average social surplus (or in our approach, the 'relational quasi-rent') the network yields and to the variance in individual pay-offs; (2) the direct connections and neighbourhoods by their density, range and symmetry (i.e., whether the connections are unequal); (3) the generic graph properties, such as the average path length, the average cliquishness, and so on; and (4) the spatial correlation of network connections.

The network is not only a means of structuring the economic transactions but also – and most importantly – a medium for the diffusion of economically relevant information. As we have already seen, in neoclassical theory the information processing and diffusion apparatus is the price mechanism and these processes are a-temporal and a-spatial. In real mesoeconomic systems, however, the diffusion of information does not take place in an isotropic space but is structured and determined by the topological characteristics of the information-diffusion medium – usually complex adaptive networks of variable architecture. These networks exhibit a capacity to diffuse information faster and more efficiently according to their index of complexity: Several studies of social network models conclude that by increasing the network connectivity, the information diffusion speed also increases, though different types of connections may have different effects.[47]

3.3 The plexus as a complex adaptive system

3.3.1 The CAS hypothesis

In this section we show that the examination of the systemic properties of mesoeconomic plexuses reveals considerable analogies with the aggregate properties of complex adaptive systems we identified in Section 1.3.2. On the basis of these analogies we formulate the hypothesis that the mesoeconomic plexus, as defined in this chapter, is a complex adaptive system.

3.3.1.1 Nonlinearities and complex dynamics

Firms and other organizations within a mesoeconomic plexus exhibit different types of behavioural patterns determining and determined by, among others, their niche in the relational structure of the plexus, that is, the external division of labour that glues the plexus together. These heterogeneous agents are boundedly rational, adaptive, local optimizers with a limited knowledge of their broader economic environment, constrained by their cognitive capacities and by their information input. Many studies, both empirical and theoretical, point to that individual firms are adaptive agents and in themselves complex adaptive systems consisting of lower-order adaptive agents, the firms' employees.[48] The mesoeconomic plexus is, therefore, a multiagent dynamical system consisting of a large number of heterogeneous adaptive agents.

The heterogeneity in the behavioural patterns of adaptive agents within a multiagent system is a sufficient condition for the existence of nonlinearities in the formal representation of the system.[49] Mesoeconomic plexuses are, therefore, nonlinear dynamical systems. Agents' heterogeneity and nonlinearities are a potential sources of endogenous novelty: as Lansing (2002) observes, systems of heterogeneous agents with limited knowledge of their environment and bounded rationality may exhibit emergent properties of self-organization and order. This is related to the fact that, while a linear system can be fully analysed by being decomposed to its elements due to the additivity of the elements' functional forms, in a nonlinear system the interaction between the constituent elements generate results that do not allow the decomposition of the system; bifurcations, for instance, which are a usual phenomenon in nonlinear systems, have as a result that a marginal change in the parameters of the system causes qualitative change in the system's aggregate properties.

Nonlinear dynamics are not always complex (Class 4) dynamics; they can be simply chaotic (Class 3). This seems not to be the case, however, with evolving mesoeconomic plexuses: The evolutionary trajectories of these formations exhibit novel and unpredictable, non-chaotic localized patterns, which lie in the domain between order and chaos known as *life at the edge of chaos* (see Box 3.4).

3.3.1.2 *Self-organization, emergence*

A plexus is an open system in constant exchange of factors of production, commodities and information with its environment. By exchanging capital, labour, commodities and information with its environment and depending on its life-cycle stage, a plexus normally becomes more organizationally complex as the number or the size of constituent firms increases: an emergent plexus is, therefore, strongly **dissipative** and in a **far-from-equilibrium** state. Such a formation expands its internal structure rapidly and increases its complexity (or equivalently, reduces its entropy) by developing interdependencies between firms. This process is equivalent to the accumulation of 'social capital' that occurs in parallel to the usual process of (human and physical) capital accumulation at the level of individual firms. By contrast, an established, or even more a declining, plexus becomes increasingly 'entropic' as a result of increasing diseconomies or technological lock-ins. Moreover, as we show later on, a mesoeconomic plexus is a dissipative system that transforms information flows it receives from its environment into new structured knowledge stocks, that is, cumulable cognitive capital. These are genuine indications of **self-organization**.

In previous paragraphs we observed that the *differentia specifica* between productive plexuses and common agglomerations is an additional aggregate and collective structure related to both traded and untraded interdependencies and social capital, which generates an external division of labour and is responsible for the fact that plexuses cannot be fully analysed into their generative components. This relational-cognitive structure is decentralized and spontaneous and emanates directly from the process of self-organization. A number of very significant economic phenomena, which are often present in mesoeconomic plexuses, such as increasing returns, collective efficiency, enhanced competitiveness and innovativeness, are phenomena specific to plexuses but not necessarily present at the level of the constituent lower-order agents, that is, the individual firms; clearly, these are emergent systemic properties. In a similar fashion, the usual aggregate phenomena that are present in this type of systems, such as production and information externalities and the related knowledge spill-overs, can also be seen as emergent properties of the systems under discussion. In this context, externalities, which were considered as forms of market failure at the level of individual microeconomic units, can now be seen as emergent properties of an ontologically different unit of economic analysis, the plexus, that contribute to its strong competitive advantage.[50] These are clear indications of **emergence**.

3.3.1.3 *Universality and phase transition*

In complex socio-economic systems systemic fitness is not directly affected by or even associated with individual fitness. In the case of mesoeconomic plexuses, an equivalent statement would be that the competitiveness of the plexus as an entity remains unaffected by the competitiveness of individual firms: while individual firms decline and cease to exist, the plexus keeps living and even expanding – another illustration of what Schumpeter called 'creative destruction'. Moreover, while inter-firm links may repeatedly change and the relational structure be in a state of constant flux, the plexus retains its cohesion and its aggregate properties – given that it is sufficiently big and complex. This is an indication of the **universality** property of complex adaptive systems: changes in the micro-specification of the system, such as its composition in terms of firms and inter-firm links – or in network terms, the vertices and edges of the network, does not affect the system's generic properties.

In many respects **phase transition** is a mirror property to that of universality: Under the former, small shifts in the higher-order (aggregate) parameters of the system cause drastic changes in the qualitative characteristics of the system, including leaps from one *attractor basin* to another and regime shifts. Under the latter, the higher-order properties of the system remain unaffected by changes in its lower-order elements. Economic history provides ample evidence that mesoeconomic systems such as regions, industrial districts, cities, social networks, but also macro-economic systems such as whole countries or, indeed, the global economy may undergo *phase transitions*: the sudden wane or wax of these meso- and macro-economic formations in terms of growth dynamics or the shifts in their techno-economic regimes instigated by minor historical contingencies are all indications that these formations exhibit phase transition.

3.3.1.4 *Path dependence, time-irreversibility and symmetry-breaking*

An increasing number of studies in the field of economic geography identify **path dependence** as an essential feature of mesoeconomic formations, such as industrial districts, regional clusters, regional networks, or more generally, the regions. Dynamic increasing returns, the irreversibility of past investment and sunk costs, agglomeration economies, technological lock-in, institutional inertia and cumulative causation are among the factors that have been identified in related literature as sources of path dependence in economic geography, and in economic history in general.[51] This rich theoretical and empirical evidence supports the view that the evolutionary trajectories of mesoeconomic plexuses exhibit the properties of **nonergodicity**, **time-irreversibility** and **symmetry-breaking**.

3.3.2 Increasing returns to complexity

We have already observed that mesoeconomic plexuses exhibit collective increasing returns that cannot be attributed either to agglomeration and network externalities or to individual increasing returns in the constituent microeconomic units. This is another indication of an emergent systemic property emanating from the complex division of labour in such formations. We refer to this property as **increasing returns to complexity** in distinction to the common notion of increasing returns to scale.

In our view, the concept of increasing returns to complexity reflects much more faithfully the Smithian ideas with regard to increasing returns and the division of labour contained in the first three chapters of *The Wealth of Nations* than the idea of scale economies:[52] considering the value-chain as a network of production units, the greater the network complexity and density is, the greater the specialization and the division of labour among these units, and hence the increasing returns. Indeed, there are two ways of generating increasing returns in production, an extensive and an intensive one: the first consists in increasing the size of the production units (e.g., the factory size, the amount of physical capital, etc.); the second in increasing the degree of the division of labour, and, therefore, of specialization of the production units. Considering the production process in network terms, this change would be equivalent to increasing the network density, that is, the number of vertices and/or edges of the network. The first case is a linear expansion of the production scale; the second is a nonlinear one. Similar conclusions also apply to the phenomenon of diminishing returns: beyond a certain threshold of complexity, **diseconomies of complexity** may begin to set in.

In the knowledge economy where the most important factor of production is intangible – technological knowledge – increasing returns are not necessarily a result of the scale of production units but, more likely, of their degree of specialization (in the case of the integrated mode of industrial organization) or of the network density (in the case of an external division of labour). Increasing returns to complexity are indeed particularly prominent in knowledge-intensive economic activities. As we show later in this volume, a potential source of these increasing returns in non-hierarchical complex adaptive systems, such as the mesoeconomic plexus, is their capacity for asynchronous information processing, distributed cognition, and endogenous and spontaneous novelty.

Conclusions

The market is not the principal regulatory mechanism in the interactions of microeconomic agents. Interactions of economic agents do not take place in the isotropic and structureless space of neoclassical economics, in which agents interact only through equilibrium price signals. The real limitations in the cognitive capacities of agents, that is, bounded rationality, imperfect and asymmetric information, volatility of preferences, and so on, mean that agents cannot be global hyperrational optimizers; they are local adaptive optimizers. Moreover, instead of a priori impersonal interactions through the market mechanism, microeconomic agents are conditioned by a relational structure, which resembles a complex dynamic network of variable architecture and of variable degree of intensity of inter-agent links. The market mechanism itself is an emerging phenomenon of this relational structure rather than its principal regulatory apparatus. We defined the mesoeconomic level to be the analytical level that corresponds to this relational structure and the mesoeconomic plexus to be its fundamental unit, that is, the minimum resilient network of agents that permits an extensive division of labour; plexuses are mesoeconomic systems exhibiting a quasi-integrated mode of industrial organization. We have seen that this extensive division of labour is the source of their competitive advantage, as it generates increasing returns to complexity, especially in the knowledge-intensive segments of the economy.

From a systemic point of view, mesoeconomic plexuses exhibit the aggregate characteristics of complex adaptive systems. These multi-agent systems have endogenous innovation capacities as a result of complex nonlinear dynamics that emerge among their constituent elements, the heterogeneous adaptive agents. Besides its very important theoretical implications the assumption that mesoeconomic plexuses are complex adaptive systems allows the development of a radically different methodological approach to quantifying and modelling mesoeconomic systems and to construing the mesoeconomic processes of innovation and technological knowledge generation: first, new indicators can be developed, based on the measurable aggregate properties of plexuses as CAS; second, agent-based computational models can be used for the simulation of the macroscopic behaviour of mesoeconomic plexuses and of their evolutionary trajectories; and third, important new normative conclusions with implications to policy making can be drawn on the basis of this new approach.

Notes

1 *Cybernetics* is a term coined by Norbert Wiener and is a precursor to *general systems theory*, founded by Ludwig von Bertalanffy, and to the more recent *science of complexity*, initially developed by the Santa Fe Institute. The scope of complexity science overlaps with that of the *theory of complex adaptive systems*. Two of the pioneers in this field are John Holland and the Nobel laureate Murray Gell-Mann.
2 Kreps (1990), p. 3.
3 Nelson and Winter (1982).
4 As Mas-Colell et al. (1995), p. 620 observe, 'a characteristic feature that distinguishes economics from other scientific fields is that, for us, the equations of equilibrium constitute the center of our discipline. Other sciences, such as physics or even ecology, put comparatively more emphasis on the determination of dynamic laws of change.'
5 Necessary conditions for existence of Walrasian equilibrium are the continuity, strict convexity and strong monotonicity of preferences. As the

Sonnenschein-Mantel-Debreu theorem has demonstrated, additional restrictions will be required to ensure uniqueness and stability.

6   The influential critique by Kaldor (1972) focuses on the neoclassical assumption of non-increasing returns to scale. Other critiques range from the assumed independence of individual behaviour of economic agents by Kirman (1989), to the instability problem generated by the *tâtonnement* assumption.

7   Hodgson (1993), p. 4.

8   See Section 1.3 and Box 3.3 for an explanation of these terms.

9   This doctrine is also related to *reductionism* and to *positivism*.

10   Schumpeter (1939).

11   Schumpeter (1939).

12   As Barro and Sala-i-Martin (1995), p. 11 observe, 'we end up with a model of growth that explains everything but long-run growth, an obviously unsatisfactory situation.'

13   Endogenous growth models include Uzawa (1965); Romer (1986; 1990); Lucas (1988); Aghion and Howitt (1992), etc.

14   Vega-Redondo (1996), p. 1.

15   Vega-Redondo (1996), p. 127.

16   Holland (1996), p. 79 observes that 'evolution "remembers" combinations of building blocks that increase fitness. The building blocks that recur generation after generation are those that have survived in the contexts in which they have been tested. These contexts are provided by (1) other building blocks, and (2) the environmental niche(s) the species inhabits.'

17   Tesfatsion (2005).

18   The mechanical equilibrium should not be confused with the statistical notion of *thermodynamic equilibrium*.

19   Allen (1997), p. 10.

20   Wilson (1974).

21   The first four properties are taken from Durlauf (2001).

22   Allen (1997), p. 22.

23   *Negentropy* is a term coined by the French physicist Léon Brillouin.

24   Markose (2005), F167.

25   This is an equivalent to *non-simulability* that relates to the insolvability of Hilbert's *Entscheidungsproblem*, independently proven by Church and Turing, and Gödel's famous *Incompleteness Theorems*.

26   Rosen (1999), p. 292.

27   Wolfram (1984), p. 1.

28   Markose (2005), F163.

29   In some cases regions are themselves part of a plexus, in others the boundaries of a region coincide with those of a single mesoeconomic plexus, and in others the region is an entity with autonomous governance structures that contains several plexuses, and thus resembles a national economy. All these cases can still be examined in the light of the theory formulated here.

30   For the concept of *national system of innovation*, see, among others, Lundvall (1992), and Nelson (1993). For that of *regional innovation systems* (RIS), see Cooke (1992), and Braczyk et al. (1998).

31   Introduction by P. Cooke in Braczyk et al. (1998).

32   Autio (1998); Cooke (2002).

33   Observatory of European SMEs (2002), p. 14.

34 As the cases of many 'industrial districts' demonstrate (for instance, the case of some Italian industrial districts), a plexus can be innovative without being *science-based*, *hi-tech*, or *R&D-driven*.

35 With regard to the latter, Krugman, following the analysis of industrial districts by A. Marshall, distinguishes three predominant 'sources of industry localization', namely *labour market pooling*, availability of *intermediate inputs*, and *technological spillovers*. See Krugman (1991), pp. 35–54.

36 The terms *inter-firm* and *external* division of labour will be used interchangeably. The same applies to the opposite terms *intra-firm* and *internal* division of labour.

37 Mas-Colell et al. (1995), p. 352.

38 Schmitz (1999), p. 469.

39 Storper (1997), p. 5.

40 These modern economic terms correspond to what Alfred Marshall used to call 'an industrial atmosphere' that was supposed to be present in the English industrial districts of Lancashire and Yorkshire studied by Marshall.

41 The usual entry barriers are product differentiation and economies of scope, absolute cost advantages and economies of scale.

42 Schmitz (1999), p. 466.

43 Audretsch and Feldman (1996).

44 According to Klein et al. (1978), p. 298, 'the quasi-rent value of the asset is the excess of its value over its salvage value, that is, its value in its next best use to another renter.'

45 Powell (1990), p. 313.

46 Powell (1990), p. 313.

47 See Midgley et al. (1992). Other extensive studies on the impact of network structure on information diffusion dynamics include Goyal and Janssen (1996), and Chwe (2000).

48 Studies treating firms as complex adaptive systems include Dooley (1997), and Fuller and Moran (2000; 2001).

49 Modelling a system with heterogeneous agents will require *agent-based simulation* methods, many of which involve the use of *genetic algorithms* for the representation of the behavioural patterns of populations of adaptive agents in *fitness landscapes*.

50 A similar idea in a different context and with a different formulation is found in Schmitz (1999), p. 475: 'The view that external economies cause underinvestment arises from mainstream analysis focusing on a single enterprise in a static fashion. Once we study interlinked enterprises in a dynamic way, the outcome is more open-ended and the enabling features of external economies become apparent.'

51 This extensive literature includes Saviotti and Metcalfe (1991); Krugman (1991; 1996); Storper (1997); Garud and Karnøe (2001); Fuchs and Shapira (2005); and many others.

52 Smith (1904).

References

Aghion, P., and P. Howitt (1992), 'A model of growth through creative destruction', *Econometrica*, Vol. 60, No. 2, pp. 323–51.

Allen, P. M. (1997), *Cities and Regions as Self-Organizing Systems: Models of Complexity*, Gordon & Breach Science Publishers, London.

Aoki, M. (1986), 'Horizontal versus vertical information structure of the firm', *The American Economic Review*, Vol. 76, No. 5, pp. 971–83.

Audretsch, D. B., and M. P. Feldman (1996), 'Innovative clusters and the industry life cycle', *Review of Industrial Organisation*, Vol. 11, pp. 253–73.

Autio, E. (1998), 'Evaluation of RTD in regional systems of innovationt', *European Planning Studies*, Vol. 6, pp. 131–40.

Barro, R. J., and X. Sala-i-Martin (1995), *Economic Growth*, McGraw-Hill, New York.

Braczyk, H.-J., P. Cooke, and M. Heidenreich, eds. (1998), *Regional Innovation Systems. The Role of Governances in a Globalized World*, UCL Press, London.

Carayol, N., and P. Roux (2003), 'Self-organizing innovation networks: When do small worlds emerge?', *Cahiers du GRES 2003–8*.

Chwe, M. S.-Y. (2000), 'Communication and coordination in social networks', *Review of Economic Studies*, Vol. 67, No. 1, pp. 1–16.

Cooke, P. (1992), 'Regional innovation systems: Competitive regulation in the new Europe', *Geoforum*, Vol. 23, pp. 365–82.

Cooke, P. (2002), *Knowledge Economies. Clusters, Learning and Co-Operative Advantage*, Routledge, London.

Dooley, K. J. (1997), 'A complex adaptive systems model of organization change', *Nonlinear Dynamics, Psychology, and Life Sciences*, Vol. 1, No. 1, pp. 69–97.

Durlauf, S. (2001), 'A framework for the study of individual behavior and social interactions', *Sociological Methodology*, Vol. 31, 47–87.

Flake, G. W. (2000), *The Computational Beauty of Nature: Computer Explorations of Fractals, Chaos, Complex Systems and Adaptation*, The MIT Press, Cambridge, MA.

Fuchs, G., and P. Shapira, eds (2005), *Rethinking Regional Innovation and Change. Path Dependency or Regional Breakthrough?* Springer, New York.

Fuller, T., and P. Moran (2000), 'Moving beyond metaphor: Towards a methodology for grounding complexity in small business and entrepreneurship research', *Emergence*, Vol. 2, pp. 50–71.

Fuller, T., and P. Moran (2001), 'Small enterprises as complex adaptive systems: A methodological question?', *Entrepreneurship and Regional Development*, Vol. 13, pp. 47–63.

Garud, R., and P. Karnøe, eds (2001), *Path Dependence and Creation*, Lawrence Erlbaum, London.

Goyal, S., and M. Janssen (1996), 'Interaction structure and social change', *Journal of Institutional and Theoretical Economics*, Vol. 152, No. 3, pp. 472–95.

Hodgson, G. (1993), *Economics and Evolution. Bringing Life Back into Economics*, Polity Press, Cambridge.

Holland, J. H. (1996), *Hidden Order. How Adaption Builds Complexity*, Basic Books, New York.

Kaldor, N. (1972), 'The irrelevance of equilibrium economics', *The Economic Journal*, Vol. 82, No. 328, pp. 1237–55.

Kirman, A. (1989), 'The intrinsic limits of modern economic theory: The emperor has no clothes', *The Economic Journal*, Vol. 99, No. 395, Supplement: Conference Papers), 126–39.

Klein, B., R. G. Crawford, and A. A. Alchian (1978), 'Vertical integration, appropriable rents, and the competitive contracting process', *Journal of Law and Economics*, Vol. 21, pp. 297–326.

Kreps, D. M. (1990), *A Course in Microeconomic Theory*, Harvester Wheatsheaf, Hemel Hempstead .

Krugman, P. (1991), *Geography and Trade*, The MIT Press, Cambridge, MA.

Krugman, P. (1996), *Peddling Prosperity. Economic Sense and Nonsense in the Age of Diminished Expectations*, Norton, New York .

Langton, C. (1992), 'Life at the edge of chaos', in C. Langton et al., *Artificial Life II*, Addison-Wesley, Reading, MA.

Lansing, J. S. (2002), '"Artificial societies" and the social sciences', *Artificial Life*, Vol. 8, No. 3, pp. 279–92.

Lewontin, R. C. (1983), 'Gene, organism, and environment', in D. S. Bendall, ed., *Evolution from Molecules to Men*, Cambridge University Press, Cambridge, pp. 273–85.

Lucas, R. E. (1988), 'On the mechanics of economic development', *Journal of Monetary Economics*, Vol. 22, No. 1, pp. 3–42.

Lundvall, B. Å. ed. (1992), *National Systems of Innovation: Towards a Theory of Innovation and Interactive Learning*, Pinter, London.

Markose, S. M. (2005), 'Computability and evolutionary complexity: Markets as complex adaptive systems (CAS)', *The Economic Journal*, Vol. 115, No. 504), F159–F192.

Markusen, A. (1996), 'Sticky places in slippery space: A typology of industrial districts', *Economic Geography*, Vol. 72, No. 3, pp. 293–313.

Mas-Colell, A., M. D. Whinston, and J. R. Green (1995), *Microeconomic Theory*, Oxford University Press, New York.

Maynard Smith, J. (1989), *Evolutionary Genetics*, Oxford University Press, Oxford.

Midgley, D. F., P. D. Morrison, and J. H. Roberts (1992), 'The effect of network structure in industrial diffusion processes', *Research Policy*, Vol. 21, No. 6, pp. 533–52.

Nelson, R. R., ed. (1993), *National Innovation Systems: A Comparative Analysis*, Oxford University Press, Oxford.

Nelson, R. R., and S. G. Winter (1982), *An Evolutionary Theory of Economic Change*, Harvard University Press, Harvard, NJ.

Observatory of European SMEs, ed. (2002), *Regional Clusters in Europe*. DG Enterprise, European Commission.

Powell, W. W. (1990), 'Neither market nor hierarchy: Network forms of organization', in *Research in Organizational Behavior*, Vol. 12, Elsevier, Nottingham, pp. 295–336.

Romer, P. M. (1986), 'Increasing returns and long-run growth', *The Journal of Political Economy*, Vol. 94, No. 5), 1002–37.

Romer, P. M. (1990), 'Endogenous technological change', *Journal of Political Economy*, Vol. 98, No. 5 (Part 2: The Problem of Development: A Conference of the Institute for the Study of Free Enterprise Systems), S71–S102.

Rosen, R. (1999), *Essays on Life Itself*, Columbia University Press, New York.

Saviotti, P. P., and J. S. Metcalfe, eds (1991), *Evolutionary Theories of Economic and Technological Change*, Harwood Academic, Reading.

Schmitz, H. (1999), 'Collective efficiency and increasing returns', *Cambridge Journal of Economics*, Vol. 23, pp. 465–83.

Schumpeter, J. A. (1939), *Business Cycles. A Theoretical, Historical and Statistical Analysis of Capitalist Process*, McGraw-Hill, New York.

Smith, A. ([1776] 1904), *The Wealth of Nations*, Methuen, London.

Storper, M. (1997), *The Regional World. Territorial Development in a Global Economy*, The Guilford Press, New York.

Tesfatsion, L. (2005), 'Agent-based computational economics: A constructive approach to economic theory', in Judd, K. L. and Tesfatsion, L. eds, *Handbook of Computational Economics*, Vol. 2: Agent-Based Computational Economics, North-Holland Press.

Uzawa, H. (1965), 'Optimum technical change in an aggregative model of economic growth', *International Economic Review*, Vol. 6, No. 1, pp. 18–31.

Vega-Redondo, F. (1996), *Evolution, Games and Economic Behaviour*, Oxford University Press, New York.

Weibull, J. W. (1998), *Evolutionary Game Theory*, MIT Press, Cambridge, MA.

Williamson, O. E. (1979), 'Transaction costs economics: The governance of contractual relations', *Journal of Law and Economics*, Vol. 12, No. 2, pp. 233–61.

Williamson, O. E. (1985), *The Economic Institutions of Capitalism: Firms, Markets, Relational Contracting*, Basic Books, New York.

Williamson, O. E. (2005), 'The economics of governance', *American Economic Association Annual Meeting: 'Expanding the Frontiers of Economics'*, Philadelphia, PA.

Wilson, A. G. (1974), *Urban and Regional Models in Geography and Planning*, Wiley, London.

Wolfram, S. (1984), 'Universality and complexity in cellular automata', *Physica D: Nonlinear Phenomena*, Vol. 10, No. 1–2, pp. 1–35.

4

Technological Knowledge Through the Looking Glass: Distributed Cognition and Co-Adaptation in Mesoeconomic Plexuses

George Chorafakis[a,b] *and Patrice Laget*[b]
[a] *University of Cambridge, Department of Geography, Cambridge, UK*
[b] *European Commission, DG-JRC, Institute for Prospective Technological Studies, Seville, Spain*

Alice looked round her in great surprise. 'Why, I do believe we've been under this tree the whole time! Everything's just as it was!'

'Of course it is,' said the Queen, 'what would you have it?'
'Well, in *our* country' said Alice, still panting a little, 'you'd generally get to somewhere else – if you ran very fast for a long time, as we've been doing.'

'A slow sort of country!' said the Queen. 'Now, *here*, you see, it takes all the running *you* can do to keep in the same place. If you want to get somewhere else, you must run at least twice as fast as that!'

Lewis Carroll, *Through the Looking Glass (and What Alice Found There)*

Introduction

Technological knowledge is commonly perceived as the principal generator of macroeconomic growth and one of the main drivers of economic competitiveness, especially in the economic setting of what is often referred to as the 'knowledge economy'. The transition to the knowledge economy as a result of the intensified deployment of technological and scientific knowledge in the production process entails the rapid expansion of the technological frontier of the world economy and the restructuring of whole production systems, especially in the advanced industrial economies. This transition is reflected in the dramatic rise in R&D investment and human resources over the past half-century not only in the industrial economies but also in the industrializing ones. The socio-economic importance of this transition is now widely recognized by policy makers and the creation of new technological knowledge has become a priority target in the policy agendas of most OECD and of many newly industrializing countries. However, the analytical tools for understanding how technological knowledge is generated and how it affects economic processes and economic systems have not yet been fully developed. As a result of this, technological knowledge – especially in the context of neoclassical economic theory – remains a black box. Opening this black box requires the incorporation in economic theory of a formal and realistic theory of cognition by economic agents. For the reasons we examine in Chapter 5 and for additional reasons examine in the following paragraph, the cognitive theory that is implicitly incorporated in neoclassical economics is very rudimentary, unrealistic, and eventually does not tell us much about the way technological knowledge comes about. In this chapter we aim to contribute to the development of such a theory of cognition in the context of evolutionary and systems theories by showing the intricate relationship between cognition and adaptation in socio-economic systems.

Knowledge generation and information processing are two of the most fundamental functions of economic agents and systems. In neoclassical economics the market is an information-processing apparatus whose only purpose is to make compatible the plans of economic agents by generating price signals. The attainment of general equilibrium, through *tâtonnement* or otherwise, is an information-intensive process of adjustment, which entirely depends on the information-processing capacities of the market apparatus. Like 'Maxwell's demon' in thermodynamics, the Walrasian auctioneer is a fictional entity that possesses infinite information-processing capacities.[1] Moreover, the axiomatic assumptions of hyperrationality and perfect information underlying the behavioural model of *homo œconomicus* also implicitly attribute to microeconomic agents infinite cognitive and information-processing capacities. Despite these implicit assumptions on the cognitive capacities of economic agents and of the market apparatus, the neoclassical paradigm does not explicitly entail any consistent theory of cognition and knowledge generation by economic agents and systems: information processing and cognition are implicitly assumed as instantaneous and automatic processes that take place at a pre-equilibrium stage, and, therefore, before the economic phenomena studied by the theory occur.

In a different strand of theory, the so-called 'knowledge-based theories of the firm', the *raison d'être* of any corporate organization is to combine and co-ordinate the integration of knowledge held by individuals;[2] this is supposed to be a task that the market mechanism by itself is incapable of accomplishing, but on the contrary, the organizational structure of the firm is. According to this strand of theory, knowledge is the most valuable asset of a firm; actually, the firm itself is seen as an aggregation of cognitive assets embodied in individuals, whose competitive advantage is determined by the capability of the firm to combine and utilize them. The knowledge-based theory of the firm, however, is a rudimentary model of knowledge aggregation at the level of the firm that cannot – and is not intended to – explain the whole range of knowledge-generating capacities exhibited by microeconomic agents and mesoeconomic systems. This strand of theory focuses on a particular type of knowledge, the non-codifiable knowledge embodied in human capital, and is based on two fundamental epistemological assumptions: First, that the economic exploitation of knowledge requires its extraction and objectification with the elimination of its subjective and contextual elements, as a direct corollary of an underlying **objectivist** epistemology[3]; this process takes place through the organizational structure of the firm. Second, on the construal of knowledge as a cumulable, capital-like asset, and, therefore, as a substance, as a stock, and as a homogeneous input in the production function similar to physical capital. This assumption can be subsumed under a general class of approaches to economically relevant knowledge, which we will refer to as **substantivist**. This class of approaches is in line with orthodox economic theory and is also related to the concept of 'knowledge production function' and 'human capital'. These approaches do not examine what is the nature and the source of technological knowledge but only its effect on economic activity; as a result, the explanation of the knowledge generation process remains exogenous to all economic models founded on the objectivist-substantivist construal of technological knowledge.

In the first section we examine the relationship between technological knowledge and industrial organization from a macroscopic perspective. In the second section, however, we dissect through the 'black box' of technological knowledge by examining how adaptive agents and systems of agents utilize information and generate cognition in an evolutionary and complex-theoretical framework. The former approach, the macroscopic perspective, takes knowledge as given and as a firm-specific asset, and it can, therefore, be considered as substantivist. The latter approach examines how cognition is generated as a result of adaptation and co-evolution and will be referred to as **constructivist** for reasons that will become clear in the following paragraphs.

4.1 Technological knowledge and industrial organization

4.1.1 Appropriability and embeddedness of technological knowledge

Even when examined from a 'substantivist' perspective, technological knowledge cannot be considered as a homogeneous input to the production process as it takes a number of forms with different effects on economic activity. These forms of technological knowledge are determined by the following criteria: the degree of appropriability of its economic effects by individuals and, therefore, its economic exploitability; by its codifiability and, therefore, by the degree of its embodiment in economic agents and its 'extractability' and 'objectifiability'; and finally, by the degree of its local (spatial and geographical) embeddedness.

First, there is a type of formal and codifiable but non-rival and non-excludable 'scientific' knowledge, which functions as a public good. This is the case, for instance, of the product of basic research that takes the form of scientific publications. This type of knowledge is directly objectifiable by formal means of representation and, therefore, non-embodied in economic agents, and it is rapidly and easily transferable through supra-local networks of scientific communities. It has a positive external effect on overall economic activity and is socially beneficial, but, as a result of its very strong external and spill-over effects, it is not directly economically exploitable on a private basis. It is, therefore, non-appropriable by individuals and also locally non-embedded. As a result of its non-appropriability, private economic agents underproduce it and public institutions will have to step in for the benefit of the society at large.

Second, there is a type of codifiable, non-rival but partially excludable 'patented knowledge, which is a quasi-public good.[4] This type of knowledge is also not embodied in economic agents, it is relatively easily accessible, and can be economically exploitable on a private basis. It is usually the result of applied research leading to patent grants. The process of generating this type of knowledge is often – but not necessarily – geographically concentrated, but its utilization is usually not. Codified knowledge, in general, does not need to be generated or utilized *in situ*. It can be produced through collaborative efforts organized in remote rather than agglomerated networks, and then tapped and acquired by companies who have good access to the network structure. As aconsequence, the results of investing in knowledge-creating mechanisms of this type are not necessarily locally exploitable.

Third, there is a type of potentially or partially codifiable but non-patented, privately owned and protected, and thus rival and excludable, 'organizational' knowledge. This type of knowledge is semi-formal and objectifiable, but it remains embodied in organization structures, and it is exploitable only by its owners. It is a private good, which confers 'technology rent' and monopoly power to the organizations that own it, at least for a certain period of time, until it becomes accessible to others through its embodiment in tradable goods and services and reverse-engineering. The generation of this type of knowledge is usually localized but it is partially transferable through intra-organization networks and, therefore, its utilization is not entirely locally embedded.

Finally, there is a type of non-codifiable, partially non-extractable and non-objectifiable, 'tacit' knowledge that remains embodied in economic agents in the form of know-how and skills, and can be developed through learning-by-doing, vocational training or formal education. This type of technological knowledge is both rival (an employee can normally work for one company at a time) and excludable, and, as a result of these properties, it is a private good. This type of knowledge is highly localized both in its generation and its utilization due to the physical and institutional limitations in labour mobility.

4.1.2 Technological knowledge and modes of industrial organization

Irrespective of the ontological view one adopts with regard to the nature of knowledge, it is commonly understood that technological knowledge and the process of technological cognition are collective and not individualistic phenomena. The generation of technological knowledge, which we will refer to as 'innovation', is a strongly synergetic and systemic process.[5] The synergetic nature of innovation does not entail that the economic agents involved in the process actually share the ownership and the management of their cognitive assets, but rather that they combine them in order to produce new, potentially economically exploitable knowledge or to engage existing knowledge in the economic activity: Both at the micro- and at the mesoeconomic levels heterogeneous, as to their cognitive assets, agents combine them for productive purposes and eventually integrate them in a common operational context.

The way economic agents combine their cognitive assets for productive purposes determines and is determined by the mode of industrial organization of the economic systems in which they operate: In the cases of vertical and horizontal integration the cognitive assets are under a single ownership and management scheme. The firms have the incentive to invest in R&D and to take the risk of their investment, and possess the resources to this aim. In the extreme – and not any more realistic – case of relying exclusively on its own R&D, these firms will have to invest heavily on innovation-specific activities but in the case of success, they will appropriate the whole technological rent. These firms usually have specialized R&D departments, and they protect their cognitive assets by restricting their use within the confines of the firm or by patenting.

By contrast, according to Leborgne and Lipietz (1992), 'quasi-integration minimizes both the costs of coordination (because of the autonomy of the specialized firms or plant), and the costs of information/transaction (because of the routinized just-in-time transactions between firms). Moreover the financial risks of R&D and investments are shared within the quasi-integrated network.'[6] In the case of horizontal quasi-integration, a group of firms linked by partnership and strategic alliance jointly undertake innovative projects and share the risk. This mode of industrial organization favours symmetric distributions of knowledge within the network and a symmetric appropriation of the relational quasi-rent of innovative activity. Their knowledge is shared and, therefore, transferable, and their knowledge creation efficiency is optimal. In the case of vertical quasi-integration, which corresponds to 'hub-and-spoke' architecture, the dominant partner, the 'hub', possesses technological knowledge asymmetrically and 'has at its disposal the know-how of the subcontractor';[7] this means that the subcontractor is locked in a particular technology and dependent on the customer. The distribution of knowledge is asymmetric and so is the allocation of the relational quasi-rent. Finally, in the case of oblique quasi-integration, the subcontractor possesses the know-how and the technology to produce according to the customer's order.

Leborgne and Lipietz (1992) argue that the more horizontal quasi-integration is the more efficient the mesoeconomic system becomes, and, subsequently, that 'the upgrading of the partner increases the efficiency of the whole network.'[8] The validity of this assertion is debatable, given that different types of industrial organization accommodate optimally different types of economic agents and inter-agent relational structures, and there is clearly a need for an empirical investigation of the efficiency of the different modes of industrial organization under different techno-economic contexts. However, in the particular case of technological knowledge creation, there is sufficient empirical evidence that firms in transition to the post-Fordist, knowledge economy exhibit the tendency to externalize R&D components of their activities by subcontracting, and thus to increasingly rely on technological knowledge produced outside their organizational structure: Many firms – including large corporations – are shifting from vertical integration to more flexible modes of industrial organization with regard to R&D activity – such as quasi-integration – in order to exploit technological spillovers, to avoid technological lock-ins, to pool the risk of investment in new and often uncharted territories of technological knowledge, to share the high costs of research, but also to take advantage of the potentially increased efficiency of networks in generating and diffusing new technological knowledge compared to hierarchical organizational structures.

Even when large corporations have the resources to invest in uncertain research projects, radical innovations are sometimes introduced in small start-up firms, which are not locked in existing firm routines. Empirical evidence shows that firms in knowledge-intensive industries, no matter how big they may be, increasingly rely on subcontracting in order to innovate. Small start-up firms with specialized cognitive assets that occupy very specific technological niches can play a vital role in the innovation process. These small firms can also act as intermediaries between institutionalized research in universities and public research centres and large corporations. Saxenian (1994) argues, for instance, that the small firms of Silicon Valley have been more innovative than the large East Coast firms because of their ability to develop multiple connections in dense networks of knowledge, which allows rapid transfer of information and innovative ideas. On the other hand, there is evidence that in some sectors of the economy quasi-integration, especially among low-tech SMEs, is not conducive to the generation of radical technological discoveries, and that technological lock-in is not an unusual phenomenon in mature quasi-integrated systems of this kind; incremental innovations in such cases are more usual than radical innovations (see Table 4.1).

There is a need for further empirical research on the relationship between the different types of technological knowledge – following the classification of the previous paragraph – and the modes of industrial organization that these types are related to Table 4.2). However, it is reasonable to assume that the first type of technological knowledge, that is, the formal and fully codifiable 'scientific' knowledge, is predominantly produced within globally networked scientific communities, due to its lack of local specificity and its perfect transferability. The second type of technological knowledge, that is, the codifiable, patented 'applied' knowledge, would be expected to be produced in both quasi-integrated and integrated systems. The third type of technological knowledge, that is, the partially codifiable but non-patented 'corporate' knowledge, is almost exclusively produced in vertically integrated systems that internalize the accruing technology rent. Finally, the fourth type of technological knowledge, that is, the non-codifiable, 'tacit'

Table 4.1 Modes of industrial organization and knowledge integration

Mode	Knowledge integration	Incentive structure	Rent distribution
Vertical integration *Horizontal integration*	Cognitive assets under single ownership and management	Authority	Full appropriation of technological rent
Vertical quasi-integration	Dominant partner possesses know-how of subcontractor	Control	Asymmetric allocation of relational quasi-rent
Oblique quasi-integration	Subcontractor possesses know-how to produce according to customer's order	Control; competition	Quasi-symmetric allocation of relational quasi-rent
Horizontal quasi-integration	Distributed knowledge	Trust, partnership	Symmetric allocation of relational quasi-rent

Table 4.2 Types of technological knowledge and industrial organization

Knowledge types	Characteristics	Modes of Industrial organization
TYPE I: *Scientific*	• Formal, objectifiable, codifiable, non-embodied in economic agents • Non-rival, non-excludable, 'public good' • Non-appropriable, generating externalities, privately under-produced • Transferable through supra-local networks, non-localized	Horizontal quasi-integration
TYPE II: *Patented*	• Codifiable, patented, non-embodied in economic agents • Non-rival, partially excludable but generally accessible, 'quasi-public good' • Appropriable • Transferable, locally produced but supra-locally utilized	Vertical integration Horizontal, vertical and oblique quasi-integration
TYPE III: *Organizational*	• Semi-formal, objectifiable, partially codifiable, non-patented, embodied in organizational structures • Rival and excludable, 'private good' • Appropriable, generating technology rent when protected • Transferable through intra-organizational networks, partially localized	Vertical integration
TYPE IV: *Tacit*	• Partially non-objectifiable, non-codifiable, tacit and contextual, embodied in economic agents • Rival and excludable, 'private good' • Acquired through learning-by-doing and training • Non-transferable, highly localized	All

knowledge that is embodied in human capital in the form of know-how and skills, is certainly found in all micro- and mesoeconomic systems and all types of industrial organization.

4.1.3 Red Queen dynamics: innovation as co-evolutionary strategy

The shifting frontier of inter-firm competition in the knowledge economy leads to the intensification of product differentiation by innovation and to the subsequent shortening of the product life-cycle. By innovating, firms constantly create new niches of absolute advantage and temporarily secure their market power and share against potential imitators. This has become a generalized corporate strategy aiming at rendering mature products obsolete and thereby reducing their profitability, so that potential market entrants are not able to compete in terms of production costs with incumbent firms. The phenomenon of innovation-based (instead of price-based) competition among firms in a continuous effort to simply maintain market shares and to avert product imitation by rivals evokes the **Red Queen principle** from evolutionary biology: In the capitalist arms race, innovation is used as a survival strategy. This term was introduced by the evolutionary biologist Van Valen (1973), according to whom 'for an evolutionary system, continuing development is needed just in order to maintain its fitness relative to the systems it is co-evolving with'. The result of this competitive co-evolution process is a zero-sum game, as the relative fitness of the competing systems remains the same. As Markose (2005) observes, by this principle 'the rivalrous co-evolution of species is seen to be a spur to the evolution of complexity itself, manifesting, however, no net gains in relative fitness.'[9]

The innovation arms race transforms the nature of competitive advantage and, consequently, the organizational structure of the firm: traditionally, the competitive advantage of the firm is based on cost reduction and economies of scale, or product differentiation and economies of scope. By contrast, innovation-based competition is based on flexibility and rapidity in searching, tracking down, tapping, transforming and utilizing new knowledge, intensive specialization, and 'economies of complexity'. Whereas the realization of economies of scale and scope requires vertical and horizontal integration respectively, economies of complexity are better attained under the quasi-integrated mode of network structures. This mode – as we argued in a previous paragraph – not only enables economic agents in knowledge-intensive sectors to better exploit technological spillovers, but also better positions them in the complex division of labour of the innovation process, in which a high degree of specialization and asset specificity is required.[10]

4.2   Cognition in complex adaptive systems

4.2.1   Cognition by adaptive agents

4.2.1.1   *Structure of adaptive agents*

The black box of technological knowledge in complex economic systems can only be opened by examining the intricate relationship between cognition and adaptation, first at the level of individual adaptive agents and then at the level of adaptive multiagent systems (complex adaptive systems). Despite the significant progress in the field of artificial intelligence, cognitive theories of adaptive agents are still in their infancy. For the purposes of our study, the exploration of the topic will not extend beyond the fundamental understanding of the causal relationship between adaptation and cognition; in this study we will not, therefore, explore the ontological dimensions of knowledge.

An **adaptive agent** is an entity that interacts with its environment and tries to accomplish a set of goals – such as the maximization of his pay-off function or the increase of his fitness; in other words, it is an entity that conducts *search in a fitness landscape in order to optimize his objective function*. The adaptive agent interacts with his environment in two fundamental ways: he can sense the environment through his **detectors** and act upon the environment through his **effectors**. These two functions are mediated by the agent's internal information-processing and decision-making mechanism. As the capacities of his information-processing apparatus are limited and the information signals he receives from his environment are noisy, the adaptive agent cannot function as a hyperrational global optimizer with perfect foresight. For this reason, the adaptive agent needs an internal, finite representation of reality, which functions as an inference-making apparatus and provides him with anticipatory and predictive capacities. An element of this apparatus is the capacity to store structured information in 'memory', in the form of 'knowledge' that is recalled and used during the inference-making process and the formation of expectations. This apparatus is referred to as **internal model** in Holland (1996) or **schema** in Gell-Mann (1994).[11]

4.2.1.2   *Schemata, cognitive theory and constructivism*

The notion of mental 'schema' is essentially drawn from modern cognitive theory.[12] This strand of theory considers that knowledge stored in memory is structured as a set of discrete schemata, that is, mental representations of types of objects or events of the environment reached through the sensory apparatuses. Knowledge is, therefore, an internalized representation of reality constructed by the agents and not simply acquired from the environment – hence the term **constructivism** to refer to this strand of theory. The process of filtering the sensory stimuli received from the environment, and structuring and storing their information content in memory is known as

bottom-up processing. The use of knowledge already stored in memory for inference-making purposes is known as **top-down processing**. Schemata operate as top-down processing apparatuses that have been generated and are updated through bottom-up processing.

Schemata are internalized models of 'reality'. These models are not necessarily 'correct' or optimal and for this reason they are constantly revised as a result of the accumulation of new experiences and of learning. Learning is the process by which the symbolic representations of reality become embedded into memory and by which new experiences are incorporated in existing cognitive structures. The updating of the schemata is the quintessence of the process of adaptation through learning: The agents' success in achieving their goals, in increasing their fitness (i.e., the number of offspring in biological terms) and, eventually, in surviving depends on their ability to improve their internal models through the process of learning. According to Holland (1996), an agent's performance system is a collection of rules with a given syntactic structure and a mechanism for updating the relative strength of the rules according to their pay-offs, called credit assignment. This is essentially a fundamental learning process based on trial-and-error.

4.2.1.3   *Schemata, adaptation and evolution*

Schemata are not exhaustive representations of reality but rather a set of generic rules that can be evoked and applied contingently to external stimuli. These schemata have a modular structure: they consist of simpler **modules** or as Holland (1996) calls them, 'building blocks'. The updating of schemata is essentially a process of recombination of existing modules or, much less frequently, the discovery of new ones. In socio-economic systems the adaptation of an agent's schema by recombining existing modules would correspond to incremental innovation, while the introduction of new modules correspond to radical innovation. In a biological context, the first process corresponds to crossover, while the second corresponds to mutation. The fitness of an agent endowed with a particular schema can be calculated by genetic algorithms that make use of the two genetic operators, namely the crossover and the mutation operator, together with a fitness function.[13] In this context, the cognitive functions of the agent can be represented by information processing models, whose updating rules are given by algorithms.

4.2.2   Distributed cognition in complex adaptive systems

4.2.2.1   *Cognition, co-adaptation and emergence*

Adaptive agents can in themselves be complex adaptive systems consisting of lower-order adaptive agents: So for instance, the agents at the microeconomic level – the firms and the households – are aggregations of individuals who themselves are adaptive agents; the agents at the mesoeconomic level, the plexuses, are collections of firms; and finally, the macroeconomy is an aggregation of firms and households from the neoclassical point of view, or of interacting mesoeconomic plexuses from the theoretical perspective we developed in Chapter 3. Higher-order aggregations of adaptive agents are often referred to as **meta-agents**.[14] As a result of emergent aggregate properties, meta-agents are ontologically different from lower-order agents and have their own emergent schemata, which determine their operational regimes: a multicellular organism, for instance, is ontologically different in its properties and behaviour from the single cell or the monocellular organism. A meta-agent's schema is not simply an aggregation of the schemata of its constituent lower-order agents. A challenging issue in the study of complex adaptive systems is to understand and model the way these schemata and, more generally, the operational macro-regimes of meta-agents emerge from that of lower-order agents.

We distinguish two very general types of meta-agents according to their internal architecture: first, hierarchical networks with unitary architecture and predetermined or fixed macro-structure, such as corporations, or, in biology, multicellular organisms, which we will refer to as **integrated systems**. Lower-level agents in such formations are fully and irreversibly specialized with fixed in-between links. Second, non-hierarchical (also called 'heterarchical') networks with open architecture and evolving macro-structure, which we will refer to as **distributed systems**. Such formations include mesoeconomic plexuses, cities and industrial districts considered as complex adaptive systems, or, in biology, colonial organisms and other local symbiotic ecosystems. In these systems, lower-order agents are semi-specialized and semi-autonomous with relatively stable but flexible in-between links. These links are made possible by complementarities in the schemata of lower-order agents that favour symbiotic relationships.

Complementarities are the result of **co-adaptation** and **co-evolution**. In the case of biological systems, the development of complementarities is a long-run inter-generational co-evolutionary process that involves the mechanisms of selection and inheritance. In the case of socio-economic systems, complementarities are mainly generated by co-adaptation. The transmission of behavioural patterns from one individual to another is a short-run, intra- and inter-generational process that takes place through imitation and communication. More specifically, communication is the means of transmitting the explicit, codifiable elements of the agents' schemata.

4.2.2.2   *Intersubjective knowledge and distributed cognition*

In the previous section we saw that knowledge can be construed as the subject-matter of the schemata of individual adaptive agents; in this context, technological knowledge, in particular, would be the equivalent of the subject-matter of economic agents' schemata. This traditionally cognitivist approach explains how knowledge accrues to individual agents; it does not explain, however, how knowledge accrues to multi-agent systems. As we have already observed in a previous paragraph, technological knowledge is by nature predominantly systemic and not individualistic; a theory that explains how systemic knowledge accrues is, therefore, essential for understanding the nature of technological knowledge.

The knowledge accumulated in an agent's schema consists of three distinct subsets, which we will refer to as **cognitive domains**, depending on the degree to which this knowledge is relevant to the agent as individual or to the system where the agent belongs: there is a subset of the agent's schema, a cognitive domain, that is not reproduced in other agents' schemata and, therefore, is relevant exclusively to the agent as individual; this is the domain of **subjective** knowledge. There is a cognitive domain that is replicated in all agents' schemata within a given multiagent system; this is the subset of the codifiable and reproducible type of knowledge that we will refer to as the domain of **objective** knowledge. Finally, there is a cognitive domain in an agent's schema that is 'topologically' mapped on similar domains of other agents' schemata without being replicated in them; this is the domain of **intersubjective** knowledge. This domain consists of tacit, non-codifiable elements of the agents' schemata, which are systemically integrated despite the fact that they cannot be directly replicated and transmitted. There is a clear correspondence between these three cognitive domains and the types of knowledge we identified in Section 1.1 [see Table 4.3].

Systemic knowledge, according to this classification scheme, involves the cognitive domains of objective and intersubjective knowledge. With regard to intersubjective knowledge, a fundamental question is how this vital type of knowledge is 'extracted', or more accurately, 'externalized' and integrated in the operational regime of a multiagent system, that is, how it becomes systemic. The answer to this question is that intersubjective knowledge is integrated through the process of co-adaptation: We have already observed that co-evolutionary dynamics shape complementarities among individual

Table 4.3 Cognitive domains and types and sources of technological knowledge

Cognitive domain	Type of technological knowledge	Main source
Objective	Scientific	Distributed systems
	Patented	Integrated systems
Intersubjective	Organizational	Integrated systems; distributed systems
	Tacit	Distributed systems
Subjective	Tacit	Individual agents

agents. These complementarities consist in topological mappings between the correspondent cognitive domains of adaptive agents – the domains of intersubjective knowledge.

Related to the question how knowledge is integrated in multiagent systems is the theory of **distributed cognition**:[15] This is a branch and a new paradigm of cognitive science that examines how cognitive processes are distributed across social groups and how internal (such as the schemata) and external (environment, cognitive artefacts, etc.) cognitive structures are co-ordinated. In the case of socio-economic multiagent systems, distributed cognition emanates from the integration of intersubjective knowledge through the division of labour. Distributed systems are par excellence capable of distributed cognition and asynchronous information processing. In such systems the collective schema is the result of emergence and self-organization, and, as such, it has a decentralized and open-ended architecture. Knowledge generation in such systems is a multilevel emergence process: It involves complex networks of adaptive agents interacting at several different ontological levels, extending from that of the neurons of the nervous system of individuals, to groups of individual researchers in organizations, to innovative plexuses of firms and other organizations, and finally, to the global network of innovative plexuses. At each one of these levels there is emergence with multiplicative effects on the knowledge output. Knowledge creation in these systems is, therefore, a genuinely complex synergetic process determined by the level and the architecture of the relational structure in which it has effect rather than by individual agents.

4.2.2.3   Knowledge as embedded information

The next step in understanding cognition in complex adaptive systems is to explore the fundamental relationship between information and knowledge from a macroscopic systemic perspective. Information, construed as a flow, has an important impact on the structure of dissipative complex adaptive systems: First of all, it is a stimulus that effects adaptive agents and causes their reaction, which eventually leads to their adaptation to changing external conditions and to the updating of their schemata. At the systemic level, information flows reduce systemic informational entropy ('Shannon's entropy'): Dissipative systems capture information flows and use them to increase their internal complexity. This process consists in using 'free' information for reordering the lower-order building blocks of the collective schema of the system, and thus transforming free information into systemically embedded and structured information; technological knowledge is exactly this systemically embedded information that allows the reordering or the discovery of new building blocks employed in economic activity. Ordering a disordered system, such as a pre-equilibrium or out-of-equilibrium market, requires a considerable amount of information proportional to the entropic state of the system. In the case of adaptive systems, homeostasis – the preservation of structure against entropic degradation in the direction of the thermodynamic equilibrium – and adaptation – the rearrangment of the structure vis-à-vis a changing environment require capturing and utilizing information in the way analysed above.

Conclusions

Information processing and knowledge creation are fundamental functions of mesoeconomic plexuses. These systems are adaptive meta-agents and, as such, they possess own cognitive schemata, which are the result of self-organization and emergence out of the schemata of lower-order agents, and not a simple aggregation of these schemata in an additive fashion. The cognitive schemata of mesoeconomic plexuses have an open architecture and an evolving macro-structure that is shaped by the co-evolutionary dynamics of lower-order adaptive agents. Co-adaptation, as part of these dynamics, plays a crucial role in the integration of the intersubjective domains of knowledge in the schemata of lower-order agents, that is, the individual firms and organizations that form the plexus.

Compared to the closed and hierarchical architecture of integrated systems, such as the large 'Fordist' corporations, the flexible open architecture of these non-hierarchical, quasi-integrated multiagent systems, the mesoeconomic plexuses, is favoured by the macro-regime of the 'post-Fordist' knowledge economy. The plexuses are capable of capturing information, processing it and converting it into new knowledge; they are also capable of internalizing knowledge spill-overs more efficiently than other mesoeconomic formations with more rigid organizational structures. However, they are more efficient in specific types of knowledge rather than others: Their efficiency is contingent upon the type of knowledge they are handling, and in particular on the potential of this technological knowledge to generate appropriable rent. Vertically integrated innovation systems perform better when they handle knowledge that generates a directly appropriable technology rent with little spill-overs. In the knowledge economy, however, the main volume of knowledge produced does not necessarily fall under this category – a fact that favours quasi-integrated network-like innovation systems.

The macro-regime of the knowledge economy is characterized by the rapid expansion of the technological frontier due to a 'Red Queen'-type of co-evolutionary dynamics. As a result of these dynamics, the appropriable technological rent is minimized: firms compete in terms of innovation just for survival and in order to preserve their market shares, which are under constant challenge by new discoveries and by the competitive pressures from new specialized firms or expanding incumbent firms. This macro-regime favours 'economies of complexity' rather than economies of scale; the mesoeconomic plexus is the par excellence mesoeconomic formation that generates the former rather than the latter.

Notes

1   *Maxwell's demon* is a fictional intelligent being, which can observe the state of the molecules in a system of gas in equilibrium and to separate them according to their speed, thus reversing the system's entropy. The *Walrasian auctioneer* is also a fictional entity, who matches supply and demand in all markets costlessly, thus making feasible the instantaneous attainment of general equilibrium without transaction costs.

2   See Kogut and Zander (1992); Grant (1996); Spender (1996).

3   Bonifacio et al. (2003).

4   By *partially excludable* we refer to the fact that there is free access to patented knowledge, but the use of this knowledge for economic purposes is protected by property rights for a certain period of time, and is, therefore, not free. Technically speaking, a non-rival but excludable good is called *collective*. Patented technological knowledge can be considered as a collective good.

5   The conceptualization of innovation as a systemic process is common in the long literature of 'Systems of Innovation', such as in Dosi et al. (1988); Lundvall (1992); Edquist (1997); and others.

6   Leborgne and Lipietz (1992), p. 341.

7   Leborgne and Lipietz (1992), p. 341.

8   Leborgne and Lipietz (1992), p. 399.

9   Markose (2005), F178.

10   The distinction between technological spill-overs – an unintended by-product of technological knowledge creation – and the complex division of labour of the innovation process is similar to that between externalities and the external division of labour will be observed in Chapter 5.

11   In a not so different epistemological context, the notion of *schema* is first introduced by Kant in his *Kritik der reinen Vernunft*. This notion is further developed in a structuralist context by the influential Swiss psychologist Jean Piaget. See Piaget (1970; 1971).

12   Modern cognitive theory is mainly based on Piaget's theory of cognitive development, and has also received strong influence from Gestalt theory, Chomsky's structuralism in linguistics and Broadbent's information processing model.

13   Flake (2000) gives the following definition for *genetic algorithms* (GA): 'A method of simulating the action of evolution within a computer. A population of fixed-length strings is evolved with a GA by employing crossover and mutation operators along with a fitness function that determines how likely individuals are to reproduce. GAs perform a type of search in a fitness landscape.' A simple genetic algorithm combining crossover with mutation is given by Holland's (1996) '*schema theorem*'.

14   See Holland (1996), p. 11.

15   The concept of *distributed cognition* was introduced by Hutchins and Norman (1988). A pioneer of the distributed cognition paradigm, however, was Vygotsky (1978), later followed by Minsky (1985). The *distributed processing model* is also directly related to the concept of *parallel distributed processing* and *connectionism* – the strand of cognitive science that treats cognitive processes as emergent phenomena of *neural networks*. A standard reference in the theory of parallel distributed processing is McClelland and Rumelhart (1988). More recent references in distributed cognition theory include Rogers and Ellis (1994).

References

Bonifacio, M., P. Bouquet, G. Mameli, and M. Nori (2003), 'Peer-mediated distributed knowledge management', *University of Trento, Technical report DIT-03-032*.

Dosi, G., et al., eds (1988), *Technical Change and Economic Theory*, Pinter, London.

Edquist, C., ed. (1997), *Systems of Innovation: Technologies, Institutions and Organizations*, Pinter, London.

Flake, G. W. (2000), *The Computational Beauty of Nature: Computer Explorations of Fractals, Chaos, Complex Systems and Adaptation*, The MIT Press, Cambridge, MA.

Gell-Mann, M. (1994), *The Quark and the Jaguar: Adventures in the Simple and the Complex*, Freeman, New York.

Grant, R. M. (1996), 'Toward a knowledge-based theory of the firm', *Strategic Management Journal*, Vol. 17, pp. 109–22.

Holland, J. H. (1996), *Hidden Order: How Adaption Builds Complexity*, Basic Books, New York.

Hutchins, E., and D. A. Norman (1988), 'Distributed cognition in aviation: A concept paper for NASA (Contract No. NCC 2-591), Department of Cognitive Science, University of California, San Diego.

Kogut, B., and U. Zander (1992), 'Knowledge of the firm, combinative capabilities, and the replication of technology', *Organization Science*, Vol. 3, No. 3, pp. 383–97.

Leborgne, D., and A. Lipietz (1992), 'Conceptual fallacies and open questions on post-Fordism', in Storper, M. and Scott, A. J., eds, *Pathways to Industrialization and Regional Development*, Routledge, London, pp. 332–48.

Lundvall, B. Å. ed. (1992), *National Systems of Innovation: Towards a Theory of Innovation and Interactive Learning*, Pinter, London.

Markose, S. M. (2005), Computability and evolutionary complexity: Markets as complex adaptive systems (CAS), *The Economic Journal*, Vol. 115, No. 504, F159–F192.

McClelland, J. L., and D. E. Rumelhart (1988), *Explorations in Parallel Distributed Processing*, MIT Press, Cambridge, MA.

Minsky, M. (1985), *Society in Mind*, Simon & Schuster, New York.

Piaget, J. (1970, *Structuralism*, Harper & Row, New York.

Piaget, J. (1971), *Biology and Knowledge*, University of Chicago Press, Chicago.

Rogers, Y., and J. Ellis (1994), 'Distributed cognition: an alternative framework for analysing and explaining collaborative working', *Journal of Information Technology*, Vol. 9, No. 2, pp. 119–28.

Saxenian, A. L. (1994), *Regional Advantage: Culture and Competition in Silicon Valley and Route 128*, Harvard University Press, Cambridge, MA.

Spender, J. C. (1996), 'Making knowledge the basis of a dynamic theory of the firm', *Strategic Management Journal*, Vol. 17, pp. 45–62.

Van Valen, L. (1973), 'A new evolutionary law', *Evolutionary Theory*, Vol. 1, No. 1, pp. 1–30.

Vygotsky, L. S. (1978), *Mind in Society: Development of Higher Psychological Processes*, Harvard University Press, Cambridge, MA.

5
Evolution of the Bangalore ICT Cluster: A Stage Theory Based on the Crystal Growth Model

Mathew J. Manimala
Indian Institute of Management, Bangalore

Industrial clusters have been recognized as an important tool for the economic development of a region. Research has hence focused on the identification of the essential ingredients of an innovation ecosystem that would support and sustain a business cluster, so that such clusters could be promoted by creating the relevant ecosystem. Having studied well-developed clusters, researchers often come out with a comprehensive list of such ecosystem ingredients such as: geographical proximity of firms, sectoral specialization within the cluster, close inter-firm interactions, access to investment funds and financial services, infrastructural facilities, favourable government policies, business support services, technology sources and support, and social capital and formal/informal networks among entrepreneurs. An often-unstated inference from these findings is that such ingredients are the cause of cluster formation, and therefore the best way to promote a business cluster is to create such institutions in the proposed region. What is often forgotten is the fact that many of these institutions or characteristics are consequences, rather than causes, of cluster development. An evolutionary study of the Bangalore ICT cluster has shown that there are at least four distinguishable stages of cluster development, namely: incubation, nucleation, agglomeration and attrition, with each of them being supported by a different type of ecosystem. The chapter discusses the characteristic features of these stages, and makes broad inferences of the support required for each stage. In general, it may be stated that the first two stages constitute one phase of cluster development, and will be helped by building the general capabilities of the region through the creation of physical and intellectual infrastructure and the promotion of openness and interaction with the external world. The last two stages constituting the second phase are characterized by industry-specific institutions, which initially arise as a consequence of cluster development and later become the cause of further clusterization.

Introduction

The 'secrets of the industry are in the air', wrote Alfred Marshall (1890) more than one hundred years ago. He made this apparently intriguing statement while discussing the phenomenon of industrial clusters, specifically the Sheffield Cutlery Cluster. Some modern scholars interpret his words (see, for example, Feldman 2001) as referring to the non-tangible non-pecuniary factors that constitute the social capital of a region (Coleman, 1988; Nahapiet and Ghoshal, 1998; Burt, 2000; Liao and Welsch, 2005; Myint et al., 2005) that facilitate the free flow and sharing of ideas and information, and thereby stimulate the clustering of specific types of businesses in certain regions. Such interpretations may often be dismissed as 'retroactive clairvoyance'. Marshall was probably expressing his inability to pinpoint the specific factors that trigger the cluster formation in a particular region. Whatever that may be, the fact remains that clustering of industries is a natural phenomenon and that its explanation and replication is seen as a major tool for bringing about economic development especially for depressed regions. The difficulty, however, is in identifying these factors and establishing their links with economic development.

The factors identified in various studies are so diverse and often ill defined that it is almost impossible to organize and build any meaningful and productive ecosystem based on these findings. It is observed that the efforts to replicate such clusters in new places have rarely produced any spectacular successes; many such experiments, especially in developing countries, have ended up in failures, and others continue with their lackluster existence (Monck et al., 1988; Storey and Strange, 1992; Hauschildt and Steinkuhler, 1994; Manimala 1997; Perry 2005; Alecke et al., 2006). Obviously this is a testimony to the inadequacy of the current research on the ecosystem for industrial clusters. One reason for the inadequacy of research findings to support replication efforts may be that almost all these studies are conducted after the event of cluster formation, and therefore the cause–effect relationships among the variables are attributed by researchers in retrospect. Besides, if a developed cluster is seen to be associated with certain institutions, systems, conditions, they cannot be legitimately interpreted as causes of cluster development; they may very well be the consequences of it (Feldman, 2001). If one were to use a familiar simple physiological analogy, the findings from a study of the characteristics of adults cannot be directly applied to understand the characteristics of newborn babies. Similar is the case of studying the characteristics of established entrepreneurs/enterprises to understand the characteristics of start-up entrepreneurs/enterprises (Manimala, 1999). The role theory of personality (Moreno, 1977) would suggest that the personality of an individual is likely to be modified on account of the roles they play. Naturally studies conducted after the roles are enacted may not give adequate information about what the individual was before. Cluster studies too suffer from this limitation. Hence the present review of the studies on the Bangalore cluster will attempt to separate the issues relating to the different phases of cluster development and propose a 'stage theory of cluster formation'.

5.1   Characteristics of an 'innovation' ecosystem

Since the development of a business cluster involves the start-up and growth of a large number of ventures in the region, often within a short period of time, it is considered to be a product as well as a source of a large number of innovations. Hence the physical, social and intellectual characteristics of such regions are often seen as constituting an innovation ecosystem (Bahrami and Evans, 2000). Studies on such regions have emphasized different aspects of their 'innovation sponsoring capabilities', and accordingly have chosen to call these regions by different names such as 'habitat for innovation and entrepreneurship' (Lee et al., 2000), 'incubator region' (Schoonhoven et al., 1990), and 'social structure of innovation' (Florida and Kenney, 1988). The essential characteristics of such an ecosystem, as identified by various researchers and reported in the literature, are summarized below (Piore and Sabel, 1984; Miller and Cote, 1985; Krugman, 1991; Saxenian, 1994; Markusen, 1996; Rosa, 1998; Porter, 1998; Shridharan and Manimala, 1999; Feldman, 2001; Kenney and Patton, 2005; Garnsey and Heffernan, 2005).

- *Geographical proximity of firms.*   A large number of firms, predominantly small and medium-sized ones, are located in a geographically bounded space.

- *Sectoral specialization.*   The cluster as a whole specializes in a specific industrial sector. That, however, does not mean that all the firms in the cluster are competing with one another. There are, indeed, a few firms in each segment of the value chain that compete with one another. These subclusters, where members compete with one another, are called the *horizontal clusters*. But a large majority of the firms in the cluster form part of the *vertical clusters* operating in different segments of the value chain in the sector, and therefore are collaborating with one another as customers and suppliers.

- *Close interactions among firms.*   As mentioned above, such interactions may be in terms of collaboration or competition, both of which help in stimulating innovation. Collaboration helps in the sharing of ideas and in building on them, while competition helps in identifying more stimulating benchmarks and in enhancing one's competencies to outperform the benchmarks themselves.

- *Access to investment funds and financial services.* The factor of 'funding support' is almost exclusively equated with the operations of the venture capital companies in the Western literature on clusters. In developing countries like India, where the formal venture capital companies are of recent origin and are still considered an 'elitist' source of equity funds, the factor of 'funding support' should be understood in a broader sense to include any kind of equity sources such as friends and relatives, local money lenders, and angel investors. Investment is still not a professional activity in developing countries, and the average entrepreneur has to muddle his way through to making his initial investment.

- *Infrastructural facilities.* Unlike in the developing countries, the cluster literature in the developed world often ignores the role of infrastructure in supporting cluster formation. This is because most places in the developed world are provided with the basic infrastructural facilities like roads, railways, airports, telephones, the internet and other connectivities, water, power, banks, educational institutions, hospitals, and so on. Obviously these are major concerns in the developing world even in their well-developed industrial clusters.

- *Favourable Government Policies.* There is a wide range of government policies that could have direct or indirect impact on entrepreneurial activities. Some examples of such policies are those pertaining to: monopolies/reservations for the public sector and the areas of freedom for the private sector; private property and transactions; individual and corporate taxation; foreign ownership of firms, operations of foreign firms, collaborations and repatriation of profits; foreign exchange rules; import and export policies; travel and visa policies; travel and commercial activities of non-residents; efficiency of the bureaucracy and the speed of administrative clearances, and so on. In all these matters, the 'policy-in-practice' is more important than the stated policies, especially in developing countries, where there are also concerns about corruption in the administrative system.

- *Business support services.* Availability of business services (such as lawyers, accountants, technologists, trainers, management consultants, etc) at affordable costs is identified by researchers as a facilitating factor for cluster formation. However, the use of such services by small and medium enterprises in developing countries is limited and is unlikely to be a major reason for joining the cluster.

- *Social capital.*   Cluster research in recent times has given special attention to the formal and informal network structures and relations in a cluster, which is collectively designated as the social capital of the region. Networks of this kind operate at three levels: at the cognitive level, what matters is the perceptions of people about the interlinkages and preferential dealings among the individuals and units; the structural level shows the formal linkages in place; and the relational level is about the actual behavioural interactions among individuals and units. Such networks among individuals and units are found to encourage professionalism, creativity and risk-taking and thereby lead to the creation of more businesses in the region.

- *Technology sources and support.*   The units in the cluster need to have adequate sources of new technologies and get continued support for sustained innovation. The Western literature generally equates this to the presence of a university or R&D centre in the region. Such institutions may not be available in all clusters in the developing countries, or may have been developed after the cluster is formed. There are many cases where the cluster's technology needs are taken care of primarily by the business interactions with customers and suppliers, who may often be located outside the cluster, sometimes in other countries.

While all the nine factors listed above are mentioned in the literature as characteristics of industrial clusters, there is a tendency to treat the last six as the causes of clustering and the first three as the effects. However, a longitudinal analysis of cluster development would show that all of these characteristics could also emerge as consequences of cluster formation, and later serve as causes of further clustering. It would therefore imply that the 'characteristics' of the cluster-region would be different during different phases of its development, and that there might be a dominant factor or a few of them (often different for different regions and phases) affecting its development in each phase. The remaining part of this paper attempts to verify and elaborate on these hypotheses, based on an analysis of the literature on the evolution of the Bangalore ICT cluster.

5.2   Evolution of the Bangalore ICT cluster

The ICT cluster of Bangalore, aptly called the 'Silicon Valley of India', is one of the largest in the world, comprising more than 1200 software companies (of which about 125 are MNCs) with a combined turnover of about US$ 3 billion as of 2003. They offer different types of products and services such as: system software (16 per cent), application software (28 per cent), communication software (11 per cent), services (29 per cent), integrated circuit design (4 per cent), and general software (12 per cent), thus covering almost all the areas of software development and services. In addition, there are a large number of ITES and BPO companies and a few hardware companies as well. Each year there are over 100 new companies coming up in Bangalore, and the total turnover of the cluster doubles in every two years, most of which are from the export market (see www.karnataka.com; www banga-loreit.com). According to current estimates, there are more engineers in Bangalore than in Silicon Valley, the city has more engineering colleges than any other city in the world and has more than 40,000 PhDs working in its R&D institutions, which number over 100 (www.businessweek; *Economic Times* 2004).

The traditional perception that the Bangalore cluster produces 'low-cost/low-quality' products and services has also undergone a significant change. The output of the cluster is recognized as meeting world-class standards. One testimony to this comes from the fact that out of the 40 SEI CMM Level-5 companies, 29 are in India and 18 are in Bangalore! (see www.karnataka.com). It is no wonder that the United Nations has ranked Bangalore as the fourth best 'Global Hub of Technological Innovation' (see www.businessweek.com). The city has become a 'text-book' model of an industrial cluster, where there is all-round collaboration among the various players within the cluster. 'The Indus Entrepreneur' (TiE) has its largest chapter in Bangalore; so too the 'Software Process Improvement Network' (SPIN). A crowning example of the cluster's professional net-working is the annual mega event (Bangalore IT.COM) organized by the Government of Karnataka in collaboration with the industry and with participation from all over the world. The is Asia's largest IT Conference and Trade Show, which has been organized every year since 1997 and is currently attracting more than 500 IT and telecom majors from all over the world along with about 150,000 individual visitors. While the theme of the meet changes from year to year, it is essentially a forum for generat-ing business leads, structured networking and pre-arranged meetings for identifying international and domestic outsourcing partners (see www. businessweek.com).

According to most analysts, the starting point of the ICT cluster forma-tion in Bangalore is the setting up of an offshore facility in Bangalore by Texas Instruments (TI) in 1984. The fact that 'www.bangaloreit.com' (the official website of the Karnataka Government's Department of IT and Biotechnology) also mentions this as the first milestone in the evolution of the IT industry in Bangalore (see Exhibit 1) could be treated as sufficient evidence for a consensus that TI 'started' the IT boom in Bangalore. Hence an investigation, to the extent possible, into the factors that influenced TI's initial move is likely to give some insights into the phenomenon of cluster formation itself.

The immediate reason for TI choosing Bangalore as the location for its offshore facility is cited as the alumnus-connections of a high-ranking scientist of TI with the Indian Institute of Science (IISc) Bangalore, who was deputed by the company to set up the offshore facility in India (Deshmukh, 1993). It is interesting to note that the initial decision to move was influenced not so much by the attractiveness of the new location as the unattractiveness of the alternatives. In the specific case of TI, Deshmukh (1993) mentions that the decision to move part of their work out of the US was influenced primarily by the severe 'software manpower crunch' experienced in the early 1980s in the United States and Europe and the very high cost of employing those available there. India was seen as a low-cost economy, with especially low wage-costs even for the English-educated engineering graduates, who were available in plenty. While India was a natural choice for the offshore facility for the above reason, the specific location for this facility would depend on the infrastructural facilities available in potential locations.

Exhibit 1   The evolution of the IT industry and support systems in Bangalore: major milestones

1984	Texas Instruments sets up an offshore development facility in Bangalore.
1984	Indian government announces changes in its computer and software policy, recognizing software as an industry, reducing import duties on hardware and software from 135 per cent to 60 per cent, and at the same time reducing the corporate income tax exemption on net software exports income from 100 per cent to 50 per cent.
1985	Government of Karnataka sets up KEONICS (Karnataka State Electronics Development Corporation Limited) to develop IT and telecom infrastructure and to provide consultancy and training in IT.
1986	Department of Electronics (DoE), Government of India, announces a new software policy, liberalizing imports of hardware and software and increasing the export obligations of hardware importers.
1989	VSNL (Indian government-owned telecom company) commissions a direct 64-kbps satellite link to the US with a new gateway switching system that operated through Intelsat.
1991	Software Technology Parks of India (STPI) scheme was launched by the Ministry of Information Technology (formerly DoE), Government of India, with whom 100 per cent export-oriented software units could be located/registered so that they could get tax/duty exemptions; Bangalore had one of the first STPIs, which subsequently had the fastest growth in membership and was the first park (and also the city) in India to be connected to the Internet.
1992	Government of India sets up exclusive satellite international gateway for software exporters.

1993	Indian government launches the Electronic Hardware Technology Park (EHTP) scheme (similar to the STPI scheme), allowing tax and duty exemptions to 100 per cent export oriented units registered with them.
1997	Government of Karnataka becomes the first state in India to announce its IT policy.
1999	Government of Karnataka establishes Indian Institute of Information Technology (IIIT-B) in collaboration with the IT industry for conducting advanced and industry-oriented courses in IT related subjects.
1999	KITVEN Fund (Karnataka Information Technology Venture Capital Fund) is established jointly by the Karnataka State Industrial Investment Development Corporation (KSIIDC), Karnataka State Financial Corporation (KSFC), and Small Industries Development Bank of India (SIDBI).
2001	NASDAQ opens its office in Bangalore.
2003	The number of software units registered with STPI in Bangalore grows to 1154 (with an export turnover of US\$ 2.67 billion), while those registered with EHTP in Bangalore grows only to 31 (with an export turnover of US\$ 0.30 billion).

(Compiled from www.bangaloreit.com, Basant 2006 , and the websites of specific schemes and agencies mentioned in Exhibit 1)

Considering the availability of international airports and direct data communication links in cities like Mumbai and Delhi, the few predecessors of TI went to these cities. However, on account of the high cost of real estate in these cities, the labour cost advantage was not being fully realized. Besides, there were some political movements in these cities, especially in Mumbai, which were hostile to the entry of foreign MNCs into India (Interview data). TI's search for alternative locations brought them to Bangalore through the project champion's links with IISc. They were happy with the availability and diversity of the managerial and professional talent in Bangalore, which had a special advantage of being located at the boundary of Karnataka state and therefore had labour force pools flowing in from the neighbouring states of Tamil Nadu, Andhra Pradesh and Kerala, which along with Karnataka constitute South India and is the educationally more advanced part of India (Interview data). The influx of technically trained manpower from these and other states of India into Bangalore was facilitated by the setting up of a large number of technology-based firms and research organizations by the Government of India during the three decades immediately following Independence. These organizations were in the areas of defence, space, telecom, aeronautics, machine tools, heavy electricals and equipment, and other high-tech and high priority areas of research and manufacturing, which had liberal funding support from the Central Government and thus could attract and retain the best talents in the country, who created a technology culture and ambience in the city. One of the reasons given for the choice of Bangalore as the location for the defence and space related institutions is that the city is located away from the country's borders (Lateef, 1997). This explanation is only partially true, as it does not explain the setting up of other types of large organizations in Bangalore by the Central Government. A possible reason for this could be the political equations of the state governments of Tamil Nadu and Karnataka with the Central Government. For a long time after Independence, Karnataka had governments by the same party as the one ruling at the Centre, whereas Tamil Nadu lost that status within the first decade of Independence. Naturally therefore the institutions planned for the South were located in Bangalore ignoring the claims of Madras (now Chennai), which was and still is the largest city of the South (Interview data).

One other factor that was mentioned in favour of Bangalore is its mild and 'salubrious' climate (Balasubramanyam, 1998; Lateef, 1997). Though this may be dismissed as a trivial factor by the professionally trained decision maker, our interviews show that it is apparently not so trivial. It is obviously a serious consideration for Western visitors anticipating a long stay. It was also mentioned as important by the cost-conscious, quality-seeking Indian entrepreneurs as well, of course for a different reason. Since electronic systems and equipment could be damaged by excessive heat and dust, these entrepreneurs, especially the small and medium ones, believe that a mild climate will help them reduce the cost of air-conditioning as well as the damages due to heat and dust. One of the entrepreneurs who moved to Bangalore from Baroda during the early 1990s narrated his experience of the location search thus: 'After visiting the four metro cities during the summer months, we came to Bangalore and stepped out of the aircraft to find hardly any difference between the temperatures inside and outside. There and then we decided that Bangalore is the place!' (Interview data).

5.3   Stages of cluster formation: the Crystal Growth Model

IISc connection, diverse and low-cost professional talent, and the climate – would these constitute the 'ecosystem for innovation' and trigger the cluster formation process? They would not, if one were to go by the descriptions of such systems in the research literature. Where are the infrastructure facilities, policy support, venture capital companies, enterprise support services, and the like? In fact, in the early 1980s Bangalore was woefully lacking in a critical piece of infrastructure needed for the IT industry – the direct connectivity for data transfer (Deshmukh, 1993), which was provided only in 1989 (see Exhibit 1). The same may be said about most other ingredients of the ecosystem, as may be observed from Exhibit 1. It seems that in the initial stages of cluster formation, the enterprises are chasing the support system rather than the other way round. There has to be one or more dominant factor(s), based on which a pioneering entrepreneur or entrepreneurial organization makes the first move. The synergistic conditions (gravity) created around the place then attract other players into the locality and together they create or bring in the other ingredients of the ecosystem. For Bangalore, as we have seen, it was the technical ambience/talent pool and the climate. The process is similar even for older clusters, as may be seen from the following examples of two Indian clusters. When Jamshedji Tata laid the foundations of India's steel city at Sakchi (now Jamshedpur), there was nothing in that 'jungle' other than the raw material (Piramal and Herdeck 1985). Similarly, the textile cluster of Ahmedabad owes its origin to the adventurous entrepreneurial spirit of Ranchodlal Chhotalal, who had to import the machinery to Kandla port and transport it in bullock carts in knocked down condition to Ahmedabad, where there was no textile industry-specific infrastructure or institutions other than the raw material and the 'unskilled' workers (Tripathi, 2004).

It becomes clear that the evolution of an industrial cluster is an interactive process among enterprises and institutions, where the initial impetus is from the 'crystallization' of the entrepreneurial enthusiasm of an individual or a company due to their experience of the business environment outside the region and one or more dominant characteristics of the region. The process may be compared to the chemical process of crystal formation and growth. Just as the chemical process goes through certain stages such as saturation, nucleation, growth, agglomeration, and attrition, business clusters also develop through a few comparable stages. These stages may be defined as: (1) Incubation, (2) Nucleation, (3) Agglomeration, and (4) Attrition. In the ensuing part of this section we will briefly describe these four stages with special reference to the Bangalore ICT cluster.

5.3.1 Incubation

The incubation of Bangalore for its future ICT cluster started in the pre-Independence period. Since the establishment of the Cantonment by the British in the eastern part of Bangalore in 1809, it remained a divided city till 1949, as the western part was under the rulers of Mysore. Though such division was then a cause of occasional tension, which later extended to the other regional and ethnic groups flowing into this border city (Nair, 1999), the people-to-people level interactions helped all the groups to develop a multicultural perspective of city life, which sowed the seeds of the famed diversity and tolerance among the Bangalore labour force and has later contributed in no small measure to the development of an industrial cluster of global scope and operations.

While the western side of the city concentrated on traditional industries like textiles, the east had the industries that came with the British, like breweries, tanneries, weaponries and tobacco. This relatively diverse industrial base (and the presence of a diverse workforce) was responsible for bringing even more diversity in the city's industries. The active presence of the British in the city for over a century and a half established a life-style acceptable to Europeans at least in one part of the city. This is probably why, when the German MNC, Bosch, wanted to come to India in 1951, they chose Bangalore for establishing a subsidiary of Bosch, Motor Industries Company (MICO) Limited, which along with the various government and public sector enterprises and R&D organizations mentioned above (whose employment, according to Pani, 1988, was more than 300,000 in the mid-1980s), helped in creating a technology culture and diversity for the Bangalore workforce. Though diversity of workforce in Bangalore is often discussed in terms of ethnic, regional and linguistic groups, one should not forget to emphasize the gender dimension of this factor as well. Ironically, it was the 'traditional' textile industry that has brought about a culture of women's employment in the city. Today there are about 80,000 people employed in Bangalore's garment industry, most of who are women (Nair, 1999). This is no mean achievement in a society, which is known to be conservative about women's employment, and has paved the way for large-scale employment of women (who, according to STEM 2000, were about 21 per cent in 1997 in the IT sector) in IT and BPO companies, so much so that the Government of India recently had to amend the law regarding the employment of women at night.

It is clear that the pattern in the process described above is that it is the enterprise of people that pushes the policy and public support in their favour, not the other way around. This is true of the subsequent stages also, as we have realized when tracing the evolution of the Bangalore cluster (see Exhibit 1). In the earlier phase of incubation, it was the 'enterprising' struggle to control the city by different groups (provided the struggle is accommodative rather than destructive) that brought diversity in its workforce and thereby diverse types of industrial enterprises, which then pushed for institutional/policy support and reforms. It is often mentioned that the role of the Indian Institute of Science (IISc) in promoting and supporting industry in Bangalore (we have seen how it became instrumental in bringing TI into the city) is an example of the causal influence in the reverse direction from institution to industry. Indeed, the accomplishments of IISc in this regard are quite impressive, as the following brief sketch of its 'history' unambiguously demonstrates.

The Indian Institute of Science (IISc), Bangalore, is rightly called the technology incubator for the Bangalore ICT cluster. This pioneering institute was established as early as 1909 in the pre-Independence period at a tripartite initiative (quite uncharacteristic of that period) of J. N. Tata, a private industrialist, the Maharaja of Mysore and the government of British-ruled India, mainly for conducting research in the frontier areas of science and technology. Starting with just three departments (one of them, rather prophetically, was the Department of Electrotechnology), it now has more than 30 departments, 15 centres and 2000 active researchers working on cutting-edge technologies. As we have seen above, the first IT MNC to start operations in Bangalore in 1984 – Texas Instruments – operated through an employee of theirs, who was an alumnus of IISc, which was probably a reason for their choosing Bangalore as the location (Deshmukh, 1993) and illustrates the seminal role of IISc in bringing the IT cluster to Bangalore. As a special initiative for promoting industry interaction, in 1991 IISc created an autonomous agency within itself called the Society for Innovation and Development (SID), which now has joint R&D projects with almost all major companies in Bangalore including the MNCs (such as Texas Instruments, Intel, Nokia, Philips, Hewlett Packard, Motorola, Nortel, and so on) and holds several patents jointly with them (Basant, 2006). IISc has also spun off a few technology-based ventures through SID.

The story of IISc is indeed fascinating, and illustrates how institutions can stimulate and support industry. What is often forgotten is the first part of this story – how IISc came into being as a result of the enterprise of a private individual and his willingness to collaborate with several agencies including public ones to create this institution. J. N. Tata, the entrepreneur, was an 'outsider' to Bangalore, and in some sense, even to India (he was born in Navsari, Gujarat, in a community that migrated from Persia, now Iran, long ago and lived in the periphery of the mainstream Indian society for over 1000 years), and had most of his enterprises in Central and Western India. Tata's roots in different cultures were reinforced by his 15-year-long travel and stay in different countries, where he picked up his industrial and scientific outlook. He was willing to interact and learn from all quarters and collaborate with anyone who had something to contribute to his projects, not excluding even the hostile Viceroy of British India – Lord Curzon (Lala, 2004). And, who were his partners in the IISc venture? The local maharaja and the British rulers. Thus, the 'Bangalore's own' IISc was the product of interaction among at least three cultures (most of them non-Bangalorean), not counting the ones that Tata had absorbed in his travels.

The significant finding of this analysis as well as that of the city itself is that the development of a region happens primarily through its interaction with other cultures, and such development is the most important part of the incubation process that enables the region to receive and support the entrepreneurial initiatives when they arrive. In other words, *a culture that is endogamous and xenophobic cannot incubate and support entrepreneurial initiatives.* Though the interaction of cultures may occasionally lead to some clashes among them, their eventual integration will lead to the development of newer ideas and an enterprising spirit among competing cultures and thereby help the development of the region. An analysis of the development of regions and civilizations amply demonstrate the importance of inter-cultural interaction for development. For example, the Hindu civilization and culture of India, which supported the development of the region in ancient times, emerged from the interaction (and integration) of Aryan culture with the native culture. Subsequently, in modern times, the better-developed regions of the country are the ones that came into direct contact with the British. Even the English culture and the development of the region are linked to several invasions by the Germanic, Norwegian, Danish and French warlords. The language originated when three Germanic tribes invaded the Celtic settlers in the fifth Century AD, and the monarchy, which steered the country's achievements in modern times, was founded by William the Conqueror in the eleventh Century AD. Nearer our times, and in the context of cluster development, the best example of inter-cultural interaction promoting regional development is the Silicon Valley itself. Based on an analysis of Dun and Bradstreet data, Saxenian (1999) states that in 1998 there were 2001 Chinese-run and 774 Indian-run businesses in Silicon Valley, which employed more than 58,000 people and generated USD 16.8 billion in wealth.

It was against the background of the Silicon Valley experience (mentioned above) that some European countries attempt to encourage venture creation by foreign nationals. In the United Kingdom, for example, even though they do not allow foreign students to take up employment in the country, there is a rule allowing a foreign student to stay on if he/she could start a new enterprise in the country within 18 months after completing the course. While the intention of this rule is laudable, it shows a lack of understanding of the 'incubation' process necessary for such start-ups. It may be noted that most of the students from developing countries will be on heavy loans while pursuing their studies, especially in the Western developed countries. Naturally, they cannot think of starting an enterprise until they have worked for sometime and have repaid the loans and saved enough money for the initial investment. Besides, the work experience would also help the potential entrepreneur to understand the market and identify the right opportunity as well as develop the social capital required to nurture and grow the new business. In other words, asking foreign students to start ventures without allowing them to take up employment in the country will not serve the purpose. It may be noted that most of the immigrant entrepreneurs of Silicon Valley took the 'employment route' to entrepreneurship. *An important implication of this experience is that the openness to other cultures and ideas that would facilitate the incubation process has to be of a general and welcoming nature rather than conditional and restrictive.*

5.3.2   Nucleation

The entrepreneurial event that triggers the start-up of a series of enterprises of the same industry sector in a region may be called the nucleation of the cluster phenomenon. As noted above, the arrival of TI is recognized as the nucleation point of the Bangalore ICT cluster. There are such discernible points for other clusters too, which was mentioned above about Jamshedpur and Ahmedabad in India, for example. An important point to remember about the success of nucleation is the adequacy of the incubation process in the preceding phase. To paraphrase the words of Louis Pasteur ('fortune favours the prepared mind'), one could say that the cluster settles on the prepared ground. This preparation, as we have seen, is about the region's openness to new ideas/cultures and receptiveness to entrepreneurial initiatives, which in turn has helped in developing the general capabilities of the region. Nucleation efforts without such prior preparation (planned or evolutionary) are likely to end in failure, as has been demonstrated by several initiatives of governments and public agencies to develop industrial clusters (van Dijk and Rabellotti, 1997; Craig, 2000). Interestingly, Bangalore itself offers an illustration of the differential impact of such promotional efforts in different 'incubation' conditions. The Government of India launched the Software Technology Parks of India (STPI) in 1991 and the Electronic Hardware Technology Park (EHTP) scheme within just two years in 1993, with similar facilitation for the 100 per cent export-oriented units located within these parks. Though Bangalore was one of the first cities to take advantage of both the schemes, there is an almost inexplicable difference in the growth of units under these two schemes in Bangalore. By 2003, STPI had a membership of 1154, whereas EHTP had only 31 (see Exhibit 1). Apparently the 'ecosystem' that would support the software units may not be adequate to support the hardware units. For example, hardware units would require larger investments than those for software units. Similarly they would need more sophisticated manufacturing skills for making high-precision products that were increasingly getting miniaturized. Moreover, the export (transfer) of software could be easily carried out through the wire, whereas for exporting hardware one has to have excellent infrastructural facilities and logistical systems for the physical movement of products. Bangalore is obviously deficient on all these. No wonder, EHTP lagged behind while STPI surged ahead. The implication is that there has to be a fitment between the ingredients of the ecosystem and the requirements of the industry concerned, without which the ideology-induced cluster-development initiatives would not have any impact. This is why in this chapter we devoted a fairly long section on the incubator phase of cluster formation, which is probably the most critical of all phases.

It is interesting to note that the nucleation phase of cluster formation is almost always linked to dynamism in the environment, which is also true of the biological as well as the chemical processes. In the chemical process, the sudden cooling of the external environment of a saturated solution is one of the most commonly observed causes of crystal formation. Similarly, the role of the sudden and turbulent changes in the global business environment in the nucleation of the Bangalore ICT cluster cannot be over-emphasized; these were the shortages and high cost of software manpower in the West and the high real-estate cost and nationalist militancy in the other eligible Indian cities. This special feature of the nucleation process offers a useful lesson to planners and interventionists involved in cluster development. After initiating appropriate measures to build the general capabilities of the region, they should institute mechanisms for constantly scanning the environment for the relevant developments and, accordingly, facilitate suitable entrepreneurial initiatives.

5.3.3   Agglomeration

In the crystallization process, there is a distinction made between the growth stage and the agglomeration stage. This is because the tiny crystal has to achieve a certain level of growth before it can form an agglomeration with other crystals. In the case of business clusters, there are three models in operation (1), where the agglomeration happens after the growth of the nuclear unit; (2), where the growth of the nuclear unit and the agglomeration take place simultaneously; and (3), where the nuclear unit is already in a 'grown up' stage and immediately starts attracting other firms to the region to form an agglomeration. In this paper, the use of the word 'agglomeration' should be understood as including the growth of the nuclear unit wherever applicable.

As in the case of the crystal agglomeration process, there is hardly any need for special efforts or interventions in bringing about the agglomeration if the region is already a 'prepared ground' having gone through a proper incubation phase. The natural ease with which this process has taken place in Bangalore is described by Deshmukh (1993) in the following manner: 'TI became a beacon for attracting hi-tech companies like Digital, HP and Motorola. When Motorola, for example, was selecting a location for its first joint venture in India, the presence of TI, HP and Digital in Bangalore became a key factor in relieving the anxieties of Motorola's top brass in Schaumberg, Illinois' (p. 20). For the MNCs operating in developed countries, there will naturally be some anxiety in going to a new place in a developing country. There is nothing more effective in relieving such anxiety than the demonstration effect of someone of their own ilk having done it. Besides, one will have the professional atmosphere that is necessary for high-tech operations. Even if the experience is going to be miserable, there will be comfort, as the old saying goes, in having 'miserable company' around. In other words, one would not be worse off than one's competitors on account of the decision to make this move.

Agglomerations based on the considerations mentioned above fall in the category of 'horizontal clusters'. There are equally good or better reasons for the formation of 'vertical clusters'. The larger players would attract many other enterprises to the region in different roles such as customers, suppliers, subcontractors, distributors, intermediaries, infrastructure providers, consultants, trainers, service providers, and so on. Since the cluster gets noticed at this stage as a phenomenon to be reckoned with, most researchers start describing all those players as the essential ingredients of the innovation ecosystem. We have, however, explained above the differences in the ingredients of this ecosystem in different stages, which reinforces the need for a stage theory to understand the cluster phenomenon.

5.3.4 Attrition

Though the Bangalore ICT cluster is currently in the agglomeration stage, there are minor signs of attrition from the cluster. The attrition stage is comparable to the 'decline' stage identified by organizational life cycle theorists (Kimberly and, Miles 1980; Quinn and Cameron, 1983; Mintzberg, 1984; Jawahar and McLaughlin, 2001), which is a natural process for any organic, organizational or social system. Business clusters are no exception. Take for instance the cotton textile cluster of Manchester, which was so flourishing once upon a time that the city had lent its name to other textile clusters in the world (as in 'Manchester of India' for Ahmedabad, and 'Manchester of Japan' for Osaka). But there aren't many cotton textile mills in Manchester today. The few survivors are seeking financial support from the European Union and technical support from universities. The only consolation for the city is that the knowledge and skills generated by the cluster is being used in some other related industries (Parsons and Rose, 2005). This (the flexible recycling of cluster-generated resources) is indeed not a small consolation, and should be the most desirable consequence of the inevitable attrition/decline of a business cluster.

The attrition process may be initiated by factors internal or external to the cluster. The population ecology theorists generally identify the internal factors with density related issues (especially the struggles and costs) of *legitimation* and *competition* (Hannan and Freeman, 1977 and 1989; Brittain and Freeman, 1980; Singh et al., 1986; Hannan and Carroll, 1992; Peli et al., 1994). *Legitimation* is the index of how the various elements of the ecosystem would welcome a new entrant into the cluster. Obviously, they would get a warmer welcome in the initial stages of cluster formation when the players are fewer and they bring prosperity to the area. As the number of players increases, there will be severe constraints on resources and growing inequalities among the different socio-economic classes of people, which would result in increasing hostilities to the new entrants and thereby reducing the legitimacy of their entry. While legitimacy decreases with cluster growth, *competition* increases (as may be seen from the graphs in Figure 5.1).

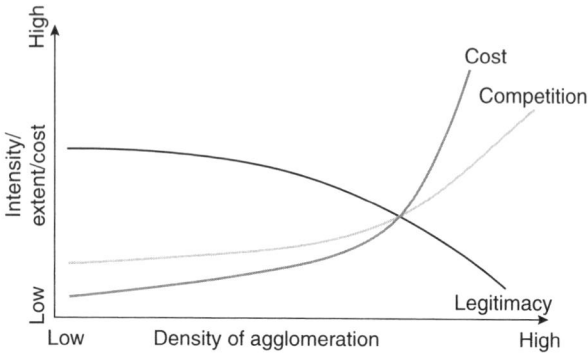

Figure 5.1   Trends in legitimacy and competition with increasing agglomeration

In either case, whether one is dealing with disparities and struggles or competing for scarce resources, there will be an upward push on the costs. In
other words, beyond a certain level of density (which is region-specific and
can be expanded to some extent with appropriate facilitation and support),
the transaction costs (in terms of real estate, professionals, support services,
etc.) and legitimization costs (appeasements, general welfare, social responsibility, accommodation of less meritorious groups, training for the under-
privileged, etc.) would increase in a disproportionate manner so that even
the firms that are already in the area would think of alternative locations,
not to speak of new firms coming into the area. What it means is that *the
process of agglomeration itself would contain the seeds of attrition, and the former
would inevitably lead to the latter.*

A recent instance of Apple Computers closing its shop in Bangalore (except
for sales and services), apparently due to or anticipating high cost of operations
in Bangalore (Tejaswi et al., 2006), could very well have a prognostic character
of the shape of things to come. Many are the newspaper and conversational
reports about the stupendous increases in the costs of other factors that make
operations unviable in Bangalore. For example, hotel tariffs in Bangalore have
become one of the highest in the world so that visitors find it more economical
to stay in the nearby city, Chennai, and commute by flight. Transport and
power are the other 'sore points' periodically being mentioned by industry
leaders. Though the transportation costs are not at all high in absolute terms,
the poor road conditions, the overcrowding and lack of traffic discipline are
making companies waste much of their professional time on the roads.
Similarly, while the power tariffs are not particularly high, the shortages, irregularities and discontinuities in supply are forcing companies to make alternate
captive arrangements at enormous costs. Though there are frequent mentions
in the media about the narrowing of professional costs between India and the
West, especially in the middle and senior levels, it is the salaries that still give

an advantage to Bangalore. According to the findings of a recent survey (Tejaswi et al., 2006), India continues to be the cheapest among the ten major outsourcing destinations in the world; the salaries here are 85–90 per cent lower than those of the United States. But the gap is closing fast, as rival contenders are emerging in other parts of the world, such as the Philippines (80–85 per cent), Brazil (75–80 per cent), Mexico (70–75 per cent), Malaysia (70–75 per cent), Czech Republic (70–75 per cent), and so on.

Changes in the attractiveness of other places and/or the business conditions in general would constitute the external factors that could work in conjunction with the internal ones to speed up the process of attrition. As for the Bangalore cluster, there is probably a greater threat from other regions within the country than from outside. This is because there are many other centres in the country that have the similar intellectual and infrasturctural conditions as in Bangalore (except of course the weather, whose advantage is progressively getting offset by the costs associated with the cluster-induced internal developments in Bangalore). The increasing facilitation of IT industries in other Indian cities, especially in terms of the physical, communications and energy infrastructure, could wean away some major projects to those cities. The recent decision to locate the 'Fab-City' project (for the manufacture of hardware components) in Hyderabad in preference to Bangalore is a case in point. Similarly, for the location of the 'SMART-City' project (under the Dubai Internet City's ambitious expansion plans in India), the places being considered are Cochin, Kolkata, and Hyderabad (not Bangalore).

Thus, the greater threat of attrition to the dominant cluster would be from 'virtual attrition' (i.e., newer entrants ignoring the dominant cluster) than from 'actual attrition' (i.e., existing firms in the dominant cluster closing down or moving away). Indications of such attrition are being reported periodically. For example, according to the software export data of Indian states released by the Electronics and Computer Software Export Promotion Council (ESC), Andhra Pradesh (which includes the Hyderabad cluster) had the highest growth in software exports (51 per cent), with Karnataka (which includes the Bangalore cluster) being pushed to eighth place with 34 per cent, behind the Punjab, Delhi, Uttar Pradesh, Haryana, Rajasthan, and Maharashtra (*TOI*, 2006). It should, however, be noted that a higher percentage on a lower initial volume need not indicate higher performance in absolute terms. In fact, it does not in the present case. Karnataka's software export volume is more than double (INR 3700 million) that of the second highest volume (INR 1550 million) exporter (Maharashtra), and it has a 37 per cent share of total software exports from India. And yet the higher growth rates at other places are often interpreted as indications of alternative clusters for future development as potential rivals to the dominant cluster. While the alarm being raised by researchers and analysts about the possibility of companies moving out of Bangalore and/or new companies going elsewhere because of sky-rocketing property prices, poor conditions of road/rail/air transport and communication infrastructure, inadequacies and irregularities of power and water supplies, rising salary costs, bureaucratic hurdles and corruption, inadequate domestic markets, divisions and struggles among different segments of people, and the like (Lateef, 1997; Nair, 1999; Saxenian, 2000) is fully justified, these developments (i.e., the virtual and actual attrition from the dominant cluster) should also be understood as part of a natural process in the life-cycle of a cluster, which can be delayed for some time but not deferred for ever. What is needed is the facilitation of the flexible recycling of the knowledge and skill resources generated by this cluster so that they could be used for the creation of more advanced productive systems in the region by the time the dominant cluster reaches the 'wrong' side of its maturity stage.

Conclusion

This chapter made an attempt to understand the 'innovation ecosystem' that would facilitate the formation and development of business clusters, with special reference to the Bangalore ICT cluster. It was found that the prescriptions in the literature are at variance with what is happening on the ground. This is because most studies have looked at the cluster as a 'state' rather than at cluster development as a 'process'. Research studies of the former kind are the more common, as it is only a developed cluster that would look like a cluster and therefore merit the attention and explanation. Naturally, all that is seen around the cluster are described as part of the ecosystem that has promoted the cluster. However, an evolutionary perspective of cluster development is necessary to bring out the different types of requirements at different stages of cluster development and the directions of causation among the ingredients of the ecosystem. Our analysis of the evolution of the Bangalore ICT cluster has brought out the following issues, among other things, about the cluster development phenomenon.

- The development of a business cluster passes through different stages that are comparable to the stages of the chemical process of crystal formation and growth. These stages are *incubation, nucleation, agglomeration,* and *attrition.*
- Each stage has its own characteristic ingredients for its ecosystem. Among these it will almost always be a single factor or a limited number of factors that would be guiding the decision makers. In general, therefore, the cluster phenomenon could be explained by what I call a *dominant factor theory.* As the perceived relevance of such a dominant factor would depend on the geophysical, socio-cultural, legal-political, infrastructural and economic environment of the specific time-period, the presence of such a factor under a different set of circumstances may not necessarily

lead to the replication of the cluster experience in a different region or even in the same region at a later period.

- If one were to characterize the nature of the ecosystem ingredients in different stages, one could regroup the four stages into two broad phases. Accordingly, during the first phase comprising the first two stages, the focus of action will be on *building the general capabilities of the region based on openness to and collaboration with external ideas, people and cultures.* During the second phase comprising the third and fourth stages, however, the focus will be on *building industry-specific infrastructure, institutions, and policy support.* It is interesting to note that in the first phase, the ecosystem ingredients act in conjunction with the external environment to *cause the cluster formation*, whereas in the second phase, they emerge as a *consequence of cluster formation* and later *becomes the cause* of further agglomeration and sometimes attrition.

- As the precipitating event leading to the nucleation of a cluster is often generated through the impact of a dynamically changing business environment outside the region on the 'incubated' characteristics of the region, policy makers and implementers will have very little control over the event itself. Their role in the first phase, therefore, should be that of *taking 'proactively open' measures for building the general capabilities of the region* by promoting educational institutions/initiatives especially in the new and emerging areas of technology, facilitating the travel and movement of people of different cultures in and out of the region (for 'brain circulation' à la Saxenian, 2000), creating infrastructural facilities of world class systems and standards, attracting knowledge-based industries in new technology areas preferably from the countries that pioneered them, and so on. In the second phase, however, their role has to change to that of *being 'sensitively supportive' in creating industry-specific policies, infrastructure, institutions, and service agencies in collaboration with the industry as per their emerging requirements.*

- One of the mistakes that is commonly made in cluster development initiatives is to ignore the importance of the incubation stage, which is perhaps the most critical of all stages but is not counted in most reckonings, as it is not possible to perceive its influence as direct and tangible, as is the case with other factors. Obviously it is as foolish and disastrous as building an edifice without proper foundations for the ostensibly 'sound' reason that much of it in any case goes under the ground and therefore is not 'seen'. Though the analogy is powerful enough to bring out the folly involved in such actions, mistakes of this kind are much more common than expected, not only in cluster development initiatives but also (and rather more prevalently) in entrepreneurship development in general, as was pointed out by Manimala (forthcoming) while discussing the dual role of education in promoting entrepreneurship (see Figure 5.2) based on the findings of an earlier study (Manimala, 2005) that changes in the

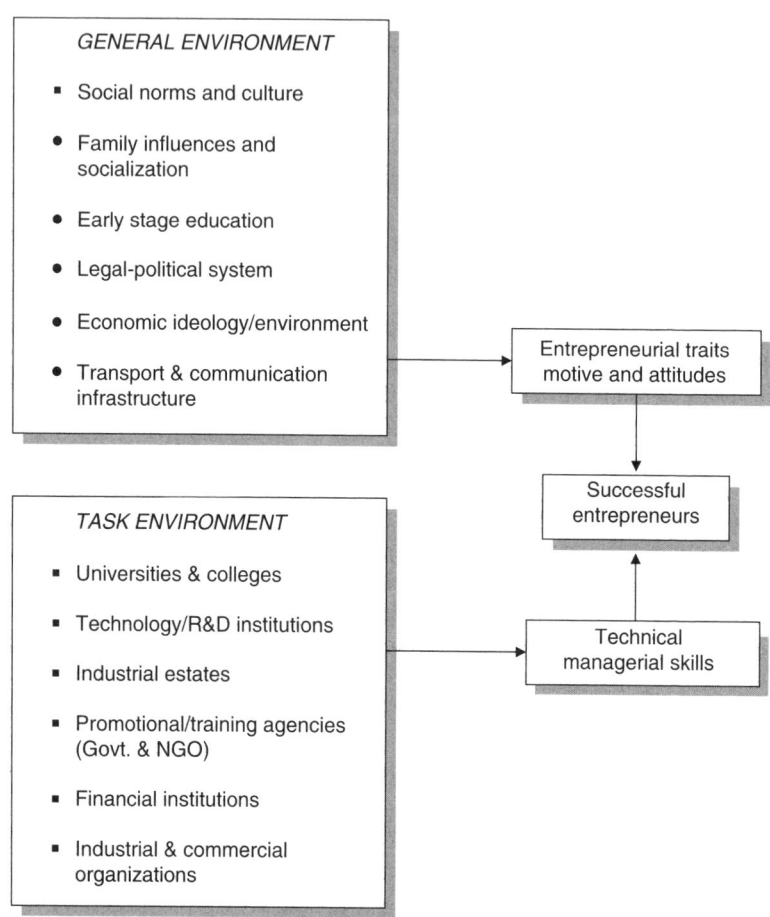

Figure 5.2   A model showing the dual role of education in promoting entrepreneurship
Source: Adapted from M. J. Manimala (forthcoming).

task environment without corresponding changes in the general environment did not have any impact on the emergence of innovative enterprises. As the task environment is seen as having immediate linkages with business operations, it is natural for policy makers to give exclusive priority to those issues and institutions, as it has happened in many developing countries in the past, which was later found to be totally ineffective. Similar have been the experiences of some cluster development initiatives in developing countries, where the governments went ahead with the creation of later-stage institutions without first assessing the 'incubation-status' of the respective places for sustaining these newly created institutions and enterprises. Obviously, we cannot ignore Pasteur's words: 'fortune favours the prepared mind!' *The most important task for governments is to prepare the grounds and people's minds, and the rest will be taken care of by the prepared minds themselves.*

• Finally, it should be noted that stage theory would help us in adopting a more constructive attitude towards 'attrition'. The understanding that attrition is the inevitable final stage in the life-cycle of biological, social or organizational systems would enable us not to be unduly alarmed by it when it has to occur, but to think of the possible positive outcomes of this eventuality. History is replete with innumerable cases of business clusters that flourished and perished. Of course, we should not allow a flourishing cluster to meet with premature death because of our carelessness and apathy. The right attitude should be that of the medical sciences: do everything possible to sustain and extend the productive life, but if the inevitable has to happen, leave it to the forces of nature. And, nature does not waste anything. It conserves every ingredient and recycles it into more advanced forms of evolution. So the discussion on the final stage of cluster development should not end up with a tragic note. We should actively facilitate the 'flexible recycling of firms' (Bahrami and Evans, 2000) and create more advanced forms of business models, products and services, and even newer forms of more viable clusters using the knowledge, skills and resources left behind by the cluster that has admirably served its purpose in its particular context.

References

Alecke, B., Alsleben, C., Scharr, F. and Untiedt, G. (2006), 'Are there really high-tech clusters? The geographic concentration of German manufacturing industries and its determinants', *The Annals of Regional Science*, Vol. 40, No. 1, March, pp. 19–42.

Bahrami, H. and Evans, S. (2000), 'Flexible recycling and high-technology entrepreneurship', in Kenney, M., ed., *Understanding Silicon Valley*, Stanford University Press, Stanford, CA, pp. 165–89.

Balasubramanyam, V. N. (1998), 'Bangalore is where the action is', Paper presented at the International Technical Seminars of 'Bangalore IT.COM', hosted by International Technology Park Limited (ITPL) and held at National Aeronautical Laboratories (NAL), Bangalore, 1–5 November.

Basant, R. (2006), 'Bangalore cluster: Evolution, growth and challenges', Working Paper No. 2006-05-02, (May), Ahmedabad: Indian Institute of Management.

Brittain, J. W. and Freeman, J. H. (1980), 'Organizational proliferation and density-dependent selection', in Kimberly, J. R. and Miles, R. H., eds, *Organizational Life-Cycle*, Jossey-Bass, San Francisco, pp. 291–338.

Burt, R. (2000), 'The network structure of social capital', *Research in Organizational Behaviour*, Vol. 22, No. 2, pp. 345–423.

Coleman, J. S. (1988), 'Social capital in the creation of human capital', *American Journal of Sociology*, Vol. 94, pp. 95–120.

Craig, J. (2000), 'Developing a regional industry cluster: A possible generic process', Centre for Policy and Development Systems, Brisbane.

Deshmukh, V. (1993), 'Bangalore: India's hi-tech birthplace', *Economic Reform Feature Service*, Article No. 3, Center for International Private Enterprise, Washington, DC.

Economic Times (2004), 'What is Bangalore's secret?', 22 June.

Feldman, M. P. (2001), 'The entrepreneurial event revisited: Firm formation in a regional context', *Industrial and Corporate Change*, Vol. 10, No. 4, pp. 861–75.

Florida, R. L. and Kenney, M. (1988), 'Venture capital, high technology and regional development', *Regional Studies*, Vol. 22, pp. 33–48.

Garnsey, E. and Heffernan, P. (2005), 'High technology clustering through spin-out and attraction: The Cambridge case', Regional Studies, Vol. 39, No. 8, pp. 1127–44.

Hannan, M. T. and Carroll, G. R. (1992), *Dynamics of Organizational Population: Density, Legitimation and Competition*, Oxford University Press, New York.

Hannan, M. T. and Freeman, J. (1977), 'The population ecology of organizations', *American Journal of Sociology*, Vol. 82, No. 5, pp. 929–64.

Hannan, M. T. and Freeman, J. H. (1989), *Organizational Ecology*, Harvard University Press, Cambridge, MA.

Hauschildt, J. and Steinkuhler, R. H. (1994), 'The role of science and technology parks in NTBF development', in Oakey, R. P., ed., *New Technology-Based Firms in the 1990s*, Paul Chapman, London, pp. 181–91.

Jawahar, I. and Mclaughlin, G. (2001), 'Toward a descriptive stakeholder theory: An organizational life cycle approach', *Academy of Management Review*, Vol. 26, pp. 397–414.

Kenney, M. and Patton, D. (2005), 'Entrepreneurial geographies: Support networks in three high-technology industries', *Economic Geography*, Vol. 81, No. 2, April, pp. 201–28.

Kimberly, J. and Miles, R., eds, (1980), *Organizational Life Cycle*, Jossey-Bass, San Francisco.

Krugman, P. (1991), *Geography and Trade*, MIT Press, Cambridge, MA.

Lala, R. M. (2004), *For the Love of India: The Life and Times of Jamsetji Tata*, Viking Penguin Books India, New Delhi .

Lateef, A. (1997), 'Linking up with the global economy: A case study of the Bangalore software industry', Discussion Paper, International Institute of Labour Studies, International Labour Organization, Geneva.

Lee, C.-M., Miller, W. F., Hancock, M. G., and Rowen, H. S. (2000), *The Silicon Valley Edge: A Habitat for Innovation and Entrepreneurship*, Stanford University Press, Stanford, CA.

Liao, J. and Welsch, H. P. (2005), 'Roles of social capital in venture creation: Key dimensions and research implications', *Journal of Small Business Management*, Vol. 43, No. 4, pp. 345–62.

Manimala, M. J. (1997), 'Higher education-enterprise cooperation and the entrepreneurial graduate: The need for a new paradigm', in Mitra, J. and Formica, P., eds, *Innovation and Economic Development: University-Enterprise Partnerships in Action*, Oak Tree Press, Dublin, pp. 95–118.

Manimala, M. J. (1999), *Entrepreneurial Policies and Strategies: The Innovator's Choice*, Sage Publications, New Delhi.

Manimala, M. J. (2005), 'Innovative entrepreneurship: Testing the theory of environmental determinism', in Manimala, M. J., *Entrepreneurship Theory at the Crossroads: Paradigms and Praxis*, 2nd edn, Wiley-Dreamtech, New Delhi, ch. 2 (pp. 21–43).

Manimala, M. J. (forthcoming), 'Entrepreneurship education in India: An assessment of SME training needs against current practices', Forthcoming in the Special Issue of *International Journal of Entrepreneurship & Innovation Management* on the Role of Universities for Entrepreneurship Development.

Markusen, A. (1996), 'Sticky places in slippery space: A typology of industrial districts', *Economic Geography*, Vol. 72, pp. 294–314.

Marshall, A. (1890), *Principles of Economics*, Macmillan, London.

Miller, R. and Cote, M. (1985), 'Growing the next Silicon Valley', *Harvard Business Review*, Vol. 63, No. 4, July–August, pp. 114–23.

Mintzberg, H. (1984), 'Power and organizational life cycles', *Academy of Management Review*, Vol. 9, pp. 207–24.

Monck, C. S. P., Porter, R. B., Quintas, P. R., Storey, D. J. and Wynarczyk, P. (1988), *Science Parks and the Growth of High Technology Firms*, Croom Helm, London.

Moreno, J. L. (1977), *Psychodrama*, Vol. 1, 4th edn, Beacon House, New York.

Myint, Y. M., Vyakarnam, S. and New, M. J. (2005), 'The effect of social capital in new venture creation: The Cambridge high-technology cluster', *Strategic Change*, Vol. 14 (May), pp. 165–77.

Nahapiet, J. and Ghoshal, S. (1998), 'Social capital, intellectual capital, and organizational advantage', *Academy of Management Review*, Vol. 23, No. 2, pp. 242–66.

Nair, J. (1999), 'Battles for Bangalore: Reterritorializing the city', SEPHIS (South-south Exchange Programme for research on the HIStory of development) paper, Digital Publications, kb 79, International Institute of Social History, Amsterdam, p. 21.

Pani, N. (1988), 'A demographic and economic profile of Bangalore', *Bangalore 2000*, Times Research Foundation, Pune, pp. 20ff.

Parsons, M. and Rose, M. B. (2005), 'The neglected legacy of Lancashire cotton: Industrial clusters and the UK outdoor trade 1960-1990', *Enterprise and Society*, Vol. 6, No. 4, pp. 682–709.

Peli, G., Bruggeman, J., Masuch, M. and O'Nullain, B. (1994), 'A logical approach to formalizing organizational ecology', *American Sociological Review*, Vol. 59, No. 4, pp. 571–93.

Perry, M. (2005), 'Clustering small enterprise: Lessons from policy experience in New Zealand', *Environment &Planning C: Government & Policy*, Vol. 23, No. 6, December, pp. 833–50.

Piore, M. J. and Sabel, C. F. (1984), *The Second Industrial Divide: Possibilities for Prosperity*, Basic Books, New York.

Piramal, G. and Herdeck, M. (1985), *India's Industrialists*, Vol. I, Three Continents Press, Washington, DC.

Porter, M. (1998), 'Clusters and the new economics of competition', *Harvard Business Review*, Vol. 76, No. 6, November–December, pp. 77–90.

Quinn, R. and Cameron, K. (1983), 'Organizational life cycles and shifting criteria of effectiveness: Some preliminary evidence', *Management Science*, Vol. 29, pp. 33–51.

Rosa, P. (1998), 'Entrepreneurial processes of business cluster formation and growth by "habitual" entrepreneurs', *Entrepreneurship Theory and Practice*, Vol. 22, No. 4, Summer, pp. 43–61.

Saxenian, A. (2000), 'The Bangalore boom: From brain drain to brain circulation', in Kenniston, K. and Kumar, D., eds, *Bridging the Digital Divide: Lessons from India*, National Institute of Advanced Study, Bangalore.

Silicon Valley's New Immigrant Entrepreneurs, Public Policy Institute of California, San Francisco, CA.

Saxenian, A. (1994), *Regional Advantage*, Harvard University Press, Cambridge, MA.

Schoonhoven, C. B., Eisenhardt, K. M. and Lyman, K. (1990), 'Speeding products to market: Waiting time to first product introduction in new firms', *Administrative Science Quarterly*, Vol. 35, pp. 177–207.

Shridharan, L. and Manimala, M. J. (1999), 'Promoting industrial clusters in India: Lessons from Europe and East Asia', *Journal of Entrepreneurship*, Vol. 8, No. 2, pp. 165–93.

Singh, J. V., House, R. J. and Tucker, D. J. (1986), 'Organizational change and organizational mortality', *Administrative Science Quarterly*, Vol. 31, pp. 587–611.

STEM (2000), 'Bangalore's IT industry: A techno-economic profile', *Information Today & Tomorrow*, Vol. 19, No. 4, December, National Information System for Science and Technology (NISSAT), Department of Scientific and Industrial Research (DSIR), Government of India, pp. 8–10.

Storey, D. J. and Strange, A. (1992), 'Where are they now? Some changes in firms located on United Kingdom science parks in 1986', *New Technology, Work and Employment*, Vol. 7, No. 1, pp. 15–28.

Tejaswi, M. J., Raghavendra, R. and Bhashyam, S. (2006), 'Is Indian IT getting too expensive?', *The Times of India*, Bangalore edition, 23 June, p. 18.

TOI (2006), 'State (Karnataka) tops in software exports, but Andhra Pradesh clocks the fastest growth rate of 51%', *The Times of India*, Bangalore edition, 19 June, p. 17.

Tripathi, D. (2004), *Oxford History of Indian Business*, Oxford University Press, New Delhi.

Van Dijk, M. P. and Rabellotti, R. (1997), *Enterprise Clusters and Networks in Developing Countries*, Frank Cass, London.

6

A Model of an Innovation System with a Position Regulation of Science and Technology Parks within Innovation Networks

Holger Graf [a] *and Randolf Margull* [b]
[a] *Friedrich-Schiller University, Germany*
[b] *Technology and Innovation Park, Jena, Germany*

Introduction

The sources of innovation are often found rather between firms, universities, research laboratories, suppliers and customers than inside them (Powell, 1990). Firms engage in co-operation not only to share the costs and risks of research activities but also to obtain access to new markets and technologies and make use of complementary skills (Kogut, 1989; Hagedoorn, 1993; Eisenhardt and Schoonhoven, 1996; Mowery et al., 1998). In rapidly developing industries, where competition might be seen as a learning race, it is almost inevitable to engage in inter-firm collaboration to identify new opportunities and learn about new technology (Powell, 1998). Accordingly, Teece (1992) argues that complex forms of co-operation are necessary for competition on a level of high technological sophistication especially in fragmented industries.

The co-ordination pattern which underlies these bilateral informal or weak formal co-operative relations is called a network organization. The functionality of networks is based on the principles of complementarily and reciprocity. This means that firms will only participate in these networks if they expect to learn from other network members (complementarity) and if the transfer of knowledge is bi- or multilateral (reciprocity) (DeBresson and Amesse, 1991). In contrast to enforceable market contracts, networks are often more stable, in the presence of interdependent preferences, than market relations, but more flexible than labour contracts.

Networks of innovating firms are identified in different configurations: supplier-user networks, networks of pioneers and adopters, regional inter-industrial networks, international strategic technological alliances, and professional inter-organizational networks (DeBresson and Amesse, 1991). Despite these organizational arrangements, the physical interaction takes place between people. Interpersonal networks are considered an important channel for the diffusion of knowledge and information (Zander and Kogut, 1995; Zucker et al., 1998; Sorenson, 2003). Sorenson (2004) shows that the importance of these transmission channels depends on the complexity of the underlying knowledge-base and, in particular, that knowledge complexity limits the rate at which knowledge diffuses across geographic boundaries.

These aspects of interactive innovation are at the core of what we refer to as a local innovation system. Besides the transfer of knowledge between existing firms and research organizations, an important function of such a system is to be able to attract actors from outside the region to avoid the risk of lock-in situations (Bathelt et al., 2004; Storper and Venables, 2004) and to generate new firms through spin-off from existing firms and academic start-ups out of the academic sphere.

We study the innovation system of Jena – a city which stands out of the mass of communities in the eastern part of Germany as a technologically and economically successful region (OECD, 2001; Cantner et al., 2003b). Within this local innovation system, we focus on the specific role of the Technology and Innovation Park, Jena, in fostering both a firm foundation and communication between local actors. Finally we develop a model of the integration of a science and technology park within a functioning system of innovation.

6.1   The system of innovation in Jena

6.1.1   The changing nature of the Jena innovation system

Jena is situated in the Free State of Thuringia, the green heart of Germany. With 100,000 inhabitants and more than 23,000 students, Jena provides the unique combination of a beautiful setting, strong cultural and philosophical traditions, high-tech industry and, above all, a modern university landscape.

Thuringia's academic roots go back to 1392, when the University of Erfurt was founded. In the fifteenth century almost a quarter of the students in Germany studied there. In 1558 Jena founded its own university. In the second half of the seventeenth century the University of Jena developed into a school of national and international reputation. Many professors were fascinated by the modern applications of their specialities and led their students on regular tours to factories and tried to improve technical processes. In the eighteenth century the 'storehouse of knowledge and science' – as Goethe referred to Jena – attracted not only famous professors and students such as Schiller, Hegel, Fichte und Leibniz but also businessmen.

At this time a new industry grew, when the first glassworkshop was built in Thuringia. The heavily forested uplands had all the necessary raw materials – quartz sand, chalk and soda. Charcoal and water for the further processing of the glass were also available. Later on, glass formed the basis for a new branch of industry – optics. The development of the optical industry in Jena is a particularly well-illustrated example of fruitful co-operation between tradition and progress, theory and practice.

In the late nineteenth century, three men – Carl Zeiss, Ernst Abbe and Otto Schott – came together in Jena and formed the first 'competence cluster'. The engineer Carl Zeiss faced bad economic times in the mid-1800s. In 1846 Carl Zeiss founded the Zeiss Works for Precision Engineering and Optical Products. He had just a few employees and made only about 20 microscopes per year because he had an almost 'trial and error' approach to the development and production of the lenses and microscopes.

The physicist Ernst Abbe, called to the university as associate professor in 1870, created an image formation of the microscope and found a way to build microscopes following a plan. His contractor was Carl Zeiss, who advanced making optical instruments to ever-higher standards of perfection in his private workshop. Carl Zeiss realized that the application of Abbe's scientific research results could radically improve the design and production of optical components for microscopes. Therefore, Carl Zeiss sold a third of his own business to Ernst Abbe.

Otto Schott, the third man in this alliance, was a specialist in the field of production and characterization of glass and together with Carl Zeiss and Ernst Abbe founded a 'Glass technical laboratory' – later called 'Jenaer Glaswerk Schott & Genossen' – to melt the required special glasses for Carl Zeiss's optical instruments.

In 1886 Carl Zeiss employed 250 workmen and delivered the ten-thousandth microscope. By 1900, 12 years after Carl Zeiss died, the Zeiss firm already employed 1070 people. Ernst Abbe improved the academic and research resources, but he was also very interested in social reforms. He founded the 'Carl-Zeiss-Stiftung' to ensure that both of the firms ZEISS and SCHOTT follow the social vision of its founders. The employment benefits were uncommonly good for their day – these included an eight-hour workday, paid holidays, health benefits, profit sharing and a retirement plan.

The common work of Zeiss, Abbe and Schott created a very close link between science and economy and was the basis for the development of the German optical and glass industries in the twentieth century. The synergistic combination of the artisan, scientist and materials specialist still serves even today as a valid model for modern start-up companies.

On 3 October in 1990 a period of rapid change started with the reunification of Germany. At first it seemed Jena would lose its outstanding position as a centre of research and industry. More than 20,000 employees of Carl Zeiss Jena lost their jobs and more than 30,000 employees lost their jobs in subsidiary firms. In 1990 Carl Zeiss Jena employed only 1700 members of staff. But as in Zeiss's time, science and economy again formed new alliances. The companies Carl Zeiss Jena Schott Jenaer Glass and Jenapharm opened up the economy region with their traditional roots and developed new high-tech enterprises with, at that time, visionary technologies. Highly qualified workplaces, worldwide co-operations, an export quota of over 40 per cent in the industry, fully developed infrastructures and a growing economy potential justify Jena's reputation as a high-technology centre.

Today Jena is a centre of different innovation networks primarily in the fields of optics, nano-and biotechnology. The effective co-operation of science and economy brought Jena a top position in the latest ranking of German growth regions with high potential.

6.1.2   Industry structure and innovative actors in Jena

Besides these large firms mentioned above, a vital industrial structure has developed over the last decade. To characterize the local industry, we refer to a recent study of 93 manufacturing and knowledge intensive service firms within the innovation system of Jena (Cantner et al., 2003a). Their sample of firms characterizes Jena as a city deeply rooted in the historical traditions of Zeiss, Abbe and Schott sketched above.[1] Looking at the number of firms, the dominating industry is optics with 28 firms, followed by services and data processing with 22 and 15 firms respectively. Other relevant industries present are chemicals, metal products, metals and machinery. Figure 6.1 shows the share of industries in number of firms (dark coloured) and their employment shares (light coloured). Optics and data processing also dominate

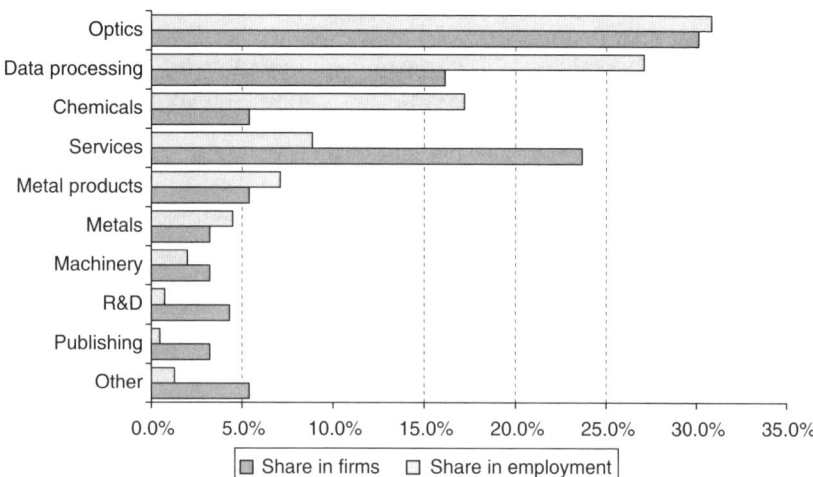

Figure 6.1   Industry structure in Jena

Source: Cantner et al. (2003a).

in employment with a share of over 50 per cent. Firms within services are significantly smaller (13.2 employees per firm) than in chemicals (112 employees per firm) and therefore these industries switch ranks.

Within the last 15 years, well-known research institutes have established themselves around the Friedrich Schiller University and the Science Campus Beutenberg. The campus, with its science and technology, is providing an interdisciplinary base for innovative research fields with great potential for applications. It is an international competence centre for certain fields in biology and physics. The different fields are prepared to address issues of totally new quality and implication.

Concepts and methodologies of both fields meet. Different materials and methods for nanofabrication and tests on the atomic scale supplement each other. At the edge of cell biology, genetics, molecular medicine and the physics of Microsystems, -optics and mechanics, the Science Campus Beutenberg is concentrating its research and is promoting innovative products by developing advanced research tools.

Box 6.1   Institutes and incubators on the Science Campus Beutenberg

Hans-Knöll-Institut für Naturstoff-Forschung e.V. (HKI)
Natural products as base for new drugs

Institut für Molekulare Biotechnologie e.V. (IMB)
Stability and instability of the genome

Friedrich-Schiller-Universität
Institute für Virologie und antivirale Chemotherapie
Fight viruses and bacteria – help patients

Max-Planck-Institut für chemische Ökologie
Chemical signals exchanged between organisms and enviroment

Max-Planck-Institut für Biogechemie
Chemical and biological cycles on world scale

Institut für Physikalische Hochtechnologie e.V. (IPHT)
Research and technology for innovative systems

Institut für Angewandte Physik der Friedrich-Schiller-Universität
Tools for light – light as a tool

Fraunhofer-Institut für Angewandte Optik und Feinmechanik
Thin films for optics, characterization technology, micro-optics, precision mechanics

BioInstrumentezentrum
Biotechnology orientated start-up enterprises

Technologie- und Innovationspark
Technology orientated start up-enterprises

Together with many new-founded biotechnology orientated enterprises, the institutes and incubators form a bio-instruments cluster combining technical and scientific abilities. Innovation for medicine, biology and biotechnology are created particularly from the areas of optics, apparatus engineering and mechatronics. BioRegio Jena e.V. has been co-ordinator of the biotechnology network since 1996.

OptoNet e.V. in Jena is the competence network for optical technologies in Thuringia. It combines business enterprises, research and educational institutions with the aim of actively participating in the international development in the field of optical technologies.

The development of systems for diagnosis and therapy of eye diseases occupies another important position. Enterprises throughout the region have combined in the competence centre 'OphthalmoInnovation'. The network provides a continuous chain of research in medicine and medical engineering as well as the industrial implementation of systems for new treatments.

The accelerated conversion of scientific development achievements to new marketable products is the aim of the Technology and Innovation Park founded in 1991. In co-operation with our partner Thuringian Entrepreneurship Network, we have already supported here more than 135 enterprises in the area of communications and software development, laser and micro-system engineering (see Figure 6.2).

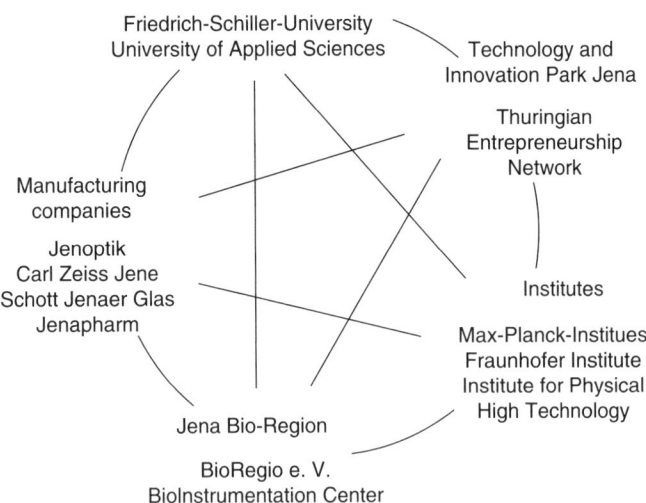

Figure 6.2   Integration of Technology and Innovation Park Jena in the local network

On around 5000 m² of production and office space more than 50 enterprises with up to 250 employees find the best possible conditions for their starting and stabilization phases. The incubator enhances the knowledge exchange, offers various activities in technology-orientated networks and provides a wide range of contacts.

Close networking of fundamental research and applied research is characteristic for the work of the Technology and Innovation Park Jena between the different institutes, two universities and many new enterprises. Scientific know-how is realized again and again in new products and proceedings and, last but not least, new jobs in the field of physics and life sciences.

6.1.3 Interactive structure of the innovating actors

To get an impression of how these actors with industrial as well as scientific background are related to each other, we refer to the work of Cantner and Graf (2005). In analysing the network of patent applicants via common team membership of the inventors of the respective patents, a visualization is provided of the local network for two three-year periods (Figure 6.3 and Figure 6.4). We can observe a highly connected network in both periods, where the personal relationships either arise through co-operation (joint patent application) of the applicants (grey edges) or through the job mobility of scientists (black edges). Comparing the two networks, we find a network structure that is characterized by an increase in the average number of linkages of the innovators and an increase in centralization. With respect to the historical sketch above of economic development in Jena, we also notice

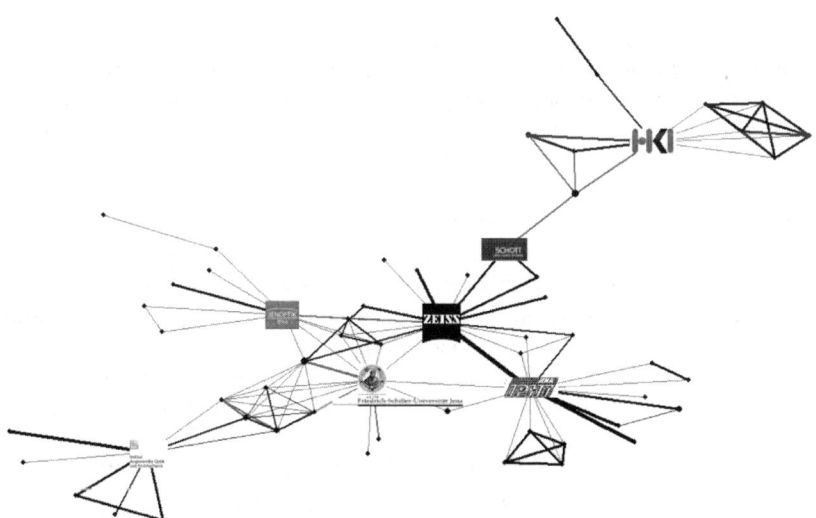

Figure 6.3   Network of innovators in Jena, 1995–1997

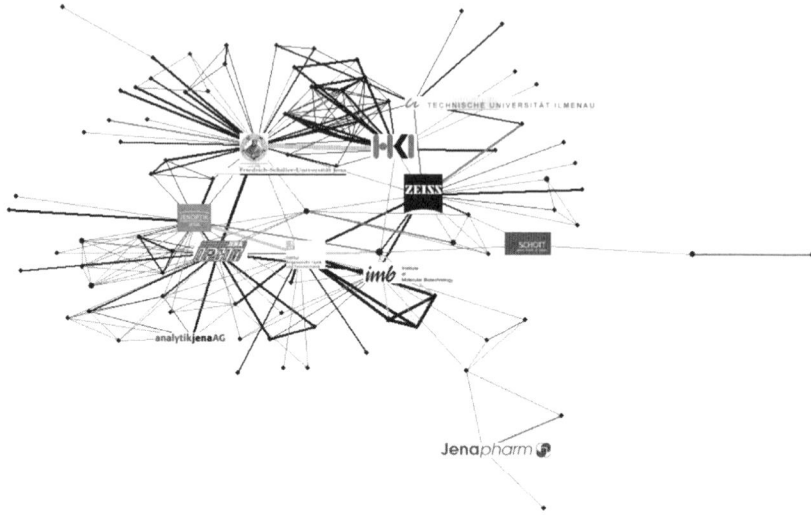

Figure 6.4   Network of innovators in Jena, 1999–2001

a more central position of the university in the network along a less central position of the successors of the VEB Carl Zeiss (Carl Zeiss and Jenoptik).

The functionality of the system also shows in the integration of public research within the network of the second period. The research institutes with a more practical focus, like the Fraunhofer-Institute, HKI, IPHT and IMB are especially well connected to local firms.

The increase in the number of actors in the innovator network indicates strong entrepreneurial activities in the local system during that period. The following section will address the question of the heritage of these new firms and their connection to incumbent actors, that is, firms, university and public research institutes.

6.1.4   Where do new actors come from?

Firm founders in general do not actively decide on the optimal location for their enterprise (Cooper and Folta, 2000). The establishment of a new firm introduces many changes in the life of the founders. Professional life and the income situation is subject to great risks. The network of personal relations might be the only constant and serve to reduce uncertainty in some aspects of founders' lives. To stay located at the place of previous employment can provide the possibility of consultations with former colleagues. Spin-off firms and academic start-ups stay where they were before, as they might have agreements with the incubator organization (firm, university) to use laboratories, contacts or other facilities (Cantner et al., 2003a). Founders appreciate these stabilizing functions and, consequently, search for alternative locations in only a few cases. Cantner and colleagues (2003a) found that only 31 per cent of the firms in Jena had actively considered alternative locations for their firms. Most of the founders had been in Jena before starting their own firm (Fornahl and Graf, 2003). They report a 93 per cent share of local foundations as compared to firms that moved or located a subsidiary to Jena.

During the period after German reunification, when the central actors of the network were the successors of the VEB Carl Zeiss, integration in the network was not a big problem. Most founders were spin-offs from the Kombinat and had therefore been in the 'market' before with good contacts to former colleagues. At a later stage of development (Figure 6.4), the university became the central actor of the network. Academic start-ups, while presumably having good contacts to academia, lack integration within the network of private firms. Besides, entrants from outside the region might have problems getting in touch with incumbent firms and becoming an active member of such a tight network.

6.1.5   Technology and Innovation Parks as incubators

The existence of an incubator is not a relevant factor for firms to locate in a specific region per se. Again drawing on the findings of Cantner and colleagues (2003a), we observe that during the process of establishing a firm, the existence of a technology park is ranked least important for location decisions, followed only by 'footloose' venture capital. Rather, factors related to interaction seem especially important. While the existence of a qualified labour force is named most relevant, the presence of other actors, like firms, universities and research institutes, as well as an existing personal social network are critical. It is worth noticing that all actors allowed to be evaluated according to their function (other firms, universities, research institutes, competing firms) were most often appreciated as a possible partner for co-operation.

The role of a technology park is therefore not only to be seen in providing production facilities but especially in fostering interaction by providing contacts to the existing system of innovation.

6.2   The position of Science and Technology Parks within innovation networks

The assessment of the factors which influence the foundation of an enterprise at a certain location is of special interest for the position regulation of Science and Technology Parks within local clusters and innovation networks:

- Availability of qualified human resources
- Existence of universities and research institutes as well as larger enterprises

- Innovation networks
- Research co-operation
- Social environment for entrepreneurship
- Image of the location

But creativity and innovation ability are also part of the factors which don't decide only on the future of a scientist or an enterprise but also on the location. Because success stories usually start with the idea for an innovative product and leads to company formation with economic success.

Policy makers consider this influence more and more in many places and react with:

- Creation and safeguarding of an internationally competitive research infrastructure
- Formation of research main emphases and competence networks
- Support of combined research plans into co-operation between enterprises and scientific research facilities of the region

The following special features of an innovation network are to be considered:

Innovation	Production and introduction of new products, production methods, organization forms in the economy
Network	Different levels of contact, interaction and face-to-face communication between different agents, the nodes in the network

Innovation networks link a large variety of agents, for example students, scientists, research work groups, employers, enterprises and business partners, policy makers and services including banks or venture capital firms. The interactions and relations between the agents of the network are relatively long lasting and voluntary.

The networks can benefit science and research as well as business in several ways:

- Providing new contacts
- Developing of new technologies
- Synergy effects in research, development and marketing
- Competence grouping
- Efficient use of technical and financial resources

It is generally appreciated that there is a direct connection between the degree of innovation in enterprises and the increase of jobs. However, if small and medium-sized enterprises have no capacities for their own research and development, also universities and research institutes can work as initiators of processes of innovation. Combined research is an example of how research institutes and enterprises work hand in hand. These investments are an essential reason for an innovative entrepreneurial atmosphere, besides the direct support of company formations.

Accordingly, the tasks of Science and Technology Parks in promoting the culture of innovation and the competitiveness of its associated businesses and knowledge-based institutions are manifold:

- Integration of new establishments in the local network and general network management
- Concentration on strengths and competencies of one's own
- Observing the international development
- Looking for co-operation between different research institutes and enterprises with the aim of generating synergy effects in science and research
- Mutual inspiration of research institutes and enterprises as a starting point for new scientific projects and regional entrepreneurial development
- Generation of start-ups and spin-offs with high potential and active support in the process of foundation and development
- Appropriation of an optimal infrastructure and accompanying services

Conclusion

We provided a description of the local innovation system in Jena which is characterized by a long lasting tradition especially in the optics and precision mechanics industries. Later developments integrate new, related technologies in the system and provide a fertile environment for the establishment of new firms. As we have seen, the innovative actors with different motivations (firms and public research) are deeply intertwined by the mobility of scientists and frequently co-operate in research and development. Despite this favourable structure, we identify some bottlenecks within the system.

The strong role of academic research and the resulting high rate of academic start-ups might pose a problem for these firms and the system in general. As these academic start-ups are generally well endowed with good technological knowledge, they often lack knowledge about relevant markets. Being related to the public research infrastructure cannot help in acquiring this type of knowledge. Rather, we find that academic start-ups should gain contacts to business firms and learn relevant market knowledge through these networking channels. A technology park, where a large fraction of new firms is located, is therefore required to offer more than just production facilities. Being connected to the local network of existing firms, the management of a technology park has to provide contacts for the new establishments and help in integrating them in the network.

Note

1   For a detailed discussion of the historical tradition in Jena, see Walter(2000) and Länger (2003).

References

Bathelt, H., Malmberg, A. and Maskell, P. (2004), 'Clusters and knowledge: Local buzz, global pipelines and the process of knowledge creation', *Progress in Human Geography*, Vol. 28, No. 1, pp. 31–56.

Cantner, U. and Graf, H. (2005), 'The Network of Innovators in Jena: An Application of Social Network Analysis, Paper presented at the 4th EMAEE Conference, 19–21 May, Utrecht, NL.

Cantner, U., Fornahl, D. and Graf, H. (2003a), *Innovationssystem und Gründungsgeschehen in Jena: Erste Erkenntnisse einer Unternehmensbefragung*, Jenaer Schriften zur Wirtschaftswissenschaft, FSU Jena, 06/2003.

Cantner, U., Helm, R. and Meckl, R. (2003b), *Strukturen und Strategien in einem Innovationssystem: Das Beispiel Jena*, Verlag Wissenschaft & Praxis, Sternenfels.

Cooper, A. and Folta, T. (2000), 'Entrepreneurship and hightechnology clusters', in Sexton, D. L. and Landström, H., eds, *The Blackwell Handbook of Entrepreneurship*, Blackwell Business, Malden, MA, pp. 348–67.

DeBresson, F. and Amesse, F. (1991), 'Networks of innovators: A review and introduction to the issue', *Research Policy*, Vol. 20, No. 5, pp. 363–79.

Eisenhardt, K. M. and Schoonhoven, C. B. (1996), 'Resource-based view of strategic alliance formation: Strategic and social effects in entrepreneurial firms', *Organization Science*, Vol. 7, No. 2, pp. 136–50.

Fornahl, D. and Graf, H. (2003), 'Standortfaktoren und Gründungsaktivitäten in Jena', in Cantner, Uwe, Helm, Roland and Meckl, Reinhard, eds, *Strukturen und Strategien in einem Innovationssystem: Das Beispiel Jena*, Verlag Wissenschaft & Praxis, Sternenfels, pp. 97–123.

Hagedoorn, J. (1993), 'Understanding the rationale of strategic technology partnering: Inter-organizational modes of cooperation and sectoral differences', *Strategic Management Journal*, Vol. 14, pp. 371–85.

Kogut, B. (1989), 'The stability of joint ventures: Reciprocity and competitive rivalry', *Journal of Industrial Economics*, Vol. 38, No. 2, pp. 183–98.

Länger, A. (2003), 'Die Entwicklung der feinmechanisch-optischen Industrie in Jena ab 1846', in Cantner, Uwe, Helm, Roland and Meckl, Reinhard, eds, *Strukturen und Strategien in einem Innovationssystem: Das Beispiel Jena*, Verlag Wissenschaft & Praxis, Sternenfels, pp. 267–89.

Mowery, D. C., Oxley, J. E. and Silverman, B. S. (1998), 'Technology overlap and inter-firm cooperation: Implications for the resource-based view of the firm', *Research Policy*, Vol. 27, No. 5, pp. 507–23.

OECD (2001), *Cities and Regions in the New Learning Economy*, OECD, Paris.

Powell, W. W. (1990), 'Neither market nor hierarchy: Network forms of organization', *Research in Organizational Behavior*, Vol. 12, pp. 295–336.

Powell, W. W. (1998), 'Learning from collaboration: Knowledge and networks in the biotechnology and pharmaceutical industries', *California Management Review*, Vol. 40, No. 3, pp. 228–40.

Sorenson, O. (2003), 'Social networks and industrial geography', *Journal of Evolutionary Economics*, Vol. 13, pp. 513–27.

Storper, M. and Venables, A. J. (2004), 'Buzz: Face-to-face contact and the urban economy', *Journal of Economic Geography*, Vol. 4, No. 4, pp. 351–70.

Teece, D. (1992), 'Competition, cooperation, and innovation: Organizational arrangements for regimes of rapid technological progress', *Journal of Economic Behavior and Organization*, Vol. 18, No. 1, pp. 1–25.

Walter, R. (2000), 'Die Ressource "Wissen" und ihre Nutzung: Ernst Abbe und der Jenaer Aufschwung um 1900', in Kodalle, Klaus M., ed., *Angst vor der Moderne*, Königshausen & Neumann, Würzburg, pp. 11–23.

Zander, U. and Kogut, B. (1995), 'Knowledge and the speed of the transfer and imitation of organizational capabilities: An empirical test', *Organization Science*, Vol. 6, pp. 76–91.

Zucker, L. G., Darby, M. R. and Brewer, M. B. (1998), Intellectual human capital and the birth of U.S. biotechnology enterprises', *American Economic Review*, Vol. 88, No. 1, pp. 290–306.

7
Knowledge Appropriation and the Complexity of Regional Innovation Systems: A Conceptual Precursor to Simulation

Michael Provance
George Washington University

This chapter explores contentious perspectives on regional competitive advantage by proposing a conceptual model of the impact of knowledge appropriation activities of firms embedded in a region's innovation system on that region's competitive advantage over time. This model provides the precursor to simulation and empirical research that may refine and integrate disparate conceptions of the dynamics of regional advantage. Perspectives of spatial economics and industrial agglomeration that have emerged over decades to explain regional economic growth (Porter, 1980; Krugman, 1994) differ on the relationship between knowledge appropriation and a region's competitive advantage (Audretsch, 1998). Regional competitive advantage (or competitiveness) is defined here as the innovative performance of a region (Saxenian, 1994; Kenney, 2000). Innovation performance is conceived throughout this study as the value extracted from innovations created and exploited in the market through innovation and production systems in a region.[1] This chapter attempts to bring parsimony to these theoretical contrasts on regional advantage by integrating them through knowledge- and complexity-based views of innovation activity in regional inter-organizational systems (Lomi and Larsen, 1996; Uzzi, 1997; Almeida and Kogut, 1999).

We draw our integrative lens comprised of knowledge and complexity from evolutionary economics (Nelson and Winter, 1982; Audretsch and Keilbach, 2004). Integrating these theoretical perspectives enables the formation of a dynamic framework that describes significant factors influencing the emergence and reinforcement of a region's competitive advantage. This framework illustrates how certain patterns of knowledge appropriation in regional innovation systems produce greater competitive advantage for regions. Further, the study adopts a regional innovation system level of analysis to explore the dynamics of three primary elements defining a firm's embeddedness in the innovation system: innovation complexity that produces specialization within the system, inter-organizational linkages, and knowledge appropriation formality. In addition to unpacking the dynamics of firm embeddedness, our contribution from the computational model below extends prior qualitative framework with a more precise explanation of variation in regional innovation performance.

This chapter specifies the propositional elements of the regional innovativeness model as a preliminary design for a simulation study. Other empirical methods may suffice to test the effects of knowledge appropriation on regional innovation performance under measurable conditions, but that context is insufficient to the problem described above. Simulation contributes to the framework described above on two important dimensions: (1) it enables the contrast of competing theoretical perspectives under ambiguous and dynamics settings commonplace in regional innovation systems, and (2) it allows a greater exploration of the behavioral characteristics of actors and dynamics of information flows that comprise the complex system described above.[2] As such, this approach is appropriate to the goals of this chapter. The remainder of the chapter outlines the underlying theory and prior work that support the proposed model of regional innovation performance. Then, it provides a preliminary, descriptive model of the simulation. Further, it presents propositions to guide future simulation and empirical work that is part of my ongoing research in this domain as well as the work of other scholars of entrepreneurship, innovation and strategy. Finally, it offers concluding discussion on the impact of these theoretical contributions.

7.1 The impact of social embeddedness on regional competitive advantage

Regional competitive advantage is a research domain that continues to consume and stir debate among scholars. This debate lodges mainly in the distinctions drawn between spatial economic interdependency (Porter, 1980; Krugman, 1994) and agglomeration of specialized capabilities and knowledge (Saxenian, 1994; Audretsch, 1998; Florida, 2005). While these theoretical lenses have converged on innovative activities as determinants of regional advantage (Audretsch and Fritsch, 2002), they remain contentiously divided on the role of knowledge spillovers in the region (Audretsch, 1998). Economic geographers such as Krugman (1994) and others argue that knowledge appropriation activities are not contained by geographic (e.g., regional) boundaries. Contrastingly, others have shown that economic knowledge is uncertain and difficult to transfer (Audretsch and Keilbach,

2004). Therefore, firms embedded within a region are more likely to exchange knowledge within the boundaries of embeddedness than beyond it (von Hippel, 1994; Almeida and Kogut, 1999).

Saxenian (1994) suggested that a region comprised of a decentralized network of smaller firms would exhibit greater competitive advantage than one that emanated centrally from one or few larger firms because of the freer flow of information in the network. Work building upon her theory of regional advantage has continued to develop the networked notion of advantage (Uzzi, 1997; Almeida and Kogut, 1999), but has largely avoided dissection of the network into fundamental dynamics that lead to this advantage.

Other scholars have offered contrarian views to the Saxenian perspective. Some examine the responsiveness of organizations and regions to environmental shocks, but do not consider the contribution of system level characteristics such as structure and content to the capacity for responsiveness (Meyer, 1982). Greenwood and Suddaby (2006) argue that under certain conditions of stability and maturity, central, dominant actors are more likely to initiate adaptive behaviours that lead to positive structural changes at the industry level. Similarly, one economic perspective of entrepreneurship in the regional economy suggests that under certain conditions it is a function of incumbent firm action and economic knowledge spillover (Audretsch, 1998; Audretsch and Fritsch, 2002; Klepper and Sleeper, 2005). A commonality across all of these perspectives that remains consistent with Saxenian (1994) is the embeddedness of firms in a greater regional structure of interaction.

Uzzi (1996, p. 674) defines embeddedness as the 'process by which social relations shape economic action.' A region's innovation system provides one context in which the effects of embeddedness emerge. The regional innovation system, as a heterogeneous network or social, economic and institutional ties within a region, serves as the substrate on which firms are embedded for the conduct of innovative activities (Asheim and Coenen, 2005). The regional innovation system provides critical structure to the development of competitive advantage (Saxenian, 1994). This system provides the conduits for the flows of knowledge that lead to firm formation, development and diffusion of product and market innovations, and institutional reinforcement of competitive dynamics (von Hippel, 1994; Audretsch, 1997; Asheim and Isaksen, 2002).

The regional innovation system may be thought of as the nexus of interdependent organizations engaged in innovative and competitive actions and 'the institutional infrastructure supporting innovation within the production structure of a region' (Asheim and Coenen, 2005, p. 1177). The nexus occurs in the context of firms and support organizations socially embedded with the knowledge flows of a region's economic activities. Asheim and Isaken (2002, p. 83) elaborate on this definition from a knowledge-based perspective:

> ... regional clusters are, thus, regarded as places where close inter-firm communications, socio-cultural structures and institutional environment may stimulate socially and territorially embedded collective learning and continuous innovation. ... the proximity between different actors makes it possible for them to create, acquire, accumulate and utilise knowledge a little faster than firms outside of knowledge intensive dynamic regional clusters.

Saxenian (1994) reflects this definition in her characterization of Silicon Valley as a strong and resilient regional innovation system, while suggesting Boston's firm-centric, monolithic culture from the 1950s to 1990s possessed a significantly weaker regional innovation system.

This variation in innovation system composition uncovered by Saxenian (1994) demonstrates dramatic differences in inter-organizational linkages, and the effects of innovation complexity and knowledge appropriation activity among firms in different innovation systems. Her characterization of regional advantage posited firm interdependence through co-ordinated decentralization of the region's innovation system, specialization of knowledge resulting from the complex chain of innovation activities, and the informal flow of knowledge between firms as the primary determinants of this advantage. Each of these determinants is examined below.

Knowledge appropriation formality. The patterns of interaction and emergence of new firms described by Saxenian (1994) reflect an underlying interdependence between two types of knowledge appropriation resident in these innovation systems: formal knowledge appropriation, and informal knowledge appropriation. Formal knowledge flows are defined as actions effected on the landscape of a regional innovation system, a signalling form of information transmission. These actions may emanate from the incumbent organizational forms (rivalry), institutions responsible for regional governance or co-ordination of the system (i.e., trade associations, regulatory bodies), or emergent organizational forms (new ventures). For example, formal knowledge flows include rivalrous actions taken by existing competitors or alliances formed by incumbents (Smith et al., 1991; Rosenkopf and Almeida, 2003), They could also be efforts to remove technological uncertainty through a standard-setting process, provide co-ordination of disparate innovation and production activities through a certification process, or protect the intellectual property of the firms within the regional system through enforcement of restrictive covenants.

Informal knowledge flows are defined as social transmission of ideas and knowledge that comprise the innovation content of a system (Saxenian, 1994; Asheim and Coenen, 2005). While they may be co-ordinated at an organizational or regional level, these informal flows occur through the interaction of individual actors participating in the system. For example, informal knowledge flows occur when engineers meet socially and discuss technological challenges or engineering advances in passing (Almeida and Kogut, 1999). They also occur through the development of relationship between firms and their buyers, suppliers and competitors (Saxenian, 1994).

Knowledge appropriation occurs within regions through the search and knowledge absorption processes of firms (Cohen and Levinthal, 1990; Almedia and Kogut, 1999). These processes are moulded by the degrees to which the firms are embedded in their task, technical, social and institutional environments (Saxenian, 1994; Uzzi, 1996). The prevalence of knowledge appropriation through informal flows is thought to increase as embeddedness of the firms in a region grows stronger (Uzzi, 1997; Almeida and Kogut, 1999). In this way, we would expect the formality of knowledge appropriation activities to play a substantial role in the competitiveness of regions (Neck et al., 2004).

Proposition 1A   Knowledge appropriation formality will exhibit a negative influence on regional innovation performance.

Interdependence.   This form of interdependence occurs at the firm level and reflects the embedded condition of the firm in its social-institutional environment. Firms embedded in the same social-institutional may develop close ties as trust between the firms' managers grows. Exchange of resources and involvement in each other's business practices become stronger in these trusted relationships (Uzzi, 1996). These bilateral exchanges have greater likelihoods of improving both firms' competitive positions and contributing to processes such as the creation of innovations.

Proposition 1B   Inter-organizational interdependence will exhibit a positive influence on regional innovation performance.

Innovation complexity.   As the innovation activities of a regional innovation system focus on increasingly complex results, the demands for specialized knowledge and complementarity of organization as involved in these activities will increase. At the same time, the co-ordination requirements of these activities and knowledge acquisition demands will become increasingly cumbersome. As a result, these counterbalancing dynamics should optimize regional innovation performance at a point where the targeted innovation results of firms within the regional system are moderately complex.

Proposition 2   Innovation complexity will exhibit an inverse nonlinear influence on regional innovation performance.

Moderating influence of interdependence on other determinants. Prior literature has suggested that firm interdependence and knowledge appropriation are more tightly intertwined in highly embedded contexts (Uzzi, 1996). Relations between firms become stronger through the growing trust that accompanies experience with and exposure to each other's business practices. Uzzi (1996) suggests that, as these trusted relationships develop, the level of involvement in each other's innovation and production activities grow deeper and more frequent. In this way, interdependence would positively influence the effects of knowledge appropriation on regional advantage.

Proposition 3A   Interdependence will increase the speed and magnitude of influence of knowledge appropriation formality on regional innovation performance.

Scholars have discussed the varied impact of strong and weak ties in the value of social network structures (Granovetter, 1973, 1985; Burt, 1992). Additional research has suggested that strong clustering of organizations within an industrial context may produce adverse results with respect to innovation as non-innovative firms within these clusters may act as constraints on the regional innovation system's performance (Beaudry and Breschi, 2003). Strong ties act to more quickly diffuse the contents of a social network. In the case of a regional innovation system one significant type of content is novel knowledge related to innovation activities. The implications of strong ties, then, are that they may have a normative effect on the behaviours of organizations within the region. These firms may be less likely to experiment or act on specialized knowledge in novel ways. Thus, as the complexity of innovation undertaken within a region increases, the demands for specialization will be reached faster as knowledge of the innovation activity moves through the system faster. Conversely, the conflict among dynamics associated with innovation complexity will also increase more rapidly, leading to the condition where an optimal point of regional innovation performance is reached earlier and with lesser impact on the overall value of the innovation. This logic suggests that early in the innovation process, interdependence may make positive contributions to regional innovation performance by speeding discovery. However, it will soon be overwhelmed by the effects of introducing co-ordination and knowledge acquisition challenges earlier into the process.

Proposition 3B   Interdependence will increase the speed and magnitude of the influence of innovation complexity on regional innovation performance.

Figure 7.1 summarizes this set of relationships between the embedded characteristics of firms and regional innovation performance.

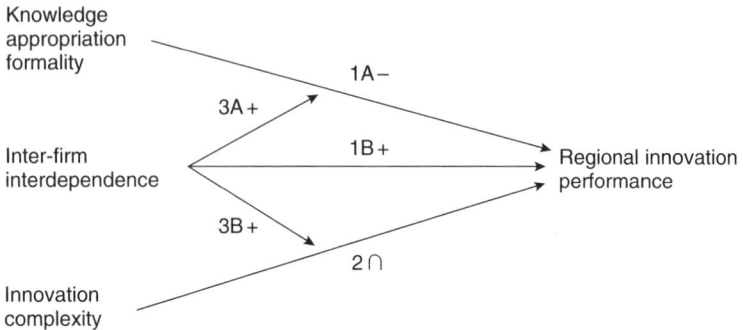

Figure 7.1 Regional innovation performance

7.2 An exploratory model of regional innovation performance

The framework presented here unpacks the primary components of firm embeddedness in the social environment of innovation (Uzzi, 1996). Specifically, we explore the influence of interdependence, innovation complexity and the formality of knowledge appropriation within the regional innovation system on the level of regional innovation performance. Our simulation model provides the means to explore these relationships. In this case, the modeller specifies a process of knowledge appropriation in which a firm acquires and transforms information into knowledge useful in its own innovation routines. The resulting model is configured by the modeller with fixed parameters that guide the computer's execution of the simulation model. The computer generates, as a part of program execution, certain parameters and imputed variables the produce variation among simulation runs.

Simulation does not provide 'realistic' results in the sense that many aspects of a firm, its innovation capabilities and routines have been simplified in order to focus attention on the key variables of embeddedness identified here: actor interdependence, product complexity and search formality. These variables reflect constructs the literature has proposed and empirically demonstrated as central to the problem of innovation outcomes at a firm or regional level (Saxenian, 1994; Uzzi, 1996, 1997). The model reflects the reality of repeated organizational search activities related to the creation of a single innovation and the objective of firms to maximize production of profitable innovations.

A simple computational model of regional innovation can be specified by three process subsystems comprising the regional innovation system, a stream of knowledge appropriation choices on a search landscape, and a set of knowledge appropriation and innovation value extraction assumptions.

7.2.1 Knowledge appropriation and innovation value extraction assumptions

The knowledge appropriation and innovation value extraction assumptions for the computational model are operationalized as parameters fixed at the beginning of the simulation run. These parameters consist of four categories: (1) simulation parameters, (2) innovation parameters, (3) firm interdependence parameters, and (4) a pay-off matrix. The simulation parameters define the scope of the simulation run. They include the number periods for which the model will run (T) and the number of firms competing in the model (I). The innovation parameters include the number of components (N) comprising an innovation configuration, the degree of inter-operability between components (K), the number of initial components allocated to the firm's innovation profile (S) and the number of components (A) acquired by the firm through any given knowledge appropriation event. The interdependence parameters include probabilities of partner exchange occurring as a result of far knowledge appropriation distance through informal mechanisms $[Pr(Exch_{FI})]$ and moderate appropriation distance through informal mechanisms $[Pr(Exch_{MI})]$ where $[Pr(Exch_{MI})] > [Pr(Exch_{FI})] > 0.5$. Interdependence parameters also include the bit string length for a partner exchange event under moderate formal search conditions (A_{MF}). The pay-off matrix provides values for successful knowledge appropriation events contributing to innovation creation under different search conditions. This value is defined as the function P, a variable determined at period t based on a pay-off matrix. An example of a pay-off matrix for this simulation model is shown in Table 7.1.

Table 7.1 Knowledge appropriation distance

	Knowledge appropriation distance		
	Near	Moderate	Far
Innovation result (search form)			
Incremental (formal)	1	2	4
Incremental (informal)	3	5	50
Radical	50	500	1,000

One of the limitations of the simulations approach discussed here is the limited realism associated with the central dynamics of the system. Knowledge appropriation between organizations provides a core explanation of regional competitive advantage. In the model we treat knowledge appropriation choices as discrete and active. This is to say, we allow each organization to make one choice regarding their innovation process in each period (including the choice not to choose any active work on its innovation). This choice is then evaluated in its 'distance' from the organization. Some literature from decision-making and information search has suggested that organizations work outward from their core in the pursuit of new knowledge (Levitt and March, 1988; Miller, 1993; Gavetti and Levinthal, 2000; Hill and Rothaermel, 2003). Other work has suggested that social context plays a more significant role in the acquisition of new knowledge (Yli-Renko et al., 2001).

7.2.2   Describing the embeddedness model

Knowledge appropriation formality.   This variable is determined computationally by the simulation for each firm in each period by choosing between formal and informal flows of appropriated knowledge. Formal mechanisms occur through discrete and overt ('official') relationships between firms. These relationships might include transactions between firms, agreements to collaborate on technology development or marketing alliances that facilitate movement of a firm's products through distribution channels to the market. Informal knowledge appropriation mechanisms occur through social relationships of employees in different organizations. These informal relationships may be coordinated through institutions on the search landscape (e.g., trade associations) or may occur more freely through other means.

For purposes of modelling in this simulation, formal mechanisms are assumed to be contractual and thus occurring at a higher cost, with greater familiarity and with lower returns (since the degree of asymmetry in knowledge post-contract is assumed to be significantly lower than for informal mechanisms). Formal mechanisms will have limitations governed by a model parameter so that they cannot occur in every period (reflecting the cost associated with the time to identify a partner, negotiate an agreement and execute a contract; periods in this simulation are scaled to months not years). The model uses three levels of the rate of formal action recurrence to test the effects of latency in the formalization of structure in the region. Informal mechanisms are modelled as random social interactions of individuals that occur more regularly (e.g., the possibility exists for informal action to occur in each period), on a smaller scale, and with lower likelihoods of success than for formal mechanisms.

Innovation complexity. Design complexity has been defined previously as the collective result of the number and inter-operability requirements of components in a system. Scholars have applied this definition to organizational design, product architecture and innovations (Henderson and Clark, 1990; Rivkin and Siggelkow, 2003; Rodgers [and Shoemaker, 1962], 2003). This computational model extends the definition to innovation configurations held in common by firms within the regional innovation system. It assumes the complexity of an innovation is consistent across firms within that system.

A region's innovation complexity is specified by a target innovation profile consisting of N components. N is determined as a fixed parameter at the initialization of a given run of the simulation and represents one dimension of degrees of freedom in the overall simulation design. Thus, every firm in the model is pursuing an innovation of identical size and composition. The configuration of the target innovation profile is a priori unknown to the firm. For example, an innovation target may be represented by a bit string, or a string of ones and zeros, specified to length N as shown in Figure 7.2.

To ensure sufficient degrees of freedom with this function of the simulation model, N is set greater than or equal to nine (9).

The interoperability of an innovation's components (bits in the bit string above) can be represented in terms of an influence matrix (Cohen, March and Olsen, 1972; Rivkin and Siggelkow, 2003) that determines which components are required to be present when the focal component is included. The modeller specifies K number of components that influence other components. K represents the degree of component inter-operability. The model allows K to range from zero (0) to N/3. At K = 0 the components are completely distinct and independent elements of the innovation. K≤N/3 ensures the innovation will consist of at least three independent modular subsystems (sets of inter-operable components). This latter limitation ensures variation will exist between the innovation processes of firms in the model; without this limitation the target innovation profile has the potential to become monolithic in the sense that a component would require all other components in order to be introduced into the firm's innovation. The influence matrix is generated by the computer randomly assigning K unique components to relate to each component to K components with which it is required to be inter-operable. Figure 7.3 illustrates a possible randomly assigned influence matrix for N = 6 and K = 2.

111 010010 1010	100 000010 1000
Target innovation profile	Initialized firm innovation profile
(a)	(b)

Figure 7.2   An innovation target representation

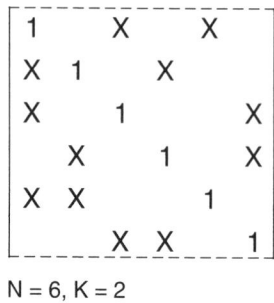

N = 6, K = 2

Figure 7.3   A possible randomly assigned influence matrix for N = 6 and K = 2

In this example, the inter-operable components are represented by Xs and relate to the focal component indicated with a '1'.

Inter-firm interdependence. In the computational simulation, interdependence is modelled by another firm's innovation process being altered by changes in the focal firm's innovation process. At the beginning of a simulation run, each firm is assigned an initial innovation position consisting of an N-length bit string in which S components are allocated to the firm at randomly assigned positions in the bit string (the firm's Innovation Bit String or IBS).

Interdependence here is defined as a partner exchange event in which both firms appropriate knowledge from each other that may contribute to respective improvements in their IBSs. When a firm's knowledge appropriation choice is a moderate distance from the firm on the search landscape (e.g., within the firm's industry sector or adjacent technology domain), the partner exchange event occurs in two ways. For formal information flows between partners at moderate distance, the exchange of knowledge reflects alliances, technology partnerships and other formalized relationships between firms in which tactical knowledge regarding innovation creation is exchanged. In this case, the computational model selects another firm randomly from the search landscape and adds A_{MF} components to that firm's IBS (if the component slots as depicted in Figure 7.2 are available).

When the knowledge appropriation choice is a far distance from the firm on the search landscape, the partner exchange event is assumed to occur through informal mechanisms such as the social interaction of engineers from firms in disparate industry sectors or technology domains (Saxenian, 1994). Formal mechanisms such as alliances are assumed in this computation model to have indirect and strategic influences on firm performance and thus do not directly contribute to changes in the partner firm's IBS. Informal mechanisms, by contrast, reflect the characteristics of social embeddedness through the interaction of individuals across organizations

(Uzzi, 1997). The probability of successful knowledge exchange occurring in a distant social interaction is low because of the stronger influence of random chance on these relationships. In the model, successful appropriation from a far search location through informal means creates potential for the transfer to a partner firm of one component (or bit) on some probability $Pr(Exch_{FI})$. If the model determines partner exchange occurs under this condition then one bit of a randomly selected 'partner' firm's IBS is updated to include the corresponding component of the innovation (toggling the bit from zero to a one in programming parlance).

Regional innovation performance. Regional innovation performance is the visible performance measure used to evaluate and compare runs from the simulation. It is modelled as an entropy measure of the concentration (an analogue of the Herfindahl Index) of value produced through the development of innovations by the simulated firms. Equation 1 describes this variable formally.

$$\text{Regional Innovation Performance} = \sum_{i=1}^{I} \left(\frac{\sum_{t=0}^{T} P_i(t)}{\sum_{i=1}^{I} \sum_{t=0}^{T} P_i(t)} \right)^2 \tag{1}$$

A Herfinahl-type measure enables the comparative evaluation of different configurations of regional innovation systems on a grand scale. It offers a preliminary means for normalizing innovation activities that would vary across industry context and regional economic conditions. Using simulation, one can then better isolate and assess the roles of knowledge appropriation, inter-organizational interdependence and innovation complexity on regional innovativeness.

Conclusion

This chapter delivers a conceptual framework for exploration of significant factors effecting the competitive advantage of regions. It contributes to theory on regional innovation systems by bridging the contentious elements of perspectives on spatial economic interdependency and agglomeration of specialized capabilities and knowledge. The model presented here illustrates the uniquely positive effect that informal exchange of knowledge between organizations can have on the performance of a regional innovative system, While the probability of successful exchange of *useful* knowledge may be low, the potential impact at the firm and regional level for this type of exchange that occurs in bowling alleys and neighbourhood bars is extraordinary. Others have characterized this single factor as a dominant explanation in the sustained competitive advantage of Silicon Valley (Saxenian, 1994; Kenney, 2000).

The model presented here extends that notion by considering the simultaneous impact of knowledge appropriation informality, interdependence among organizations in a region, and the complexity of innovations undertaken by firms in that region. The model applies a systems dynamic approach to explore how these factors may be co-evolutionary with the innovation performance of a region. While the chapter does not present a completed simulation study, its objectives were to stimulate thinking about the central factors of regional innovativeness and to promote directions for future simulation and empirical study on this question of regional competitive advantage.

Notes

1   In order to isolate the knowledge appropriation mechanisms in innovation, the region's production system and markets for innovations are assumed in the proposed model to behave with perfect efficiency.
2   Simulation provides a comprehensive approach to understanding the nature and level of interdependencies present in a system, such as the regional innovation function, that is less feasible through analytical approaches (March, 1991; Rivkin and Siggelkow, 2003; Davis et al., 2007). It also enables the researcher to expand the boundary conditions of a phenomenon beyond levels that might be reasonably expected from field research, such as the dimensionality of knowledge appropriation activities or level of interdependency between firms in a region (Cohen et al., 1972).

References

Almeida, Paul and Kogut, Bruce (1999), 'Localization of knowledge and the mobility of engineers in regional networks', *Management Science*, Vol. 45, No. 7, p. 905.
Asheim, Bjorn and Coenen, Lars (2005), 'Knowledge bases and regional innovation systems: Comparing Nordic clusters', *Research Policy*, Vol. 34, No. 8, p. 1173.
Asheim, Bjorn and Isaksen, Arne (2002), 'Regional innovation systems: The integration of local "sticky" and global "ubiquitous" knowledge', *Journal of Technology Transfer*, Vol. 27, No. 1, p. 77.
Audretsch, David (1998), 'Agglomeration and the location of innovative activity', *Oxford Review of Economic Policy*, Vol. 14, No. 2, p. 18.
Audretsch, David and Fritsch, Michael (2002), 'Growth regimes over time and space', *Regional Studies*, Vol. 36, No. 2, p. 113.
Audretsch, David and Keilbach, Max (2004), 'Entrepreneurship and regional growth: An evolutionary interpretation', *Journal of Evolutionary Economics*, Vol. 14, No. 5, p. 605.
Beaudry, Catherine and Breschi, Stefano (2003), 'Are firms in clusters Really More Innovative?' *Economics of Innovation & New Technology*, Vol. 12, No. 4, p. 325.
Burt, Ronald (1992), *Structural Holes: The Social Structure of Competition*, Harvard University Press, Cambridge, MA.
Cohen, Michael, March, James and Olsen, Johan (1972), 'A garbage can model of organizational choice', *Administrative Science Quarterly*, Vol. 17, No. 1, pp. 1–25.

Cohen, Wesley and Levinthal, Daniel A. (1990), 'Absorptive capacity: A new perspective on learning and inno', *Administrative Science Quarterly*, Vol. 35, No. 1, p. 128.

Davis, Jason, Eisenhardt, Kathleen and Bingham, Christopher (2007), 'Developing theory through simulation methods', *Academy of Management: The Academy of Management Review*, Vol. 32, No. 2, p. 480.

Florida, Richard (2005), *The Flight of the Creative Class: The New Global Competition for Talent*, Harper Collins Publishers, New York.

Gavetti, Giovanni, and Levinthal, Daniel (2000), 'Looking forward and looking backward: Cognitive and experiential search', *Administrative Science Quarterly*, Vol. 45, No. 1, p. 113.

Granovetter, Mark (1985), 'Economic action and social structure: The problem of embeddedness', *The American Journal of Sociology*, Vol. 91, No. 3, pp. 481–510.

Granovetter, Mark (1973), 'The strengh of weak ties', *American Journal of Sociology*, Vol. 78, No. 6, pp. 1360–80.

Greenwood, Royston and Suddaby, Roy (2006), 'INSTITUTIONAL ENTREPRENEURSHIP IN MATURE FIELDS: THE BIG FIVE ACCOUNTING FIRMS', *Academy of Management Journal*, Vol. 49, No. 1, p. 27.

Henderson, Rebecca M., and Clark, Kim B. (1990), 'Architectural innovation: The reconfiguration of existing,' *Administrative Science Quarterly*, Vol. 35, No. 1, p. 9.

Hill, Charles W. L. and Rothaermel, Frank T. (2003), 'The performance of incumbent firms in the face of radical technological innovation', *Academy of Management: The Academy of Management Review*, Vol. 28, No. 2, p. 257.

Kenney, Martin (2000), *Understanding Silicon Valley: The Anatomy of an Entrepreneurial Region*, Stanford University Press, Stanford, CA.

Klepper, Steven and Sleeper, Sally (2005), 'Entry by spinoffs.' *Management Science*, Vol. 51, No. 8, p. 1291.

Krugman, Paul (1994), 'Complex landscapes in economic geography', *The American Economic Review*, Vol. 84, No. 2, p. 412.

Levitt, Barbara and March, James (1988), 'Organizational learning', *Annual Review of Sociology*, Vol. 14, pp. 319–40.

Lomi, Alessandro and Larsen, Erik R. (1996), 'Interacting locally and evolving globally: A computational approach to the dynamics of organizational populations', *Academy of Management Journal*, Vol. 39, No. 5, p. 1287.

March, James (1991),'Exploration and exploitation in organizational learning', *Organization Science: A Journal of the Institute of Management Sciences*, Vol. 71. INFORMS: Institute for Operations Research.

Meyer, Alan (1982), 'Adapting to environmental jolts', *Administrative Science Quarterly*, Vol. 27, No. 4, p. 515.

Miller, Danny (1993), 'The architecture of simplicity', *Academy of Management Review*, Vol. 18, No. 1, pp. 116–38.

Neck, Heidi, Meyer, Dale, Cohen, Boyd and Corbett, Andrew (2004), 'An entrepreneurial system view of new venture creation', *Journal of Small Business Management*, Vol. 42, No. 2, p. 190.

Nelson, Richard and Winter, Sidney (1982), *An Evolutionary Theory of Economic Change*, Belknap Press/Harvard University Press, Cambridge, MA, and London.

Porter, Michael (1980), *Competitive Strategy*, 1st edn, The Free Press, New York.

Rivkin, Jan and Siggelkow, Nicolaj (2003), 'Balancing search and stability: interdependencies among elements of organizational design', *Management Science*, Vol. 49, No. 3, pp. 290–311.

Rogers, Everett (2003 [1962]), *Diffusion of Innovations*, Free Press of Glencoe, New York.

Rosenkopf, Lori and Almeida, Paul (2003), 'Overcoming local search through alliance mobility', *Management Science*, Vol. 49, No. 6, pp. 751–66.

Saxenian, Anne-Marie (1994), *Regional Advantage: Culture and Competition in Silicon Valley and Route 128*, Harvard University Press, Cambridge, MA.

Smith, Ken, Grimm, Curtis, Gannon, Martin and Chen, Ming-Jer (1991), 'Organizational information processing, competitive responses, and performance in the U.S. domestic airline industry', *Academy of Management Journal*, Vol. 34, No. 1, p. 60.

Uzzi, Brian (1996), 'The sources and consequences of embeddedness for the economic performance of organizations: The network effect', *American Sociological Review*, Vol. 61, No. 4, p. 674.

Uzzi, Brian (1997), 'Social structure and competition in interfirm networks: The paradox of embeddedness', *Administrative Science Quarterly*, No. 42, pp. 35–67.

von Hippel, Eric (1994), '"Sticky information" and the locus of problem solving: Implications for innovation', *Management Science*, Vol. 40, No. 4, p. 429.

Yli-Renko, Helena, Autio, Erkko and Sapienza, Harry J. (2001), 'Social capital, knowledge acquisitions, and knowledge exploitation in young technology-based firms', *Strategic Management Journal*, Vol. 22, No. 6/7, p. 587.

8

Product Innovation as Micro-Strategy: The 'Innovation-Based Diversification' View

Seppo Hänninen[a] *and Ilkka Kauranen*[b]
[a]*Helsinki University of Technology, Lahti Centre*
[b]*Asia Institute of Technology, Thailand*

Diversification strategy discussion has focused relatively little on the unintentional diversification caused by a product innovation which does not match the existing business strategy of a company. The objective of the study is to deepen the understanding of product-innovation-based diversification as a corporate micro-strategy. The new theory development is illustrated with a case study of a consumer electronics product innovation. One of the key findings is that the micro-view offers a way to better understand innovation-based diversification, which is an unavoidable consequence of any product innovation in a company. A second finding is that the diversification indicators operate beyond the limits of the coherent product innovation concept.

Introduction

Diversification has typically been seen as an intentional decision, which takes place under the deliberate control of corporate management (Markides, 1997). Problems have been identified in implementing the diversification decision, rather than in the diversification intention itself. Diversification is dependent, however, on the available resources and especially on the prevailing knowledge (Wernerfelt, 1984; Breschi et al., 2003; Bitencourt, 2004).

For diversification with a radical innovation in a new market, it is customarily recommended that the 'probe and learn' process be used. However, this is a slow and expensive method (Lynn et al., 1996; O'Connor, 1998). The risk of failure in diversification is highly significant, and development to a profitable level is usually slow, which is one reason why an innovation causing unintentional diversification does not typically fit well with the overall corporate strategy. The benefits of new product development are likely to be harvested in a gradual, incremental innovation development process (Hauser, 2001). Several operational instruments have been applied in managing uncertain and unpredictable product development processes, for example, feedback-loop related solutions (Hilmola et al., 2005). However, these instruments have focused on the product development process, not on the strategic process related to innovation.

Only few research studies have focused on unintentional diversification caused by a product innovation, which does not match the existing business of the company. Such product innovations often distort the existing business strategy and the potential of such innovations to be successful is vulnerable. Many innovations at the same time bear characteristics of both a radical and incremental innovation and, thus, they may be categorized as semi-incremental innovations. Such semi-incremental innovations are very common, making their implications wide-ranging. This is typically so, for example, if the product innovation is based on a product platform and if the product at the same time involves new value-adding technologies. The risk is that such a semi-incremental innovation may bring about minor but significant changes in the company's target customer groups and patterns of competition, with the consequence that the company is unable to exploit the full market potential. If the product innovation is a first product in a new product category, the difficulties inherent to the fact that the company is forced to deal with new customers and to learn new patterns of competition is even a greater threat. A possible scenario is that the investment in the innovation may ruin the financial basis of the company without opening up new business opportunities. Companies with low innovative level clearly have low learning capabilities (Heijs, 2004) but the limited learning can also cause strategy related difficulties with the innovations (Mentzas, 2004). High learning capabilities are very important in tackling the challenges of unintentional diversification.

Recent strategy discussion has had a focus on micro-strategy and micro-strategizing (Johnson et al., 2003; Salvato, 2003). A micro-perspective on company strategy is needed in order to better understand the total strategy process. Micro-strategy is the company strategy in a small scale. The actor of the company strategy is the company. The actor of the micro-strategy is, for example, a strategic business unit, a sales office, or a product development team (Johnson et al., 2003). In the present study, the actor of micro-strategy is the product innovation. However, product innovation as a micro-strategy has not yet emerged in the product development literature. Traditionally in product development literature innovations are discussed as a part of broader business strategy, not as a strategy in itself (e.g., Calantone et al., 2003). However, in a small company, the only observable strategy often is its innovation. The objective of the present study is to deepen the understanding of product-innovation-based diversification as a corporate micro-strategy. The new theory development is illustrated by a case study of a consumer electronics product innovation. This product innovation has played a key role within its product category; yet there are indications that the potential of this innovation has so far not at all been fully exploited. This product innovation is not merely an element in the company's overall product strategy, but it also constitutes in itself a micro-technology strategy, a micro-end-user strategy, a micro-brand strategy, and a micro-business strategy. An examination of this product innovation and its history can also reveal the company's innovation-driver patterns and systemic solutions.

In the present study, first knowledge bases concerning product innovation are introduced. The idea is that by understanding the relationships between product innovation and its underlying knowledge bases, diversification strategy as represented by product innovation can also be better understood and developed. Then the approach is expanded to the knowledge base debate, including the driver knowledge level, systemic knowledge level, and strategic knowledge level. Then the product innovation case study is analysed, and the solutions are discussed in relation to the international market context. Incorporating knowledge bases and knowledge levels into the discussion of product innovation constitutes a new approach, which has not previously been utilized.

8.1 Theory

8.1.1 Features of a knowledge base

The concept of a knowledge base refers to managerial and organizational cognition and concepts about the development project and its environment, and the relationships between these. In contrast to a database, a knowledge base also includes implicit knowledge, such as values, routines and stories. Cohen and Levinthal (1990) have discussed some key features of a knowledge base, which explain how one knowledge base can dominate the other knowledge bases. Typical features of a knowledge base are the demand for prior knowledge, the cumulative nature of knowledge development, filtering of knowledge, and knowledge-base-specific language.

Demand for prior knowledge. For any knowledge to be focused and to be of interest, there must be some prior knowledge. New knowledge cannot ring the alarm bells in the organization if there is no knowledge base where the new knowledge can be received. Some of the prior knowledge needed can be recruited with new professional personnel, and some of it is related in an evolutionary way to experiences, especially dramatic experiences within the organization.

Cumulative knowledge. Once a knowledge base has been established, it becomes deepened through the addition of further new knowledge. Each knowledge base consists of both explicit and tacit knowledge, which is stored in organizational routines, stories and files. Knowledge is created through the interaction of organization members and through practicing skills relevant to the organization's objectives.

Filtering of knowledge.   Part of the knowledge development process is that only knowledge supporting prior knowledge can be accepted. Other knowledge will be rejected. This filter is based on the values formed by management and specialist personnel, on the grounds of their previous experiences. For example, anyone studying a new skill knows how difficult it is to accept new, differing, viewpoints.

A knowledge-base-specific language.   One part of the filtering process is that the knowledge base needs a specific language. Specialists communicate through shared mental models and consensual concepts, which constitute large-scale concentrates of multidimensional information. Similarly, there are also project-specific and industry-specific 'languages'.

8.1.2   The four knowledge bases of product innovation

A micro-strategy should be analysed by considering the role of knowledge bases in product innovation. The role of knowledge bases in product innovation is a major topic in the innovation management literature (Tushman and Anderson, 1986; Cohen and Levinthal, 1990; Leonard-Barton, 1992; Walsh, 1995). This discussion has mainly either focused on the technological knowledge base, or the content of the knowledge base has been left undefined. The present model makes use of four knowledge bases: the technological knowledge base, the end-user knowledge base, the brand knowledge base, and the business-logic knowledge base. The four knowledge bases are illustrated in Figure 8.1. The total contribution of the four knowledge bases is more than the sum of the four when each knowledge base is considered separately.

All four knowledge bases can be shown to exist during the product innovation process, but they may remain latent. Such latency is supported, for example, by the dominance of one knowledge base. Usually any organization has at least a passive consciousness of all four knowledge bases. The view of the present chapter is that the knowledge bases are related to each other like networked computers, developing information into knowledge.

8.1.2.1   *Technological knowledge base*

The 'technological' knowledge base refers to the specific phase of technological development in which an innovation takes place, and to the potential opportunities that technology offers. Alongside a dominant technology, new alternative technologies may develop, which may lead to a new division of the market (Bower and Christensen, 1995). Enterprises need both research to expand their technological knowledge, and operations to exploit it (March, 1991). The technological environment, in which any innovation is developed, is regulated by standards and patents. An important task of product innovation is to ensure the alliance of an innovation with those technological solutions, which will best ensure its commercial success.

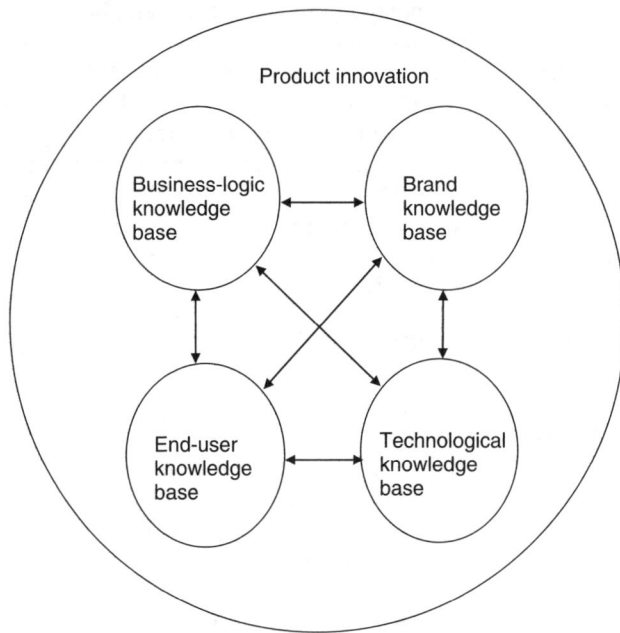

Figure 8.1 The four knowledge bases in product innovation

The advancement of technology, like that of scientific paradigms, occurs through both evolutionary processes and breakthroughs (Dosi, 1982). Technological breakthroughs may lead to the promotion, or to the collapse, of an enterprise's previous knowledge base (Tushman and Anderson, 1986; Henderson and Clark, 1990; Laamanen and Autio, 1996). The future of technology can to some extent be predicted by means of technology road-maps, which are a tool for forecasting probable future developments (Kappel, 2001). New developments in semiconductor technology and power battery technology, for example, are likely to have a significant impact on product innovation in high-technology industries in the foreseeable future. A road-map can be used in ensuring that a new product innovation utilizes the optimum technology both at the time when the technology is launched on the market and for as long as possible thereafter.

A significant proportion of technological knowledge can be expressed explicitly, by means of mathematical formulas or diagrams, for instance. This is one reason for the finding that the technological dimension easily becomes over-emphasized among different knowledge bases for technological product innovations (Leonard-Barton, 1992). It is common in product innovation to devote more financial resources to promoting technological development than to marketing (Cooper, 1975).

The function of the technology in product innovation, however, is to offer a solution to an explicit problem or a latent problem experienced by the end-user. The broader the scope, within which the technology is innovative, the less overt the needs of the end-users will be. The useful life of a product innovation will therefore be extended if several technological options can be incorporated into it. Technological options can include latent innovative features, including features, which cannot yet be used at the market launch of the product, for example, because the available infrastructure does not yet support them. However, ignoring other knowledge bases and utilizing only the technological knowledge base is much riskier.

8.1.2.2   The end-user knowledge base

The 'end-user' knowledge base refers to the ways in which a product innovation may be able to solve problems, whether explicit or latent, faced by the end-users. End-users have two roles in relation to innovation: as prospective purchasers, and as prospective users. How much influence the end-user has on the actual purchase itself will depend on the specifics of the purchasing process. Consumer goods are typically bought by the consumer. In corporate purchasing, the end-users' role is usually limited to influencing the choice, but not to making the actual act of buying.

In the end-user knowledge base, what matters about a product innovation is that it should be user-friendly and should enrich experience – in other words, it should have what the end-users will perceive as added value. User-friendliness affects users' willingness to accept and adopt innovations, but for a product innovation to gain users' commitment, it needs to have as many features as possible, which will extend their experience (Prahalad and Ramaswamy, 2003). User-friendliness and experience-enrichment are complementary, not mutually exclusive features.

Lead users are those who take advantage of new products and themselves develop them further to better fulfil their own needs. Software products can be enhanced with features, which facilitate this kind of product development by the user (Franke and von Hippel, 2003). Corporate personnel may well be enthusiastic about taking part in product innovation development processes as users, not merely as part of the product development machine. New knowledge creation by synthesizing capability through dialectical leadership is one key factor in creating customer value and succeeding in new markets (Kodama, 2005).

The end-users' knowledge base is constructed through a variety of channels such as, for example, feedback from clients, case stories, usability surveys and market research.

8.1.2.3   Brand knowledge base

The 'brand' knowledge base was presented and discussed in an editorial article by Tauber (1983). The 'brand' knowledge base describes how an innovation relates to the enterprise's brand equity (Aaker, 1991). Brand equity is constituted not merely by a range of products, but by the project's total systematic mode of operations, irrespective of the enterprise's size. Even open-source software products have a brand identity, one purpose of which is to identify the copyright holder (O'Mahony, 2003).

An enterprise's brand does not exist independently of its products; at the heart of the concept of a brand are the product innovation and the added value which the innovation creates for the end-users (Aaker, 1991). Brand can also relate to technological added value. The slogan 'Intel inside', for instance, tells us nothing about the technology deployed, but rather, promises value to the personal computer user (Ward et al., 1999). A product needs to share the same idiom with the rest of its brand. The design needs to be consistent and coherent throughout, from the innovation itself to the product's entire mode of operations. Consistency reduces costs, and concentrates the message on a coherent set of values. The construction of a brand knowledge base may well begin with the graphic design of the brand and the industrial design of the product (Schmitt, Simonsen, and Marcus, 1995). Developing a brand and brand equity is, however, very time-consuming (Aaker, 1991).

8.1.2.4   The business-logic knowledge base

The 'business-logic' knowledge base describes the status and function of an innovation within the overall context of the project's business operations. The term 'business logic' is used to describe the dominant mode of operation within a specific company or branch of business, which is constituted by the various logics of value creation within this environment and which supports commercial success. Other closely related terms and concepts include 'dominant logic' (Prahalad and Bettis, 1986) and 'strategic logic' (Kim and Mauborgne, 1997). Understanding the dominant business logic is particularly important both for radical product innovation and in mature business sectors. In hyper-competitive markets, it is very important to be able to scan the environment and learn the new changing business logic (Drejer et al., 2005).

Typically, a new product innovation is intended to replace or displace alternative substitute products from the market. Even if none of the substitute products is strictly speaking in immediate competition with the new product, all substitutes are effectively in competition for parallel roles for the end-users and for business operations (Porter, 1980). In order to avert a situation of direct competition, companies need to develop innovations, which will be capable of changing the dominant business logic (Kim and Mauborgne, 1997). Companies, which cannot alter the prevailing rules of the market, must make their products comply with the dominant logic. To challenge and alter the dominant logic is in fact one of the ways in which it is possible to challenge the status of the current market leader (Kim and

Mauborgne, 1997). If a company is not thoroughly familiar with the particular field of business, it may delegate the marketing of an innovation to another company that does know the field and is capable of carrying the financial risk (Mitchell and Singh, 1996). This is a strategy very typical of small start-up companies. Initially, the development of the knowledge bases relating to product innovation started with technological knowledge, but the understanding of product innovation has steadily expanded and these other knowledge bases relating to end-users, brands and business logic have been included. Shifts in the relative importance of the various knowledge bases in relation to product innovation development also imply shifts within corporate power structures (Normann, 1971; Henderson and Clark, 1990). A recurrent weakness relating to knowledge bases is that, for example, the branding tasks in large companies are often short-term training positions for other functions (Tauber, 1983). This means that tacit knowledge learned is lost when the person moves to new challenges.

Generally speaking, the different knowledge bases are not perceived as factors all making for change, but it is assumed that one or more of them will hold constant, and that only one of them – the technology, for instance – will change. In reality, however, each of these knowledge bases constitutes a potential platform for change. Both on the operative and the strategic level, projects need to explore the potential implications for a particular innovation of each knowledge base, without imposing constraining parameters.

Using the 'four knowledge bases approach' in product innovation favours cross-functional co-operation. The approach also suggests that problems related to the product innovation process are often caused by the relationships between knowledge bases and encountered in the exploration and exploitation of knowledge bases. Some of the most typical problems are caused by the dominance of the technological knowledge base, which is particularly common in product innovation. Other knowledge bases related to product innovation include the marketing knowledge base, manufacturing knowledge base and corporate strategy knowledge base. In a broad definition, marketing can be defined as everything other than technology. In this sense, the marketing knowledge base is a combination of end-user knowledge, brand knowledge and business logic knowledge. In the present study, manufacturing knowledge means the process knowledge related to technology. One concrete knowledge base needed is the combinative knowledge base, which is analogous to the combinative capabilities discussed by Kogut and Zander (1992). Adding more knowledge bases to the framework adds to the explanatory power of the framework but also makes the framework more complicated. At this stage of the evolution of the frameworks, the framework with four knowledge bases is investigated.

8.1.3   Knowledge levels in the product innovation knowledge bases

In the present study, the knowledge bases are seen as having four knowledge levels: the *driver* knowledge level, *product-concept* knowledge level, *systemic* knowledge level and *strategic* knowledge level. These knowledge levels are typical in analyses of companies but a new contribution can be made by utilizing this framework in the micro-strategy discussion. Some other knowledge levels are, for example, the tacit knowledge level and the explicit knowledge level, as well as the abstracted knowledge and concrete knowledge levels. The latter mentioned knowledge levels are knowledge-related and they would merit a separate discussion in further research.

The topic of knowledge levels is discussed from operational and strategic product innovation viewpoints. An operational product innovation is a solution for existing competition; whereas a strategic product innovation profoundly changes the business logic of the industry by preparing end-users for new technologies (Kim and Mauborgne, 1997). Table 8.1 illustrates the four knowledge bases and four knowledge levels of product innovation, which constitute the framework of the present study.

8.1.3.1   *Driver level knowledge in the product innovation knowledge bases*

Before a product innovation idea emerges, there must be drivers motivating its creation. Drivers can usually be explained logically afterwards, but at the fuzzy front-end phase of innovation development are often difficult to explicitly define. Driver level knowledge is in fact mostly fuzzy with strategic product innovations, though more explicit with operational innovations related to research results concerning end-users and their needs. In the concise set of knowledge bases of the present study, the main driver may be

Table 8.1   The four knowledge bases and four knowledge levels of product innovation constituting the framework of the present study

		Knowledge base			
		Technology	**End-user**	**Brand**	**Business logic**
Knowledge level	Driver	Technology drivers	End-user drivers	Brand drivers	Business-logic drivers
	Product concept	Technology options	End-user parameters	Brand identity	Business-logic solutions
	Systemic	Technology routine systems	End-user routine systems	Brand routine systems	Business-logic routine systems
	Strategic	Micro-technology strategy	Micro-end-user strategy	Micro-brand strategy	Micro-business strategy

imbedded in the knowledge base relating to technology, to end-user groups, to the brand or to business logic.

A *technological* driver creates an innovative and diversified product innovation. Important factors in technological drivers are technological learning and new frontiers in possibilities opened by advances in technologies. A successful strategic product innovation can motivate the establishment of a completely new product platform.

An *end-user* driver fits operational product innovations tailored to satisfy end-user values. Motivators, which can focus on the end-user as a driver, include a new niche market, a new user group and value creation for old users. A product innovation with the end-user driver has a special usage context or end-user value context.

A *brand* driver increases brand value in the existing target groups and in potential new end-users. The brand may also, however, act as a gatekeeper. As an illustrative example, a high-technology innovation project can be delayed until the innovation has been developed to fully offer real value to the end-user as implied by the brand of this product. This kind of product innovation can focus on full brand-value design, but with marginal technologies, marginal end-user satisfaction and marginal changes in business logic. Some brand-driver centred innovations may offer marginal benefit or marginal value for money.

Finally, a *business logic* driver increases competitiveness, for example by increasing price competitive advantages or value-chain variation. In operative product innovations, the focus is on day-to-day competition. For example, a low-cost manufacturing focus is typically driven by competitive advantage in the low-end market. Strategic product innovations, on the other hand, focus on profound changes in consumption.

8.1.3.2 Concept-level knowledge in the product innovation knowledge bases

Concept-level knowledge is implemented in and tailored to product innovation definitions. The attributes and features of product innovation for the success of any product innovation have been discussed in many highly regarded studies (Henderson and Clark, 1990). In the concise set of knowledge bases of the present study, the four knowledge bases govern design and implementation of the product innovation concept in the form of technological options, end-user experience attributes, brand identity and business models.

Technological options reach beyond the immediate technical solutions – also looking toward technological improvements in the future. *End-user experience attributes* offer more to the end-user than usability alone, which nevertheless also needs to be on a high level. The *brand identity* of the product innovation may be recognizable in its visual form, for example, but the functional logic also communicates brand values. The new *business model* of a new product innovation can change the competition rules of the whole industry.

The importance of each knowledge base differs in its operational and strategic product innovation. Profound technological knowledge, end-user knowledge, and business logic knowledge are needed in strategic product innovations. Brand knowledge and end-user knowledge can be essential in operationalizing product innovations for specific target groups. All aspects of the product innovation need to be consistent. This consistency means that various pieces of knowledge cannot be implemented in the innovation if there are still unresolved tensions between the different knowledge bases. All too often, these tensions are forgotten, and attention is focused only on the internal consistency of the technological solution.

8.1.3.3 Systemic-level knowledge in the knowledge bases

Systemic knowledge may either support or limit the success of the product innovation. In the present study, systemic knowledge is defined as routine day-to-day knowledge about transactions between the company and its environment. Operational solutions are part of this systemic knowledge. In the concise set of knowledge bases of the present study, these systemic-level knowledge bases can again be classified as technological, end-user related, brand related and business logic related.

Technological systemic-level knowledge prepares for and continues the technological solution of the product innovation. Technological routines include, for example, platform technology choices, technology development, manufacturing development, software development, component sourcing and modular manufacturing.

End-user-related systemic-level knowledge reinforces the continuous development of end-user relationships. These routines include, for example, consumer research, usability studies, dissatisfaction research and mass customizing solutions.

The objective of *brand-related* systemic-level knowledge is to increase the value of the brand. Product advertising, sales promotion, press relations and event marketing are aimed at increasing product success and also at strengthening the value of the brand.

Business-logic systemic-level knowledge pushes products into the market. Commercializing the product innovation presupposes product classification, pricing models, sales company choices, sales bonus systems and distribution channel choices, among others. Business logic routines can differ, depending on whether the product innovation is operational or strategic by nature. Strategic product innovations necessitate new business classification routines, because the existing basic rules of the business logic context are changed. The risk is that strategic product innovations, which do not match the existing routines, may be rejected by the organization. Systemic-level routines are typically based on tacit knowledge, and the transactions are well trained (Nonaka et al., 2000). The systemic-level routines can also, however, lead to inability to observe changes in the environment, for example, in end-user behaviour (Cohen and Levinthal, 1990; Bower and Christensen, 1995).

8.1.3.4   *Strategic-level knowledge in the knowledge bases*

Strategic-level knowledge is typically characterized by a few guidelines, which direct the corporate future. This knowledge is less detailed than operational or product-concept knowledge. Strategic-level knowledge is filtered from a vast amount of information collected in routines and other transactions within the operating environment. Consistently, in the concise set of knowledge bases of the present study, the four strategic-level knowledge bases of product innovation can be classified as technology strategy, end-user strategy, brand strategy and business strategy. Accordingly, we define four strategic objectives for any product innovation: taking maximal advantage of technological learning, strategic end-user learning, the strategic brand loyalty role, and the strategic business logic role.

Firstly, a product innovation can increase *strategic technological learning* (Dosi, 1982; Jolly, 1997). New technologies can be tested in new product innovations. By further developing the product innovation, new technological knowledge is also increased.

Secondly, product innovation has a potential role in *strategic end-user learning*. Once launched, a new product may have little market pull, but its main task may be to motivate end-users to learn to use the new technological opportunities enabled by new far-reaching inventions or incremental technology developments.

Thirdly, product innovation has a natural *brand loyalty role*. A product innovation represents brand values optimal for the target group. If a company is missing a product in a specific target market, this can undermine the brand loyalty already created among users of the company's other products and motivate the users to find substitutes. A brand without optimal products represents more an image than real content and value for the end-user group.

Fourthly, product innovation has a *strategic business logic role*. This means, for example, competition tasks. The product can, for example, be launched in a new context, to mount a market study measuring end-user interest in this product category (Lynn et al., 1996). Alternatively, a new product family can also be launched to satisfy the whole market potential in all target groups. For example, a Microsoft Word software package was launched to all, but AutoCAD design software was directed at specific target groups. Product innovation can easily be defined as immediate satisfaction of an end-user need without taking into account the strategic roles of the innovation. A business strategy may be an abstract game plan, without integration into product innovation-level decisions. The link from a product innovation to corporate strategy changes the early phase of product development into a frontline strategic issue.

8.2 Materials and methodology

8.2.1 Case selection

In order to evaluate the viability of the preliminary framework presented in the previous section, an explorative case study was conducted. The case study was so selected that an in-depth analysis of the four knowledge bases and four knowledge levels of the framework is possible. A very representative example of a semi-incremental product innovation, which had resulted in product innovation-based diversification was identified with the help of technology experts.

The framework introduced in the present study was utilized in one instrumental case (cf. Stake, 1995). This revelatory case was an opportunity to observe and analyse a phenomenon previously inaccessible to scientific investigation (Yin, 1989). The selected case represents behaviour where the micro-strategy development of the company had been partly successful.

8.2.2 Data collection and analyses

The material was collected by means of personal interviews with the project liaison officer and with the marketing manager of the company. All interviewed people had followed through the respective product innovation development processes in their company from the start to the end. In the interviews, open-ended questions were used. The interviews were recorded and the responses were then content-analysed for the present research study.

The interview data was supplemented by information obtained, for example, through the Internet, from written sources or from discussions with competitors, suppliers, retailers and end-users. This supplementary data must be considered almost as important as the interview data.

8.3 The case study

8.3.1 Product Innovation T

Product Innovation T was manufactured by *Company C*. Although only a few years old, *Company C* has expanded rapidly to global markets with its high-technology consumer products and it has always been among the ten most important players in its industry. This rapid growth has caused constant, severe financial difficulties to *Company C*. Newcomers from emerging economies have repeatedly challenged *Company C* in the market place.

The idea of launching the development project for *Product Innovation T* came from lead users inside *Company C* itself. They thought that such a product would be successful in the marketplace and useful for similar professionals outside. The idea was presented to the management group of *Company C*, which was the gatekeeper for radical and costly projects. After serious negotiations the project was approved.

Product Innovation T was based on a previous product platform, but the new product incorporated value-added technologies not used in any earlier products derived from the existing product platform. In this context, the term 'product platform' means that similar hardware and software solution groups had already been used in some earlier products by *Company C*. Utilization of a product platform shortened the time to market, and enabled a focus on the value-added features. The technological challenges of the added features proved, however, to be very demanding. Taming the hardware solutions to serve the product idea also meant radical changes in the software structure of the product platform.

Product Innovation T was developed for a specific target group, which was in essence very similar to the lead users inside *Company C*. Expectations of success were high, but sales results were poor. *Product Innovation T* was easy to use as a basic product, but the value-added features needed a long implementation process and a training period not typical for the original product category. From the marketing point of view *Product Innovation T* was mainly seen as a derivative product similar to other derivatives based on the same product platform. The unique selling points of *Product Innovation T* were the compact size of the unit, value-added features in a new form, and increased independence for the end-user.

Product Innovation T was then cannibalized by a new product by the same company, named here *Product Innovation T2*. The latter was in turn cannibalized by a new product by the same company, named here *Product Innovation T3*. These latter products were slightly better, but essentially similar products. This product history came about for two reasons: low competition intensity and poor market research results. *Company C's* competitors were unable to copy the technical solution or to develop viable substitutes. *Company C* was unable to identify such improvement to *Product Innovation T* that the product would awaken interest outside the immediate target group. Instead, end-users in the target group came up with several ideas for improvements to *Product Innovation T*.

8.3.2 Knowledge level analyses of the Product Innovation T

There are some reasons why *Company C's* knowledge concept for *Product Innovation T* was strategically problematic. The main question is why *Product Innovation T* has not grown to be a mass-market product. Results of the knowledge-level analyses of *Product Innovation T* are summarized in Table 8.2 and discussed as follows.

The driver knowledge level.   Rather than the needs of a highly professional target group, an important driver for *Product Innovation T* was the value-added technology, which enabled evolutionary development to meet mass-market end-user behaviour. The processor in the product was too ineffective for all the functional options offered, but it was fast enough for one feature valuable for a wide range of end-users.

Table 8.2 The knowledge bases and knowledge levels of *Product Innovation T*

		Knowledge base			
		Technology	End-user	Brand	Business logic
Knowledge level	Driver	Added-value technology for everone	Added-value technology for professional users	Create more value to the brand	Business-logic drivers
	Product concept	Added-value technology options	Professional user parameters	High-end brand identity	Only for niche market
	Systemic	Explore the added-value technology on highest levels	Test *Product Innovation T* only with professional users	Brand advertising to teenager without teenager version of *Product Innovation T*	Typical sales channel
	Strategic	Test the added-value technology with *Product Innovation T*	Serve the professional users	Expand the brand to professional target group	Stay in product group and in the business logic, don't create a new product group

The concept knowledge level. The product concept of *Product Innovation T* is clear and excellent. The professional target group was very satisfied, especially with the value-added technology of the product. Market research results confirmed that the key definitions of the product concept were well done.

The systemic knowledge level. Organizational learning in the development project of *Product Innovation T* was probably limited to the technology. The first version of *Product Innovation T* was cannibalized by the smaller, but similar *Product Innovation T2*. The latter was developed since market research showed that users of the first version of *Product Innovation T* were dissatisfied with its clumsy size. The target group, product design features and business logic definitions remained unchanged when the new version was developed.

The bonus system applied in *Company C* did not motivate national sales organizations to push *Product Innovation T* in their own markets. For example, in Portugal considerably more units of *Product Innovation T* were sold than in Spain, although Portugal has only one-quarter of the population of Spain. The national sales organizations could choose their sales targets for different consumer electronics models independently; what was important was the combined total sales result of all products.

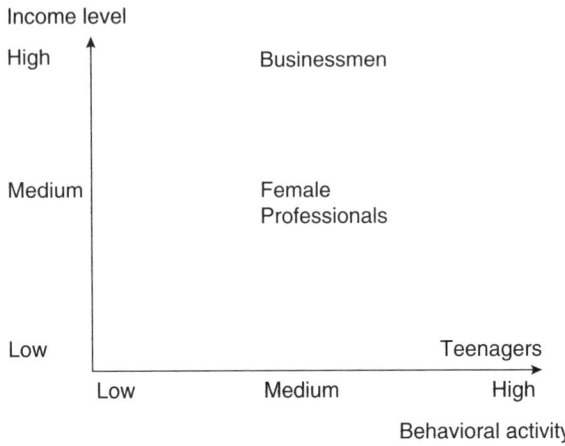

Figure 8.2 Potential user groups of *Product Innovation T*

It has been impossible to satisfy the whole end-user potential of the technology incorporated in *Product Innovation T* with only one single-price category. The most eager user group of this value-added technology has been young adults: teenagers and students; but the price category for *Product Innovation T* has exceeded teenagers' pocket money and student loan budgets. Figure 8.2 illustrates the potential user groups of *Product Innovation T*.

Company C's brand strategy in the young target group was image-oriented rather than content-oriented. For example, *Company C* supports skateboard competitions, but has not offered value-added technology products for young end-users, even though they are known to be the group with the most interest for new technologies.

The first version of *Product Innovation T* was launched as a member of *Company C's* consumer electronics product family. Many potential end-users were interested in the value-added technology, but were unable to make the relatively high investment in *Product Innovation T*. Competitors were thus motivated to develop substitutes. Figure 8.3 shows the differences between two product families.

Staged financing was applied for the *Product Innovation T* project. The results of the previous stage were evaluated each time before the next stage was financed. A more strategic financial perspective should have been used, as the stages applied were too short to suit such a diversification into a new business.

The strategic knowledge level. Rather than a new consumer electronics category, *Product Innovation T* represents an entire new class of consumer electronics products. A new product class means broad product variety for different user groups. However, in the case of *Product Innovation T, Company C's* product

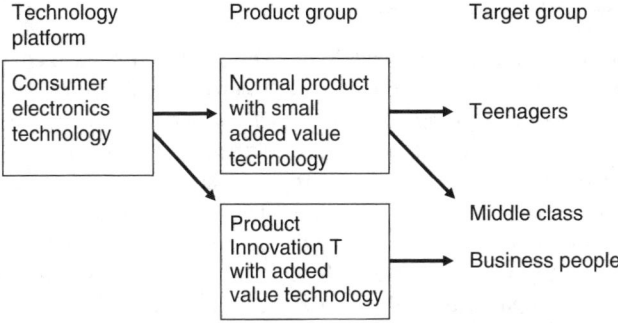

Figure 8.3 Current market base of *Company C* consumer electronics products

concept addressed only the high-end part of the product class. This is inconsistent with *Company C's* consumer electronics products, which are designed for many target groups. Three critical parameters might have been a limiting factor in the product group development: small processor capacity, small battery capacity and high-energy consumption.

The adopted solution may have limited strategic end-user learning. Learning to use consumer electronics with value-added technology prepares the end-user for the next evolutionary phase of applications based on the same technology. It can be expected that end-user learning will be a slow mass process. Potential end-users were perceiving the evolutionary phase as a revolutionary learning experience, because they had no earlier experience with this value-added technology and they had no relationship to any manufacturer representing a next technology generation.

The features of *Product Innovation T* were not optimally geared to reach critical mass. For example, most teenagers have only limited use for some features of *Product Innovation T* when they interact with their friends. In consumer electronics, being a value-added technology is not alone enough to make it become popular as a new substitute technology, because critical mass is essential in creating market pull. Especially in the young user group, end-users prefer to behave like their friends.

Company C had only limited interest in building a market for its value-added technology products. The strategy of building a new market is an alternative to the strategy of imitating, when both end-users and the required company's capabilities are new. In the case of *Product Innovation T*, there were no competitors in this value-added technology product category for five years.

It can be asked: What is the real knowledge culture in *Company C*? The above listed observations were made from outside the company, but the same basic questions, and more, should have been asked inside the company when *Product Innovation T* project was in progress.

8.4   Discussion

The key findings of these empirical analyses can be summarized as follows: First, product innovation is an emerging micro-diversification strategy of a company. For example, *Product Innovation T* was leading the company into a new business. The more radical the product innovation is, the stronger the diversification effects are, but always in the case of an incremental product innovation a new micro-diversification strategy is emerging. The product innovation process indicates how much the organizational systems support this micro-strategy. In the case of *Product Innovation T*, the micro-strategy was limited by organizational routine systems. In addition, the drivers of the product innovation and the impact of these drivers on the micro-strategy development process can be analysed, and, thus, the micro-strategy can better be redirected. The technological driver of *Product Innovation T* enabled the launching of a new product group, but the end-user driver was favoured.

Second, the diversification indicators operate beyond the boundaries of a consistent product innovation concept. Sound solutions on the product innovation level are only part of the whole truth. This could be one reason why consumer research and product testing often fail in the case of product innovation-based diversification. A broader and deeper approach, based on several knowledge levels, gives better insurance against unexpected surprises such as an underachieving innovation in an unfamiliar business logic. Product innovation-based diversification can be overlooked as minimal and, thus, operational-level misfits or unanticipated resource constraints in implementation can destroy the emerging micro-diversification strategy. This common mistake happened also in the case of *Product Innovation T* and the new product was distributed through unfit existing market channels to an unfamiliar niche market.

Third, the case study suggests that the drivers of product innovation are related to diversification mechanisms. Rather than deriving from conscious choices, in practice product innovation-based diversification typically occurs unintentionally. The risk of failure in diversification is highly significant, and development in the emerging new business to a profitable level is mostly slow. In a favourable case, normal business logic solutions can channel the innovation into a niche market. Combined with skimming pricing, a niche market can earn a satisfying profit. A less favourable scenario is that the company can lose its future, being unable to exploit the innovation in the mass market or to achieve the critical mass needed for radical change in end-user behaviour.

Fourth, the case study emphasized that product innovation-based diversification demands from the management an ability to advance in thinking from single-loop learning to double-loop learning. In the case of *Product Innovation T*, the business division management was unable to look beyond the product innovation itself, and the general management had difficulties seeing the potential of the product innovation as a micro-strategy. In other words, the business division management was limited to single-loop learning, and the general management was unable to lead the double-loop learning process; for example, by changing the rules of the knowledge absorption process. Single-loop learning means being mentally constrained to the existing product category, whereas double-loop learning means seeing beyond the borders of the existing product categories.

Fifth, the knowledge levels of a product innovation can be utilized as a basis for competitor analysis. Analyses based on knowledge levels give deeper and richer results than, for example, a conventional analysis of companies' or product innovations' strengths and weaknesses. Starting from drivers and finishing with the strategic level, both the innovation and the competing companies' strategies can be analysed and attacked. Thus, a micro-strategy-view might change the competitive position and reveal small holes in an apparently invincible castle wall. This is an approach contrary to general strategic analysis or product portfolio analysis.

8.5 Limitations and conclusions of the study

8.5.1 Limitations of the study

Some limitations of the present study should be emphasized, which also open up further research opportunities: the present study has focused on the micro-strategy level. Other strategy levels, including business division strategy and company strategy levels, must be considered in relation to a successful strategy process.

The present study does not answer the question why micro-strategies emerge in a high-technology company. The present study does offer some suggestions, which need further empirical testing.

In the present study, the analyses are restricted to four knowledge bases. The identification and empirical testing of additional knowledge bases and knowledge levels is promising. Utilizing four knowledge bases considerably enhanced the existing knowledge on how to use product innovation to optimally impact on the strategy process but adding more knowledge bases can further enrich understanding.

In the present study, the a priori concept has been discussed based on only one case study, due to the chosen research approach. This may raise concerns regarding the validity and generalizability of the findings. The results are indeed explorative, but do suggest that the findings of the present study have generalizable implications for managing product innovation-based micro-strategy in a wide spectrum of various different industries. Since at this stage the results are exploratory, there is clearly a need to test the a priori framework further with other cases, and eventually, with a quantitative approach using large samples.

8.5.2 Conclusions

The findings of the present study lead to fundamental rethinking of the existing common understanding concerning the emergence of diversification in a new business logic. The old and dominating belief that diversification is a conscious decision, and can be managed on corporate level, is obsolete. Diversification emerges on a micro-level because of relationships within the product innovation knowledge bases. Product development can, thus, lead to unintentional diversification, which needs new knowledge management tools. The attention of both academic researchers and managers must therefore be redirected towards the identification of those factors, which positively moderate the impact of innovation-based diversification on company strategy.

Knowledge-level innovation analyses introduced in the present study can be powerful tools both in academic research and in everyday management of companies. Such analyses allow companies to better exploit the strong impact of product innovations on the success of the company strategy. This present study, thus, has wide-ranging managerial implications: companies should develop product innovation-based strategies; they should allocate resources to the needs of product innovation-based diversification; and they should utilize the four product innovation knowledge bases throughout the entire innovation development process.

References

Aaker, D. (1991), *Managing Brand Equity: Capitalizing on the Value of a Brand Name*, Free Press, New York.

Bitencourt, C. C. (2004), 'Resource based theory and strategic management: The link with organisational learning', *International Journal of Innovation and Learning*, Vol. 1, No. 2, pp. 166–76.

Bower, J. L. and Christensen, C. M. (1995), 'Disruptive technologies: Catching the wave', *Harvard Business Review*, Vol. 73, No. 1, pp. 43–53.

Breschi, S., Lissoni, F. and Malerba, F. (2003), 'Knowledge-relatedness in firm technological diversification', *Research Policy*, 32:1, pp. 69–87.

Calantone, R. Garcia, R. and Dröge, C. (2003), 'The effects of environmental turbulence on new product development strategy planning', *Journal of Product Innovation Management*, Vol. 20, No. 2, pp. 90–103.

Cohen, W. M. and Levinthal, D. A. (1990), 'Absorptive Capacity: A New Perspective on Learning and Innovation', *Administrative Science Quarterly*, Vol. 35, No. 1, pp. 128–52 (Special Issue: Technology, Organizations, and Innovation, March).

Cooper, R. G. (1975), 'Why new industrial products fail', *Industrial Marketing Management*, Vol. 4, No. 4, August, pp. 315–26 .

Dosi, G. (1982), 'Technical paradigms and technological trajectories: A suggested interpretation of the determinants and directions of technical change', *Research Policy*, Vol. 11, No. 3, pp. 147–62.

Drejer, A., Olesen, F., and Strandskov, J. (2005) 'Strategic scanning in a new competitive landscape: Towards a learning approach', *International Journal of Innovation and Learning*, Vol. 2, No. 1, pp. 47–64.

Franke, N. and von Hippel, E. (2003), 'Satisfying heterogeneous user needs via innovation toolkits: The case of Apache security software', *Research Policy*, Vol. 32, No. 7, pp. 1199–215 (Special issue on open source software development).

Hauser, J. R. (2001), 'Metrics thermostat', *The Journal of Product Innovation Management*, Vol. 18, No. 2, pp. 134–53.

Heijs, J. (2004), 'Innovation capabilities and learning: A vicious circle, *International Journal of Innovation and Learning*, Vol. 1, No. 3, pp. 263–78.

Henderson, R. M. and Clark, K. B. (1990), 'Architectural innovation: The reconfiguration of existing technologies and the failure of established firms', *Administrative Science Quarterly*, Vol. 35, No. 1, pp. 9–30 (Special Issue: Technology, Organizations, and Innovation, March).

Hilmola, O. P., Helo, P., and Maunuksela, A. (2005), 'The economic nature of feedback loops in product development', *International Journal of Innovation and Learning*, Vol. 2, No. 2, pp. 197–209.

Jolly, V. (1997), *Commercializing New Technologies: Getting from Mind to Market*, Harvard Business School Press, Boston MA.

Johnson, G., Melin, L. and Whittington, R. (2003), 'Guest Editors' Introduction. Micro-Strategy and Strategizing: Towards an Activity-Based View', *Journal of Management Studies*, Vol. 40, No. 1, pp. 3–22.

Kappel, T. A. (2001), 'Perspectives on Roadmaps: How Organizations Talk about the Future', *Journal of Product Innovation Management*, Vol. 18, No. 1, pp. 39–50.

Kim, W. C. and Mauborgne, R. (1997), 'Value innovation: The strategic logic of high growth', *Harvard Business Review*, Vol. 75, No. 1, pp. 103–12.

Kodama, M., (2005), 'Customer value creation through knowledge creation with customers: Case studies of IT and multimedia businesses in Japan', *International Journal of Innovation and Learning*, Vol. 2, No. 4, pp. 357–85.

Kogut, B. and Zander, U. (1992), 'Knowledge of the firm, combinative capabilities, and the replication of technology', *Organization Science*, Vol. 3, No. 3, pp. 383–97.

Laamanen, T. and Autio, E. (1996), 'Dominant dynamic complementarities and technology-motivated acquisitions of new, technology-based firms', *International Journal of Technology Management*, Vol. 12, No. 7/8, pp. 769–87.

Leonard-Barton, D. (1992), 'Core capabilities and core rigidities: A paradox in managing new product development', *Strategic Management Journal*, Vol. 13, No. 5, 111–25 (Special Issue: Strategy Process).

Lynn, G. S., Morone, J. G. and Paulson, A. S. (1996), 'Marketing and discontinuous innovation: The probe and learn process', *California Management Review*, Vol. 38, No. 3, Spring, pp. 8–37.

March, J. R. (1991), 'Exploration and exploitation in organizational learning', *Organization Science*, Vol. 2, No. 1, pp. 71–87.

Mentzas, G. (2004), 'A strategic management framework for leveraging knowledge assets', *International Journal of Innovation and Learning*, Vol. 1, No. 2, pp. 115–42.

Markides, C. C. (1997), 'To Diversify or not to Diversify', *Harvard Business Review*, Vol. 75, No. 6, pp. 93–9.

Mitchell, W. and Singh, K. (1996), 'Survival of businesses using collaborative relationships to commercialize complex goods', *Strategic Management Journal*, Vol. 17, No. 3, pp. 169–95.

Nonaka, I., Toyama, R. and Nagata, A. (2000), 'A firm as a knowledge-creating entity: A new perspective on the theory of the firm', *Industrial and Corporate Change*, Vol. 9, No. 1, pp. 1–20.

Normann, R. (1971), 'Organizational innovativeness: Product variation and reorientation', *Administrative Science Quarterly*, Vol. 16, No. 2, pp. 203–15.

O'Connor, G. C. (1998), 'Market learning and radical innovation: A cross case comparison of eight radical innovation projects', *Journal of Product Innovation Management*, Vol. 15, No. 2, pp. 151–66.

O'Mahony, S. (2003), 'Guarding the commons: How community managed software projects protect their work', *Research Policy*, Vol. 32, No. 7, pp. 1179–98 (Special issue on open-source software development).

Porter, M. (1980), *Competitive Strategy*, The Free Press, New York.

Prahalad, C. K. and Bettis, R. A. (1986), 'The dominant logic: A new linkage between diversity and performance', *Strategic Management Journal*, Vol. 7, No. 6, pp. 485–501.

Prahalad, C. K. and Ramaswamy, V. (2003), 'The new frontier of experience innovation', *MIT Sloan Management Review*, Vol. 44, No. 4, Summer, pp. 12–18.

Salvato, C. (2003), 'The role of micro-strategies in the engineering of firm evolution', *Journal of Management Studies*, Vol. 40, No. 1, pp. 83–108.

Schmitt, B. H., Simonsen, A. and Marcus, J. (1995), 'Managing corporate image and identity', *Long Range Planning*, Vol. 28, No. 5, pp. 82–92.

Stake, R. E. (1995), *The Art of Case Study Research*, Sage Publications, Thousand Oaks, CA.

Tauber, E. M. (1983), 'Editorial. corporate wisdom: The need for "the brand knowledge base"', *Journal of Advertising Research*, Vol. 23, No. 1, p. 7.

Tushman, M. L. and Anderson, P. (1986), 'Technological discontinuities and organizational environments', *Administrative Science Quarterly*, Vol. 31, No. 3, pp. 439–65.

Walsh, J. P. (1995), 'Managerial and organizational cognition: Notes from a trip down memory lane', *Organization Science*, Vol. 6, No. 3, pp. 280–321.

Ward, S., Light, L. and Goldstine, G. (1999), 'What high-tech managers need to know about brands', *Harvard Business Review*, Vol. 77, No. 4, pp. 85–95.

Wernerfelt, B. (1984), 'A resource-based view of the firm', *Strategic Management Journal*, Vol. 5, No. 2, pp. 171–80.

Yin, R. K. (1989), *Case Study Research. Design and Methods*, 1st edn in 1984, Sage Publications, Thousand Oaks, CA.

9

'The Strength of Strong Ties': University Spin-Offs and the Significance of Historical Relations

Mattias Johansson,[a] Merle Jacob[b] and Tomas Hellström[c]
[a] *Chalmers University of Technology, Sweden*
[b,c] *University of Oslo, Norway*

This chapter investigates the relationship between universities and academic spin-offs, with special emphasis on the antecedent conditions of, and the nature of the linkages that the spin-offs form, as well as the means for sustaining them. The present research uses an instrumental case study approach, and is also an instance of a collective case study as four companies of various size and activities have been studied together. The preliminary results indicate that the network relations are characterized by a small number of strong ties to universities, with a high degree of trust and informality. Although fruitful for the transfer of complex knowledge, the strength of the ties also make them difficult to substitute, which may lead to problems as the spin-offs are highly dependent on continued basic research support. This may in turn lead to implications for policy at university, as well as higher levels.

Introduction

Recently, national governments have begun to restructure policies for funding science in order to encourage universities to commercialize their research results. As a result, academic science is increasingly being redefined by national policy makers as a contributing factor to international competitiveness. This is reflected in the rhetoric and mechanisms used by science policy agencies (OECD, 2002; Vinnova, 2002; Government of Finland, 2003), and also in the growing literature on university–industry transfer (e.g., Argyres and Liebeskind, 1998; Bozeman, 2000; Carayannis et al., 2000), and commercialization of academic research (e.g., Slaughter and Leslie, 1997; Jacob, 2003).

One of the mechanisms for transforming scientific knowledge into products and processes is the founding of new firms on the basis of results produced at universities. The closer relationship between science and technology in some areas, and the rise of science-based technologies, for example, biotechnology, has in many cases led to growing costs for pursuing research, this cost being an additional argument for capitalizing more efficiently on new knowledge, for example, through the creation of new technologies in spin-off arrangements. As new firms often lack resources, academic spin-offs based on high technology are likely to be dependent on continued relations with universities also after the initial phase of spinning off. To date, however, there have been very few studies completed on academic spin-offs that provide detailed information on the nature of firm linkages with universities (Rappert et al., 1999), and those that do have primarily taken the viewpoint of universities. Furthermore, there is a short-age of qualitative studies on how these collaborations evolved and were sustained, that is, the antecedent conditions, the process of managing the collaboration, and its academic and commercial consequences in more detail (Prabhu, 1999).

The aim of this study is to investigate the antecedent conditions, the reasons for continued relations between universities and academic spin-offs, that is, the nature of these linkages, and how they are sustained. In the first section we will provide an overview of the literature of university – spin-off linkages, in the second section we present four cases of university spin-off companies from the point of view of such linkages. This is followed by an analysis and discussion on the findings. Implications for research and policy are outlined in the final section.

9.1   Linkages between universities and spin-offs

9.1.1   Motivations for spin-offs and linkages

While there are plenty of possibilities for academically viable research to become commercialized, and vice versa, many occasions for academically valuable results to emanate from commercial activity (Rosenberg, 1982; Stokes, 1997), there often seems to be a difficulty in combining commercial and academic goals within one and the same institutional setting (Dasgupta and David, 1994, Argyres and Liebeskind, 1998). This point has been empir-ically supported by among others Goldfarb (2001), who shows that in a population of research engineers, academic goals and practical or commer-cial goals are unlikely to converge. Therefore, it is argued that external cor-porate sponsors will be unlikely to build profit-based relationships with 'purely' academic counterparts.

This would suggest that the maintenance of linkages between universities and spin-offs is to some extent dependent on benefits derived from splitting up corporate and academic activities into different institutional settings. One such benefit has been said to lie in the need to secure inventor compen-sation in a form that would be difficult in the academic setting, for example, in terms of salaries, royalty or equity, this being particularly true for public universities (Goldfarb and Henrekson, 2003). This argument is supported by Jensen and Thursby (2001) who show that the preferred relation of inventor to commercial spin-offs is one where the researcher stays in his/her lab and maintains research on the basis of corporate sponsored grants. This attitude, however, is not observed uniformly across countries and sectors (e.g., Meyer-Krahmer and Schmoch, 1998), and is likely to be related to many factors, for instance the likelihood that universities will make equity investments in start-ups in a way favourable to the academic/founder (Shane, 2002).

In a study on the differential start-up rates of US universities' technology licensing offices (TLOs), Gregorio and Shane (2003) found that a higher inventor share of royalties provides a disincentive for potential inventor-entrepreneurs by increasing the opportunity cost of starting up a new venture. Also, universities willing to take an equity stake in licensees in exchange for paying up-front patenting and licensing expenses had considerably higher start-up rates than universities that did not. From the perspective of university spin-offs there are several reasons for maintaining linkages, as well as for creating new ones, one of them of course being the endemic internal lack of an internal resources base in new ventures (Tether, 2002). Such reasons, however, are related to the content of linkages.

9.1.2   Content of linkages between universities and spin-offs

The relation between the university (e.g., department) and the spin-off firm may be of a formal or an informal nature. As examples of more formal linkages, Ndonzau and colleagues (2002) review three institutional relations between universities and spin-offs. Universities can hold some equity shares in the spin-off (financial resources), spin-offs can exploit patented technology owned by universities (intangible resources), and spin-offs can have access to some university facilities (material resources). In the case of the last two, the relation may be bi-directional and the level of informality high (Bozeman, 2000; Berglund and Hellström, 2002). Furthermore, while linkages can be of a formal character, the effects of the knowledge transferred via the linkage can be very informal. Examples of such linkages would be the employment of graduates and faculty by firms, contract research and consulting, and training of firm members (Fitzroy et al., 1994; Schartinger et al., 2002). More informal linkages may involve joint conference attendance, joint publications, joint supervision of graduate students by firm and university employees, lectures at the university held by firm members and reading of publications and patents (Fitzroy et al., 1994; Schartinger et al., 2002).

The informal linkages, apart from being important in their own right, often fill the additional function of facilitating more formal linkages (Rappert et al., 1999). In fact, informal linkages are often regarded as more important than formal ones (e.g. Meyer-Krahmer and Schmoch, 1998; Rappert et al., 1999) as they 'provide a means of receiving general and specific expertise from universities in a manner which responds to the contingencies of innovative activity' (Rappert et al. 1999, p. 886). However, these appraisals are often based on contrasting formal and informal personal contacts or way of working, that is, doing contract research compared to collaborative research, thus not paying attention to the use of equipment, patentsand so on. However, both informal and formal linkages will be of marginal relevance to overall USO competitiveness unless the USO is on the 'cutting edge' (Rappert et al., 1999), and the conditions for novel product introduction are essentially derived from basic science discovery (Powell et al., 1999).

The importance attached to either form of linkage can also be related to the perceived benefits of university-industry linkages generally. Meyer-Krahmer and Schmoch (1998) found that knowledge exchange and additional funds were the most relevant advantages seen from the point of view of universities, with emphasis differing between sectors. While additional funds can be obtained via a one-directional relationship such as, for example, contract research, for knowledge exchange to take place a bi-directional relationship involving more informal links is probably better. Rappert and colleagues (1999) found that, from the viewpoint of USOs, the general benefits were considered to be keeping abreast of university research, access to expertise, general assistance and use of instruments. Meyer-Krahmer and Schmoch (1998) also found, through patent measurement, that the content of university-industry interaction exhibits a great deal of intra-disciplinarity. In this context, the strength of linkages seems to be particularly important, as weak ties tend to enhance access to relevant findings in fields outside the core areas of the USO. Moreover, the pattern of weak and strong ties seemed to be historically determined to some extent.

9.1.3   Sustaining linkages between universities and spin-offs

A perusal of the literature will show that several factors are thought to be vital for maintaining linkages between universities and spin-offs. The existence of trust is one of these. Trust has been said to exist if both parties expect the other to work towards mutually compatible or supporting interests in a joint effort, rather than to act opportunistically and maximize their own take at the expense of the other (Das and Teng, 1998). In these types of linkages, it is especially important that the partner organization, research centre or firm is perceived: (1) to pursue compatible rather than competing interests, and (2) to be certain that firm specific knowledge is not leaked to other firms as a result of the type of knowledge sharing that may occur in the broader setting, for example, in university-industry consortia (Santoro and Gopalakrishnan, 2001). This can be facilitated by clearly articulating priorities beforehand (Burnham, 1997) and by both parties jointly assessing the interests, motivations, constraints, and potential importance of a co-operative venture (Prabhu, 1999). The existence of mechanisms for mutual monitoring, as well as channels for continuous communication, has been said to stimulate trust in similar co-operative relations (Hellström, 2003). Mutual monitoring of ongoing activities may be brought about by the existence of a common set of third-party relations, meeting places, and also by physical proximity (e.g., Saxenian, 1994; Deeds et al., 2000). Also the findings of Almeida and colleagues (2003) suggest enduring effects of geographical proximity, while the effects of mobility on external learning are particularly critical in the earliest stages of start-ups. These types of social and physical proximities provide ongoing information about projects and new relations. For example, continuous communication helps not only mutual monitoring of activities but it also enables partners to co-ordinate decision making on objectives, investments in new projects and new resource acquisitions/needs, as well as expectations with regard to technology transfer among partners (Lei et al., 1997).

Meyer-Krahmer and Schmoch (1998) found that spin-offs were likely to be associated with sustainable bi-directional interaction if the founding academic part stayed assigned with the university department. This association would presumably be supporting of trust between the firm and the university. In a survey study of 189 firms and 21 research centres in the United States, Santoro and Gopalakrishnan (2001) established that trust was indeed a key factor for this type of linkage, finding, however, that it was dependent on flexible university centre policies for IPR, patents and licences, especially regarding the extent to which the university was willing to customize contractual agreements in order to meet the spin-off firm's specific needs. Geographical proximity was also found to play a role in maintaining linkages, in particular with firms conducting basic research, however, communication to the firm concerning ongoing technology transfer activities in the university did not affect the firms' perceived strength of the linkage (Santoro and Gopalakrishnan, 2001).

Almeida et al.and colleagues (2003) and Rappert and colleagues (1999) have found size and intensity of firm R&D to be key variables in explaining high linkage activity, that is, how many and what types of linkages that are sustained. This may reflect the greater resources of larger firms, which makes them attractive to universities but also the greater awareness of larger firms as to the services available to them from these organizations. Moreover, according to Almeida and colleagues (2003) it appears that the negative effects of size, such as myopia and rigidity, become more pervasive with regard to the informal linkage mechanisms. That is, as the companies grow in size, they rely to a larger extent on formal links. This suggests a corollary to another oft-mentioned factor for sustaining linkages built on mutual exchange of knowledge, that is, the ability to learn from each other. The success of such relationships should ideally be contingent on the level of absorptive capacity (Cohen and Levinthal, 1990), a concept that is extended by Lane and Lubatkin (1998) to show that firms in a student–teacher relationship must have similarly structured relative absorptive capacities. While this points to the importance of sharing similar knowledge bases, knowledge assimilation processes, and experience in knowledge commercialization, it also suggests the importance of building a mutual language and symbols in order to foster trust, and thus to increase the likelihood of sustained collaboration (Carayannis et al., 2000).

9.2   Methodology

9.2.1   The case study approach

In qualitative research, investigators must typically think purposefully and conceptually about sampling (Huberman and Miles, 1994). The present research builds on an *instrumental* case study approach, in that the cases have been instrumental in elucidating a particular phenomenon, here university spin-off linkages (Stake, 1995). The sampling approach associated with the instrumental case study has been purposive or theoretical sampling, where actors or phenomena relevant to the research question and/or the theoretical focus at hand are actively sought out (Glaser and Strauss, 1967). The present research is also an instance of a *collective* case study approach, as several companies have been studied together with a focus on the specific and generic properties of spin-off linkages. The authors recognize that the present cases are operating within a number of contexts (financial, social, physical, etc.), and that many of the conclusions drawn are affected by situational factors. While aware of the dimensions of atypicality present in each case, it is nevertheless believed that the phenomenon of linkage activity displayed within each case is critical to understanding the general nature of the phenomenon, through presenting it in a meaningful action context. However it is important to keep in mind, that in some sense the case always represents itself, and is mainly a tool for understanding instantiation of theory (Manning, 1982).

9.2.3   The spin-off companies

All of the companies were from high-technology fields; biotech, functional foods, instrumentation and laser systems. Their age spanned from 8 to 24 years, and their size varied between 13 and 50 employees. They were all spun-out from the universities in one way or the other (see case descriptions). The locations of the spin-offs were overall very close to the sources that they had most frequent interaction with, and often also with the originating university.

9.2.4   Data collection and analysis

The participating case companies were selected through purposive sampling (Miles and Huberman, 1984) to cover a broad disciplinary spectrum, as well as to span from fairly young to older. Although all of the companies were

Swedish, geographic distribution was taken into account and companies from different university towns were selected. Founders and CEOs were contacted for face-to-face interviews. These lasted for between one and two hours, and were documented through intensive note-taking by one or two of the participating interviewers (there was an interviewee reluctance to have interviews taped). Interviews were conducted in an informal, conversational manner, during which questions were posed about founding conditions, linkages with the university and other Public Research Organizations (PROs), limitations and benefits in these regards, and plans for the future with respect to linkage activities. Interview notes were transcribed into case descriptions, which were read by all participants for coherence and accuracy.

9.3 Four cases of university – spin-off relations

9.3.1 Alfa Foods

Alfa Foods is active in the area of Functional Foods and was established in 1994. The firm has a staff of 13, equally distributed in R&D and production/ sales. Their turnaround in 2001 was around US$4 million. Alfa Foods develops, produces and to some extent distributes an oats-based milk beverage, for direct consumption, or as a foundation for other traditionally milk-based products such as ice cream, yogurt or sauces. The process technology for producing this product, as well as the basic bacteria which is central to the production, has been patented, and is the platform for a range of oats-based milk products manufactured by Alfa Foods. Alfa Foods expects to grow rapidly in the next few years, partly due to growth in the Asian and European markets.

9.3.1.1 History of the company and its links

The founder of Alfa Foods has his roots as a researcher in a university chemistry department, where he was working close to a professor who, in 1963, discovered the mechanism behind lactose intolerance. The professor also had an outspoken market orientation in his research, with links to a nearby multinational company that specialized in packaging. In 1990, on the basis of subsequent research into lactose intolerance, as well as a chance suggestion from an agricultural researcher, the founder decided to develop a non-dairy milk-replacement from oats. The company was born from this idea and the founding team consisted of four researchers. Once the company was established, the founder reduced his employment at the university to 20 per cent. The founding researchers took out an early patent for the process technology, which they funded themselves, and shortly thereafter received additional funds from a farmers' co-operative.

At this stage the only input from the university consisted of informal staffing of the company orchestrated by the founder, as well as that of the research knowledge brought over into the patent. The founder also had some experience from previous commercialization activities, among others with starting up a medical equipment company. Alfa Foods brought their product to a limited European market between 1996 and 2000. In 2001 they received new growth capital from an international venture capital firm and a private placement from the founder's brother. Some researchers from the original team were bought out during the same period. From 2001 onwards, Alfa Foods increased its research effort into health promoting oat milk products and focused on high cholesterol, intestinal functions and lowering of the glycaemic index. They have hired staff mainly from their research network, but also a new Managing Director from the private sector, who had previously worked with the founder on a university-industry development project.

9.3.1.2   *Current links with the university and other PROs*

Alfa Foods has always worked closely with the university, and considers the continuation of this connection to be critical to its future. The chemistry department from which the technology spun out is still the most important research partner, but now there are also a number of smaller research groups, loosely related to this department as well as being a research relation to clinical R&D at a university hospital. The preferred linkage to the university consists of sponsoring and supervising doctoral students on research projects of relevance to Alfa Foods' product development. This way Alfa Foods can retain a strong linkage with the university, without simply 'co-opting' new staff. They also have a considerable input on project formulation and execution. The university has traditionally been seen as a place to do research, and not as central to the later stages of Alfa Foods' business cycle (product refinement, marketing and sales). With most of the research that Alfa Foods needs located at the university in these types of co-operative arrangements, this means that Alfa Foods can focus on co-ordination of product development and commercialization in-house, and together with other companies. They have not been in contact with any of the available 'bridging organizations' in the region, simply because the need has never arisen (and partly due to the fact that they had not yet been established at the time of the founding). However, they have had help from a network at the neighbouring science park, which is a local 'meeting-place' between different kinds of academic and commercial interests. This is mainly to be seen as a network of pre- or non-competitive ideas.

During the last year, Alfa Foods has been involved in an EU-project in the agro-food area, together with three other European universities and five companies. This project is considered an important stepping-stone for future products, where the universities represent research, and new solutions are developed and tested co-operatively between the participating companies. Alfa Foods does not consider itself to be able to 'afford' more of a network presence in research or otherwise. Other public research institutes have a latent existence in the networks as indirectly connected to Alfa Foods through their university contacts, but no direct linkages have been established, or are deemed necessary. The main linkage is with the founders' 'home department', where the exchange is rich, relevant and yet low in maintenance cost. The main source of staffing is from the university, and previous contacts with the company. University contacts are considered to be a strength in potential new employees. The informal contacts are the most important: 'the company is built on people – not on written agreements'. In the future, those networks will become interesting, enabling Alfa Foods to identify new product concepts in related but more distant areas.

9.3.2   Beta Technologies

Beta Technologies is a research and manufacturing company that has been in existence since 1985. The company employed about 50 people before it was split into two separate companies in the spring of 2002. Their turnaround in 2001 was c.US$8 million. Before the split, Beta Technologies was active in two areas: laser technology, where they provide whole laser systems, and fibre optics, where they provide components for high-effect lasers. Both areas are high-technology knowledge intensive, especially the area of fibre optics where their products are based on patented knowledge. The market consists mainly of big Swedish companies for the laser systems part, and big laser systems manufacturers in Germany for the fibre optics part.

9.3.2.1   History of the company and its links

The company was spun off in the late 1970s from a government-financed research project on laser workings at a technical university. The project involved two PhD students and a professor. Halfway through the project, the professor decided to start a company due to new ideas generated in the project and the potential yield from consulting services that these new concepts could generate. The PhD students continued part-time at the university and part-time at the new company. This company came to focus on laser measurement techniques and laser systems, and in 1984 the laser systems part was spun off and formed Beta Technologies together with another company from a Swedish consortium, which contributed with the funds for its establishment. At the point of establishment, the input from the university still consisted of the ideas developed in the research programme which had formed the basis for the company, as well as academic contacts with former colleagues at the university. Over the years to come these contacts resulted in various research collaborations, and also in supervision of PhD students. Apart from structural changes in ownership relations the company remained the same until the spring of 2002 when it was decided that the two areas of activity within Beta Technologies, laser working systems and fibre optics components, were better off as two separate businesses. The reason was that since the two areas of activity are rather separate in terms of markets, chances for obtaining new investors for a coming expansion would increase if they were separated into two businesses.

9.3.2.2   *Current links with the university and other PROs*

Beta Technologies, and especially the fibre optics part, has always worked closely with the former colleagues at their 'home' university, where research into the field of their core technology has been undertaken continuously throughout the life of the company. This connection is considered to be very important for a number of reasons. One is that the 'home' university is the only one in Sweden which conducts the kind of research on which Beta Technologies' business idea is based. The second is that the technology of the fibre optics field has now developed so that within a couple of years there will be new, fundamental problems concerning materials physics and the like that will need to be solved. Even with heavy investments in R&D, Beta Technologies cannot afford to build this type of knowledge on their own. They therefore have to rely on basic research conducted elsewhere. So far the exchange with the university has been conducted through informal seminars, research collaboration and supervision of PhD students and master theses. The university and the relevant research conducted there is accessible to employees. Beta Technologies' dependence on basic research conducted at the 'home' university means that it is beginning to become concerned that declining funding for the research group on which it is dependent may affect the company's future adversely. Other university links, albeit not very strong, have been forged through participation in EU projects. Beta Technologies has participated in several such projects over the years; however, not jointly with any Swedish departments or institutes, but rather with German and French actors who contacted them and proposed collaboration. Within these projects the foreign partners deal with administrative matters. This is a requirement for Beta Technologies, since they do not perceive themselves to have the time to engage in the cumbersome bureaucracy of the EU projects.

9.3.3   Gamma Biotech

Gamma Biotech was established in 1989 and currently employs 35 persons after selling off a production unit in the summer of 2002. The turnover in 2001 was over US$2 million. The business idea is based on biotechnology, bordering on Functional Foods. Gamma Biotech's business model is to never enter the final market themselves but rather to develop concepts, verify these, securing the manufacturing process and the possibilities to make products, and then sell this to interested companies producing for end customers. The technology is built around two basic micro-organisms and the application of these to allergy and stomach-related diseases. They expect to grow rapidly in the near future.

9.3.3.1   History of the company and its links

In the mid-1980s, a professor from North Carolina State University, USA, took a sabbatical in Sweden for family reasons. Once there he began working together with a professor at the agricultural university, with whom he discovered the antimicrobial properties of the reuteri-bacteria. They patented it, and set up a company called Gamma Biotech in the Research Triangle Park area of Raleigh, NC, because the financing possibilities were at the time quite good there. The founders had some difficulty raising capital for the company in the United Statesfor a variety of reasons and began to look for alternatives and were eventually able to find new investors in Sweden. The two founders have remained on the board and act as external consultants. The company was established with little help from Swedish organizations although they had some contacts with one of the regional organizations set up to assist universities with commercialization. The main source of support throughout the history of the company has come from a biotech Centre in North Carolina. This centre has provided useful contacts, manufacturing equipment and so on. From their start they also made extensive use of the research networks of the two founding researchers, and put great effort into making themselves well known to relevant researchers and developing relationships with them. This has been especially important for Gamma Biotech since the technology on which the business idea of the company is based was not generally accepted at the time of the founding of the company. Gamma Biotech's founders were therefore forced to build acceptance and interest by involving known scientists, who in turn could spread knowledge about the technology on a broader basis as well as make it legitimate with consumers.

9.3.3.2   Current links with the university and other PROs

As mentioned above, Gamma Biotech has from the beginning worked closely with universities, and they currently have direct contact with a vast number of researchers at different universities around Sweden,. These links to universities take on various forms. They supervise PhD students at various universities, and finance them either themselves or jointly with, for example, the Swedish Agency for Innovation Systems. The more research-oriented staff at Gamma Biotech also have their own personal networks that are used for meeting up with relevant researchers to discuss issues or projects. As they have gained reputation after 10–15 years in business, researchers also contact them in order to discuss possible projects, and if mutual interests can be found, it often results in collaboration. It has, however, taken a long time and a lot of hard work to be recognized and build this network. The main factors behind it is active use of informal networks and contacts, an aim for long and lasting relations, and putting effort in finding mutual interests. Their links to academia are of vital interest for them for three reasons. Firstly, they build their business on the findings that come out of the various collaborations and projects.

Secondly, they need to spread the word and gain further acceptance for their technology, something that was especially important at the outset of their business. Due to this, they demand that researchers they collaborate with publish their findings, otherwise they are not interested in collaboration. Thirdly, they are in no position themselves to pursue all research necessary for their business, due to their limited resources being a fairly small company. There are usually no problems in the joint projects with academia as the general frameworks are explicitly set beforehand. Moreover, researchers mostly enjoy working with small companies and also have opportunities to influence the strategic orientation of the company through their findings. Other modes of interaction are conferences and seminars within academia. They almost exclusively use contacts with academia, and do not have collaborations with institutes or other organizations. Institutes are considered to make contract works and cannot add anything to the business of Gamma Biotech. Moreover, they prefer the 'free-thinking' inherent in the academic model, and are into long-term relationships, not short-term assignments.

9.3.4   Delta Sensors

Delta Sensors is active in the area of micro-sensors. They have been in existence since 1994 and merged in 1999 with a German company. Currently they employ 23 people, 11 of whom work in Sweden, another 11 in Germany, and one person in the United States. Most of the staff is in development and production, and half of them have a doctoral degree. Delta Sensors develops, produces and markets chemical sensor components and sensor modules for air quality control, and their main customers are in the automotive, heat and ventilation, air condition, and environmental care industries. Delta Sensors has recently completely refocused its business and as a consequence their turnover was approx US$279,000 in 2001. They are, however, expecting to grow rapidly in their new line of business in the next few years, with break-even in 2004.

9.3.4.1   History of the company and its links

Delta Sensors has its roots in a technical university and research on Field Effect, and started in the 1970s. In 1989 they began doing research on chemical gas sensors, building on Field Effect technology, and in 1994 there was a company spun off with an independent businessman being given the opportunity to buy the patent. Together with some of the researchers in the research group, the company was founded as Micro Instruments with a focus on developing 'electronic nose' instruments. At about the same time a German company, Micro Sensors, was founded as a couple of researchers left their research group. Micro Sensors also focused on 'electronic nose' instruments and sensor components, but based their products on other technologies; Metal Oxide Semiconductors and Quartz microbalance. In 1999 the companies decided to merge into Delta Sensors.

Before the two companies merged, they mainly had links with former colleagues at the two universities from which they had spun off, that is, the Swedish university who also provided facilities and equipment, and the German university. These contacts also remained the strongest after the merger. They also had some contacts with other universities, laboratories and research institutes, but only because these were regarded as customers or potential customers for their products and thus important for the sake of feedback. In 2000 Delta Sensors realized that they had to change focus and try to reach mass markets in order to make a profit and grow. Thus they abandoned the 'electronic nose', and instead turned to sensor components and sensor modules. In doing so they have maintained contacts with these institutes, laboratories and universities only to the extent that they still provide help or test equipment when asked for it.

9.3.4.2 Current links with the university and other PROs

They still maintain close contact with the two universities the current company spun off from, both informally in terms of personnel keeping contact with former colleagues, as well as formally in terms of research collaboration programmes. At the Swedish office, Delta Sensors participates in a formal research collaboration that is a direct co-operation between their 'home' university and about ten industrial firms, where they jointly decide upon finance and pursue different research projects. The companies in collaboration are of various sizes, and of various areas of specialization where Delta Sensors is the only firm specialized in gas sensors. The German part of Delta Sensors has a similar arrangement with the university of origin. Another important link to the university is through the financing and supervision of doctoral students. Moreover, they attend different conferences in their area of interest as well as participating in different EU projects that involves many different industries and universities throughout Europe. Altogether, the main benefits of these contacts with the universities are stated to be threefold; they acquire research results that they can develop into products, the universities are good bases for recruitment, and it is also a stimulant for the doctors working at Delta Sensors to maintain their contacts. Acquiring research results is especially important because being a small company, they cannot afford both research and development. They are thus using the university for the research part and are doing the development themselves, which leaves them with a fairly high dependence on the universities. This is sometimes a bit awkward since they can ask for research to be conducted in some areas, but in order to get it done have to rely on the university perceiving it as challenging and worthwhile to pursue.

9.4   Analysis of the cases

9.4.1   Alfa Foods

In the case of Alfa Foods, the university linkage was dominated by the fact that the initial founder group were all academic researchers, and that the founder retained a 20 per cent employment at his university department. The core technology was continuously derived and extended from the university's research, likewise the initial and continuing staffing was conducted on the basis of this linkage. Thus, intellectual capital as well as human resources was bound up in this tie. The founder and his department were the central nodes in the relation. While this is not an uncommon phenomenon, the case of Alfa Foods suggests an additional quality in the way in which these nodes become difficult to disaggregate: the department's knowledge was also the founder's knowledge, and the department's human resource base was also the founder's friends. Even the Managing Director, recruited from outside of academia, had a historical connection to the founder via a university-industry co-operative project.

For Alfa Foods, the university is not just one link among many, rather it is perceived to be critical to the very existence of the company. This observation is all the more significant considering that the nature of the link appears to be fairly informal and relaxed. Since the preferred way of sustaining this linkage appears to be the sponsoring and supervising of doctoral students, participating in research projects and so on, the actual benefits to the company will be dependent on informally acquiring knowledge through communication, 'participating by doing in the projects', and through staffing. This suggests a number of mechanisms that falls outside of traditional intellectual property regimes, and that such arrangements may even hamper or destroy informal and well-functioning knowledge transfer, that is, to weaken the strength of the tie developed (cf. Rappert et al., 1999). It is also clear that, in this process, Alfa Foods does not want to appear to 'co-opt' staff or knowledge, but must be seen to 'put something back' into the department's research. A result of this is that the company has decided to engage with academe in terms of academic imperatives for producing knowledge, that is, by doing research. Subsequent parts of the business process do not figure in the linkages with the university, but is a concern solely for Alfa Foods itself. This seems to work fine, but runs at the same time counter to innovation policy conclusions which encourage universities to engage in business development *on their corporate collaborator's behalf.* It is also clear from looking at Alfa Foods that in terms of invested time, network presence is a costly affair and that such investments must be made with prudence, especially given the high stability of the core technology.

9.4.2 Beta Technologies

Beta Technologies' historical ties to the university are very strong, in the sense that the company was in fact spun off from an actual university research project and staffed by the project personnel. The founder saw a 'personal value proposition' in the project when half way through its execution and managed to involve project members in the venture, most likely by employing his dual role as professor and entrepreneur. However, students were able to continue to pursue their degrees in their home department; a situation which is likely to have ensured a continued flow of knowledge between the department and firm. This arrangement is probably to be preferred to a situation where the company is seen as a competitor for labour with the department. This connection also enabled Beta Technologies to continuously participate in supervision of doctoral students, which is clearly a very popular and also functional type of linkage in the transfer of research knowledge (cf. Alfa Foods).

The research collaboration between Beta Technologies and the university department was not based on a 'one-shot' invention, but rather was a matter of the department continuously generating input into the company's products, that is, allowing Beta Technologies to innovate incrementally on the basis of research performed at the department. The exclusivity of this partnership is partly due to history and location, but also to the specialization of the knowledge component of the products offered as compared to the research generally available in the national science system. However, the reliance on cutting-edge research, which is conducted in only a few locations and which is also dependent on public funding, creates a problematic dependency for Beta Technologies. Innovation and survival becomes dependent on continued public funding for a particular science area: that is, a sort of 'science policy risk' is involved for the spin-off from relying on this link. One way of controlling for this risk is to forge contacts with research centres in other countries; however, this particular strategy proved to be too expensive for Beta Technologies in terms of time and other resources. This is one of the dilemmas involved in forging links with cutting-edge research collectives: the entry barriers are not only highly knowledge dependent; they are also often dependent on local professional networks, similar to the one that Beta Technologies themselves forged over many years. This may explain both why EU-project participation is somewhat restricted in terms of returns to firm innovation and that it is very contingent on available time from core activities.

9.4.3 Gamma Biotech

In the case of Gamma Biotech the ties to the initial founders, both being established researchers, have remained strong over time by the company keeping them on the board and using them as external consultants. Due to resource constraints Gamma Biotech carefully chooses the networks in which to participate, but rather than relying on only a few strong links to the university, it has worked from the outset to form more linkages, particularly through the extended networks of the founders and through recruitment. Many of these ties can be said to be strong in the sense that building many long-lasting relations has been an active strategy. In the case of Gamma Biotech, the use of many strong ties to the university could be linked to previous observations that networks are more prevalent within the biotech field generally (e.g., Powell et al., 1999). However, other aspects of their technology may also explain this. At the time of founding this was a completely new technology and, in order to create awareness and gain acceptance for it, the founders deliberately attempted to stimulate research on it on a wide institutional basis and, as mentioned above, also required researchers they collaborated with to publish the results.

Apart from creating awareness and gaining acceptance, this multitude of linkages was vital in order to maintain a broad base for staffing. An additional reason is the stated preference for the 'free-thinking' way of working in academe, which may be related to the fact that many of the employees are themselves academic researchers. The preferred linkages are collaborative research projects and supervision of PhD students. These links are formally constituted, but build on a high degree of informality and are often created through the informal ties of the research-oriented staff, often originating by university researchers approaching them with project proposals. It is also important to note that Gamma Biotech puts efforts into finding mutual interests and creating win-win situations, and sees this strategy as an important factor in making collaborative relationships work (cf. Das and Teng, 1998).

9.4.4 Delta Sensors

Of the four companies studied, Delta Sensors is the only one where the university had an active role in the spin-off process, by deciding that the time was ripe for company formation around the initial patent. Staffed by people from a research project, as well as starting out using facilities and equipment at the university, Delta Sensors' historical ties to the university were strong. As it has developed, Delta Sensors now actually consists of two spin-offs that have merged, thus leaving them with strong historical ties to two different universities.

The linkages to the two universities are very important because of a deliberate split between research and development, where the universities or research collaborations are used for the former part, while the company conducts most of the product development themselves. The reason for this division is simply that they cannot afford to have both in-house research and development to the extent needed. As in the previous cases, the preferred linkages are research collaborations and supervision of PhD students, which together with contacts with former colleagues permit knowledge to flow informally between the company and the universities. However, they also have much more formalized research collaboration, including other manufacturers as well, in the science park where they are situated as well as with other European PROs through participation in EU projects. Professional, academic historical relations, as well as to a lesser extent geographical proximities, however, constitute the strong links of this spin-off to the university.

9.4.5 Summary of the cases

Although from different sectors, of various age and size, and so on, the cases still exhibit some important similarities that are summarized below along with the more specific findings.

Table 9.1 Summary of findings

	Alfa Foods	Beta Technologies	Gamma Biotech	Delta Sensors
Origin of initiative for spinning off	Individual	Individual	Individual	University
Primary motivation for maintaining links	Research	Research	Research and to build acceptance	Research and access to equipment and facilities
Network presence	Limited. A few strong ties and more weak ties – e.g., EU projects	Limited. Mainly one strong tie and a few weak ties – e.g., EU projects	Extensive. Many fairly strong ties, as well as a number of weak ties	Limited. A few strong ties and more weak ties – e.g., EU projects, the Science Park
Nature of relations	Staffing, No. e.g., PhDs) Intangibles. Informality and bi-directionality preferred	Staffing, No. e.g., PhDs) Intangibles. Informality and bi-directionality preferred	Staffing, No. e.g., PhDs) Intangibles. Informality and bi-directionality preferred	Staffing, No. e.g., PhDs) Intangibles Informality and bi-directionality preferred, Also important with formal network
Ways of promoting sustainability	Mutual interest. Founders part time in academia. Geographic proximity, etc.	Mutual interest. Founder full time in academia. Geographic proximity, etc.	Mutual interest. Founders full time in academia.	Mutual interest. Geographic proximity.

The remainder of this chapter will now discuss these dimensions in further length.

9.5   Discussion and conclusion

Although the cases presented above are too few to make generalizations, a comparison of the cases and the literature provides enough material to form a basis for some observations which may be of use either in future research or in policy making. In three of the four spin-offs, firm formation was actualized on the initiative of the researchers and in the cases presented here, the most frequent cited reason for spinning out seems to be personal interests or value propositions rather than university policies. Delta Sensors is the exception to this rule in our sample (see Table 9.1). The fact that, in Sweden, researchers generally have the legal right to any intellectual property accruing from their research findings explains this situation to a certain extent. Incentives for individual researchers to commercialize their findings are high for would-be innovator-entrepreneurs because of the potential financial gains compared to, for instance, a smaller percentage of the possible income of a patent or licence held by the university (e.g., Goldfarb and Henrekson, 2003). According to Gregorio and Shane (2003) this should increase the likelihood of university spin-outs. However, in the Swedish case this advantage is somewhat attenuated by the costs of patenting and eventual commercialization. Thus despite the high incentives, Swedish researchers are comparably behind in rates of commercialization. This phenomenon has, not unexpectedly, been a central issue in the debate on intellectual property rights in Sweden and initially it was thought that the ownership convention was an actual obstacle to commercialization. Recent developments suggest a shift in position to a view that fits more closely with the above, that is, that the low rate of spin-outs may be more of a reflection of the costs of commercialization rather than who owns the intellectual property. In keeping with this the most recent policy proposal on this subject in Sweden proposes to keep the intellectual property rights situation intact, but allow universities to finance commercialization efforts if employees are so interested.

Another dominant trend of the cases here and the literature on the subject is that founders tend to retain their positions in academe, either part-time or full-time, in our cases it is as high as three out of four founders (see Table 9.1). This suggests that some of the vital forms of exchange, for example, transfer of research and personnel, are dependent on boundary-spanning individuals who have a 'right to belong' in the two different worlds. The reasons for retaining the linkages are many. First and foremost the researchers at the home departments are former colleagues, and likely also to be friends, between whom a strong sense of trust and lasting reciprocities has evolved, often over a long time preceding the creation of the spin-off. Another important reason noticeable in all the cases was that, like traditional SMEs, spin-offs are extremely short of resources. Initially this concern may have more to do with a need to access equipment and facilities, but over time the need to develop additional knowledge in terms of firm R&D becomes vital for purposes of competition. While previous studies have recognized the mutual dependence between universities and their spin-offs in areas such as the use of equipment and facilities (e.g., Rosenberg, 1982; Berglund and Hellström, 2002), the potentially more decisive and longer lasting effects of research dependence has not been equally well reported. There is also a need for a systematic study of this issue, both for the purposes of informing science policy as well as developing a better understanding of the R&D dynamics of small knowledge intensive firms.

In our sample, the academic spin-offs are for the most part products of research universities and the universities still provide much of the continuing research needs, while later stages of the product development process are left entirely to the company, thus turning them into some kind of 'business developers of university research'. Taken together with our earlier observations about the high level of dependence of many spin-offs on university research, a number of conclusions of interest to policy may be posited. One of the first is that the long-term consequences of continued dependence on the university for research may be problematic for the spin-off in question. As shown in one of our cases, this is a situation that already worries some companies. The vulnerability in the Swedish context, where universities are for the most part public and are dependent on the whims of policy making for their budgets, is especially high. Despite the use of the system metaphor in all policy thinking on innovation, the reality is that university research is dependent on budget allocations from the state and the ability of those who allocate budgets at this level to access information about the dependences in other parts of the system is limited, to say the least. Thus, the firm is dependent for its research on an organization that is in turn dependent on a well-meaning, but not equally well-informed benefactor. An alternative scenario, and one which policy makers may be betting on too wholeheartedly, is that spin-offs expand to the point where they can fund their own research needs either in house or through an arrangement with the university. Optimism in this regard should also be tempered with existing evidence about the R&D funding behaviour of large firms. Even in these cases, there is a critical dependence on university research and, ironically enough, just when policy makers are advocating that universities do more applied research and commercialization, such enterprises are pleading for continued public support of basic research.

Except for one case, where a wider network of weak and strong ties served as part of an active and purposeful strategy for gaining legitimacy, the academic spin-offs reviewed here are rather limited in terms of network presence, with generally two discernable types of relationship to universities. (1): a few strong ties, often related to the home departments of the spin-off, and (2) weaker ties to other universities or institutes, often mediated through EU-projects(see Table 9.1). This pattern of relatively few strong ties is supported by Liao and Welsch's (2003) findings that technology-based entrepreneurs benefit more from strong ties and a dense network than from an extensive social network. The reason is that this promotes trust and co-operation and so facilitates freer exchange of fine-grained, high-quality information and tacit knowledge. The high degree of informality that obtains in these circumstances in spite of the crucial importance of these arrangements to the firms suggests that the spin-offs are retaining the gift–market–gift cycle of exchange relations that is common in academic contexts. A corollary to this observation is that several studies have found preferences among university researchers for bi-directional, collaborative relationships rather than uni-directional relationships, like those usually found in contract research (e.g., Meyer-Krahmer and Schmoch, 1998). Our study suggests that the preference for bi-directionality also exists within the academic spin-offs and is manifested in, for example, the expressed desire for finding mutual interest, and in the strong emphasis on informality in personal contacts and knowledge exchange (see Table 9.1). This could be due to the fact that many of the employees share the same academic background and values as their academic counterparts. But this relationship is likely also promoted because of the sustainability and the development of trust involved in, and facilitated by, further knowledge transfer (Carayannis et al., 2000).

Sustainability seems to be a key characteristic of these linkages, considering the long history of many relationships and the general preference for long-term commitments. In view of the importance of knowledge transfer processes between the spin-offs and universities, this is not surprising, since such transfer is likely to require a mutual language, similar knowledge assimilation processes (Cohen and Levinthal, 1990) and again trust. The recurrent emphasis on putting efforts into finding mutual interests is also likely to promote sustainability and generate trust (Das and Teng, 1998). However, although trust and informality may be of great importance, this alone does not guarantee smooth and effective collaborations. The cases suggest that in order for these to work on a long-term basis, more hands-on practices as well as formal mechanisms may be needed. These more formal aspects may include explicitly setting up a collaborative framework beforehand, while maintaining flexibility within relationships when it comes to publication of results, IPR rights, and so on.

From the point of view of national policy, it is important to note that although policy attention emphasizes the university qua organization with regard to commercialization and knowledge transfer, it is the department, groups of researchers therein or networks of departments with which spin-offs have relations. This finding in the cases reported above is supported by studies from other countries (cf. Jones-Evans et al. 1999; Benneworth, 2001). Reasoning from this we may posit that centralized mechanisms for managing commercialization efforts may be superfluous since commercialization and follow up activities appear to take place at a lower level in the structure than that at which such services are usually placed. This is not to say that liaison offices have no place in commercialization, however. It may be that their effectiveness could be increased if they were to be restructured according to a regime that is based on co-ordinating and facilitating relations between departments and the networks that they create.

Academic spin-offs are highly dependent on a sustainable link to university research for a number of reasons, thus it should come as no surprise that their network relations are characterized by a small number of strong ties which are in turn characterized by a high degree of trust and informality. These historically, strong ties of reciprocity and location (social capital aspects), and the specificity of the knowledge transferred, can become difficult to substitute.

From the point of view of the spin-off companies, the continued need for help with research, coupled with the difficulty of substituting the strong ties, make these ties something of a two-edged sword. The cost of building and maintaining them must be contrasted with the risk of their becoming too dependent not only on one department, but also on that department's ability to attract funding from other sources. One way to mitigate this risk may be to engage in a wider network of weak ties which, in time, may be developed into strong ties. Although helpful, the development of such research collaborations does not have to involve geographical proximity (cf. Gamma Biotech); however, finding mutual interests, emphasizing informality and bi-directionality, as well as safeguarding priorities by articulating them in advance, ought not to be overlooked. One particular arrangement that seems to fulfil this to a large extent, and which was preferred by all firms in our study, was the joint supervision of PhD students. The development of such relations may also be facilitated if the founders retain a position in academia, and thereby remain able to act as boundary-spanning individuals between the two worlds.

In summary, academic spin-offs are the product of an evolution of ties between individual researchers, departments and successive generations of students. The cases above show that spin-offs have a similar relationship to universities as they have to larger research intensive companies in that they depend on universities to do the majority of the research, thus becoming enmeshed with the university in a much tighter web of social, economic and knowledge ties. This makes their dependence and vulnerability greater to shifts in national innovation and science policy trends. If the present policy trend of promoting commodification were to continue, policy makers could find that they will have to take the potential impact of research funding policies on spin-offs into account. Universities may also potentially increase their leverage in policy by pointing to the growing interdependence between departments and spin-offs.

References

Almeida, P., Dokko, G. and Rosenkopf, L. (2003), 'Startup size and the mechanisms of external learning: Increasing opportunity or decreasing ability?', *Research Policy*, Vol. 32, No. 2, pp. 301–15.

Argyres, N. S. and Liebeskind, J. P. (1998), 'Privatizing the intellectual commons: Universities and the commercialization of biotechnology', *Journal of Economic Behavior & Organization*, Vol. 35, No. 4, pp. 427–54.

Benneworth, P. (2001), 'Academic entrepreneurship and long–term business relationships: Understanding 'commercialization' activities', *Enterprise and Innovation Management Studies*, Vol. 2, No. 3, pp. 225–37.

Berglund, H. and Hellström, T. (2002), 'Enacting risk in independent technological innovation', *International Journal of Risk and Assessment Management*, Vol. 3, No. 2/3/4, pp. 205–21.

Bozeman, B. (2000), 'Technology transfer and public policy: A review of research and theory', *Research Policy*, Vol. 29, No. 4/5, pp. 627–55.

Burnham, J. B. (1997), 'Evaluating industry/university research linkages', *Research Technology Management*, January–February, pp. 52–5.

Carayannis, E. G., Alexander, J. and Ioannidis, A. (2000), 'Leveraging knowledge, learning, and innovation in forming strategic government-university-industry (GUI) R&D partnerships in the US, Germany, and France', *Technovation*, Vol. 20, No. 9, pp. 477–488.

Cohen W. M. and Levinthal, D. A. (1990), 'Absorptive capacity: A new perspective of learning and innovation', *Administrative Science Quarterly*, Vol. 35, No. 1, pp. 128–52.

Das, T. K. and Teng, B. S. (1998), 'Between trust and control: Developing confidence in partner cooperation and alliances', *Academy of Management Review*, Vol. 23, No. 3, pp. 491–512.

Dasgupta, P. and David, P. (1994), 'Toward a new economics of science', *Research Policy*, Vol. 23, No. 5, pp. 487–521.

Deeds, D., Decarolis, D. L. and Coombs, J. E. (2000), 'Dynamic capabilities and new product development in high technology ventures: An empirical analysis of new biotechnology firms', *Journal of Business Venturing*, Vol. 15, No. 3, pp. 211–29.

Fitzroy, F., Smith, I. and Acs, Z. (1994), 'High technology employment and university R&D spillovers: Evidence from US cities', CRIEFF Discussion Paper Number 9417.

Glaser, B. and Strauss, A. (1967), *The Discovery of Grounded Theory*, Aldine, Chicago.

Goldfarb, B. and Henrekson, M. (2003), 'Bottom-up versus top-down policies towards the commercialization of university intellectual property', *Research Policy*, Vol. 32, No. 4, pp. 639–58.

Goldfarb, B. (2001), 'The effect of government contracting on academic research', Discussion Paper No 00-24, Stanford Institute for Economic Policy Research.

Government of Finland (2003), 'Research in Finland', available at www.research.fi

Gregorio, D. D. and Shane, S. (2003), 'Why do some universities generate more start-ups than others?', *Research Policy*, Vol. 32, No. 2, pp. 209–27.

Hellström, T. (2003), 'Governing the virtual academic commons', *Research Policy*, Vol. 32, No. 3, pp. 391–401.

Huberman, A. M. and Miles, M. B. (1994), 'Data management and analysis methods', in Denzin, N. K. and Lincoln, Y. S., eds, *Handbook of Qualitative Research*, Sage Publications, Thousand Oaks, CA, pp. 428–44.

Jacob, M. (2003), 'Rethinking science and commodifying knowledge', *Policy Futures in Education*, Vol. 1, No. 1, pp. 125–42.

Jensen, R. and Thursby, M. (2001), 'Proofs and prototypes for sale: The tale of university licensing', *American Economic Review*, Vol. 91, 240–59.

Jones-Evans, D., Klofsten, M., Andersson, E. and Pandya, D. (1999), 'Creating a bridge between university and industry in small European countries: The role of the industrial liasion office', *R&D Management*, Vol. 29, No. 1, pp. 47–56.

Lane, P. J. and Lubatkin, M (1998), 'Relative absorptive capacity and interorganizational learning', *Strategic Management Journal*, Vol. 19, No. 5, pp. 461–77.

Lei, D., Slocum, J. W. and Pitts, R. A. (1997), 'Building cooperative advantage: Managing strategic alliances to promote organizational learning', *Journal of World Business*, Vol. 32, No. 3, pp. 203–23.

Liao, J. and Welsch, H. (2003), 'Social capital and entrepreneurial growth aspiration: A comparison of technology- and non-technology-based nascent entrepreneurs', *The Journal of High Technology Management Research*, Vol. 14, No. 1, pp. 149–70.

Manning, P. K. (1982), 'Analytic induction', in Robert B. Smith and Peter K. Manning, *Handbook of Social Science Methods: Qualitative Methods*, Ballinger, Cambridge, MA.

Meyer-Krahmer, F. and Schmoch, U. (1998), 'Science-based technologies: University-industry interactions in four fields', *Research Policy*, Vol. 27, No. 8, pp. 835–51.

Miles, M. B. and Huberman, A. M. (1984), *Qualitative Data Analysis: A Sourcebook of New Methods*, Sage Publications, Newbury Park, CA.

Ndonzuau, F. N., Pirnay, F. and Surlemont, B. (2002), 'A stage model of academic spin-off creation', *Technovation*, Vol. 22, No. 5, pp. 281–9.

OECD (2002), *STI Review*, No. 27, Special Issue on New Science and Technology Indicators, OECD, Paris.

Powell, W. W., Koput, K. W., Smith-Doerr, L. and Owen-Smith, J. (1999), 'Network position and firm performance: Organizational returns to collaboration in the bio-technology industry', in Andrews, Steven and Knoke, David, eds, *Networks In and Around Organizations*, JAI Press, Greenwich, CT.

Prabhu, G. N. (1999), 'Implementing university-industry joint product innovation projects', *Technovation*, Vol. 19, No. 8, pp. 495–505.

Rappert, B., Webster, A. and Charles, D. (1999), 'Making sense of diversity and reluctance: Academic-industrial relations and intellectual property', *Research Policy*, Vol. 28, No. 8, pp. 873–90.

Rosenberg, N. (1982), *Inside the Black Box*, Cambridge University Press, Cambridge.

Santoro, M. D. and Gopalakrishnan, S. (2001), 'Relationship dynamics between university research centers and industrial firms: Their impact on technology transfer activities', *Journal of Technology Transfer*, Vol. 26, No. 1/2, pp. 163–71.

Saxenian, A. (1994), *Regional Advantage*, Harvard University Press, Cambridge, MA.

Schartinger, D., Rammer, C., Fischer, M. M. and Fröhlich, J. (2002), 'Knowledge interactions between universities and industry in Austria: Sectoral patterns and determinants', *Research Policy*, Vol. 31, No. 3, pp. 303–28.

Shane, S. (2002), 'Selling university technology: Patterns from MIT', *Management Science*, Vol. 48, No. 1, pp. 122–37.

Slaughter, S. and Leslie, L. L. (1997), *Academic Capitalism: Politics, Policies, and the Entrepreneurial University*, Johns Hopkins University Press, Baltimore, MD.

Stokes, D. E. (1997), *Pasteur's Quadrant: Basic Science and Technological Innovation*, Brookings Institution Press, Washington DC.

Stake, R. E. (1995), *The Art of Case Study Research*, Sage Publications, Thousand Oaks, CA.

Tether, B. S. (2002), 'Who co-operates for innovation, and why. An empirical analysis', *Research Policy*, Vol. 31, No. 6, pp. 947–67.

Vinnova (2002), Effective Innovation Systems and Problem-Oriented Research for Sustainable Growth, VINNOVA's strategic plan 2003 – 2007, Stockholm, Sweden May also be downloaded at www.vinnova.se

10
Patent Strength and Diminishing Knowledge Spill-Overs: The Quest for the Optimal Patent

Andreas Panagopoulos[1]
Lancaster Management School

Introduction

Popular perception views an innovator as operating alone in the monastic solitude of her garage. This view, with notable exceptions, could not be further from reality, as innovations are seldom born in a vacuum. By contrast, clusters and networks of innovative activity are the breading grounds of innovations, a *sine qua non*, without which new ideas cannot find the nourishment they need, especially in their first stages. This is because no matter how brilliant an innovator is, standing on the shoulders of giants always enhances her viewpoint and ability to move beyond the state of the art. Metaphors aside, clusters and networks provide support to an innovator because they allow her to function having the benefit of knowing what others have already accomplished, through what is commonly known as knowledge spill-overs. Such spill-overs take various forms, word of mouth or academic journals being possible candidates.

One important way of allowing other experts a clear view of the technology embodied in a new innovation is through patent publications. Specifically, after a patent is granted, the claims of the patent (which explain in detail how the innovation functions and the scientific principles that are behind it) are published, becoming available to the public. However, for the duration of the patent, the innovator has a monopoly on the invention, which, even though it spills over to others, cannot be freely used by them. This monopoly is not self-governing; it is a property right, enforced by courts. In fact, firms frequently use patent litigation in order to protect their technological territory, as expressed by the claims of the granted patents, from innovative intruders.

Accounting for the above, various scholars have taken the view that patent litigation, stemming from a prolific control of one's technological turf, can erect fences to entrant firms, who abstain from innovating in this field, fearing retaliatory litigation by the incumbent patent holders. Lerner (1995), working on biotechnology firms, finds that this difficulty may force some entrant innovators to abstain from innovating in this particular sector.

If the above claim is substantiated, it follows (as this chapter argues) that such a reduction in innovative effort may lead to a drop in knowledge spill-overs, leading to a drop in innovative output. This idea counters the established view in the literature on patents, which are thought to act as stimuli for innovation, allowing the innovator to reap the benefits of her research. For, even though patents encourage an innovator to pursue her research in hope of an eventual patented invention, they nevertheless discourage potential entrant innovators as well, limiting the fruitful interaction that clusters and networks of innovations can bring to any researcher through knowledge spill-overs. Therefore, patents may also diminish innovative output. The importance of this issue is further highlighted by recent evidence from Lerner (2004), who, in an international analysis of the relationship between patent strength and innovation, examines 177 policy shifts in 60 countries over 150 years and finds some support for an inverse U relationship. What Lerner seems to suggest is that overly increasing patent protection can lead to a decrease in innovative activity.

Stemming from Lerner's empirical findings, this chapter aims to offer a theoretical model that accounts for the above two divergent roles of patents. My expectation is that this model will allow (under the aegis of a data set that will permit calibration) one to establish the optimal rate of patent protection; the one that maximizes the economy's innovative output and overall growth rate. Specifically, while accounting for the view that patents reward the innovator, acting as stimuli, this model will also allow an increase in patent protection to make it harder for other innovators to bypass a patent. Such a shortfall will force some innovators to abstain from innovating, reducing innovative effort and knowledge spill-overs, leading to a drop in innovative output. Therefore, in a broad way, the model concentrates on the merits of duplication, acknowledging that if many innovators work on the same technology, even though some of their work is mere duplication, they create knowledge spill-overs that can potentially affect all innovators.

The argument of this chapter will be substantiated through a static tournament model where many innovators race to create the greatest technology. The introduction of the tournament allows one to specifically model competition between innovators. In the second part of this chapter, in order to study the effect that patent protection has on output growth, this tournament model will be extended to include, similar to Loury (1979), a simple dynamic endogenous growth framework based on Aghion and Howitt (1992). It should be noted that the growth model is not essential to the chapter's results. In fact, all the important comparative statics will be proved within the static framework before I re-introduce them to the dynamic model. Nonetheless, the latter model allows one to concentrate on the following question, what is the optimal patent protection, the one that maximizes output growth? Accounting for the above, running a numerical simulation on the latter model I find that there is an inverse U relationship between patent protection and output growth.

The outline of this chapter is the following. Section 1 introduces the tournament and the way technology is generated. Section 2 displays the model's main properties. Section 3 extents the model by introducing a simple growth framework, while Section 4 contains the simulation and is followed by the conclusions.

10.1 Assumptions

In what follows the model will focus on industries such as biotechnology and pharmaceuticals. These are industries where patent protection is a successful way of protecting one's innovation, and, accordingly, patents are essential to firms. In addition, these industries face a lot of obsolescence, making the latest innovation by far the most important and useful one, both in production and as a base for further research.

I here frequently use the terms innovation, and technology. To avoid confusion, I will provide a definition of these terms. For the purpose of this chapter, technology A is the sum of many sequential individual innovations. Innovations, in turn, are defined as marketable technological advances, which are not obvious beforehand to someone skilled in the prior art. In this model, an innovation ΔA will be the result of the winning innovator's research between tournaments.

Many heterogeneous potential-innovators participate in a series of tournaments in which all the participants have full information about each other. Hence there are no trade secrets and an innovator has no option but to patent her innovation in order to protect it from imitators.[2] Innovators are assumed to be risk-neutral individuals, and their role is to form the idea that will become an innovation. In order to participate in tournament t (where t denotes the ordering of periods and tournaments), innovators must incur a sunk cost C, which represents the cost of building a laboratory and the effort to diffuse in one's research the latest findings by universities and so on. The objective of a tournament is to build a technology of the greatest possible magnitude. Hence, when a tournament ends, the winner will be the innovator who builds such a technology. Each tournament will lead to only one technology, which will be employed in the production of a consumption good. The technological advances that the remaining innovators achieved during the tournament will be treated as inventions. These inventions can be used as a base for one's future research but they will not find any marketable application, unless the innovator succeeds in winning a tournament. If an innovator chooses not to take part in a tournament, she stops her research.

In order to innovate the innovator needs to employ research workers n. These workers, who are assumed to be homogeneous, will receive a fixed percentage ε of the revenues that the innovation generates. The remaining will be the innovator's payment. The profits that an innovation ΔA_t generates are π_t. For simplicity, I will assume that π_t is a positive function of the innovation, and that research workers depend positively on the expected revenues from the innovation. In the first part of this chapter I will not offer any microeconomics structure backing these two assumptions. This will be included in the second part of the chapter.

If one is to introduce an endogenous labour market condition determining how profits are divided between the innovator and the n research workers, this must be directly or indirectly affected by the model's main variable of interest, namely patent breadth. However, there seems to be (as far as I know) no empirical evidence connecting the labour market to patent breadth. An alternative assumption would be to allow, similar to Jones (2001), the innovator to appropriate a greater part of profits as patent breadth increases. It should be stressed that working under such an assumption does not alter the chapter's results and final formulas because in the steady state the choice of n is not affected by ε.

Innovators innovate sequentially.[3] Assuming that no cross-licensing takes place, the innovation that the innovator builds in the course of a tournament adds to the technology that she had developed in the previous tournament,[4] where patents are assumed to last for two periods. If there is no (or limited) patent protection, innovators will manage to re-innovate around the winner's patent (re-innovation implies the legal development of an innovation with similar or identical capabilities). If there is patent protection, depending on how much re-innovating is allowed, the innovators will use either their own innovation, or the one that they built by re-innovating (whichever one is of larger magnitude). At the same time, since patents reveal how an innovation functions this information will spill over to all innovators.

For example, if an innovator works on catalysts, any information included in all other innovators' patents (who also work on catalysts), assists the innovator in her research effort. This could be because the innovator becomes aware of the research path that the other innovators have followed and what type of research should be avoided, or simply because the innovator has knowledge of what all the other innovators are currently working on. Nevertheless, this knowledge cannot be translated into an innovation because it is protected by a patent. Therefore, even though the innovator knows and understands the latest catalyst technology, she cannot use it without a licence. If she wants to use it, she must either pay royalties for a licence (this does not happen in this model because no cross-licensing is allowed), or attempt to re-innovate around the patent. This re-innovation will take place during the next tournament.

In light of the above, (denoting the technology of the winning innovator i, during tournament t as $A_{t,i}$ and her innovation as $\Delta A_{t,i}$), innovator j (a follower) will be able to advance her technology by $\max\{0, \Delta A_{t,j}, \lambda \Delta A_{t,i}\}$, where $\lambda \in (0.1)$ indicates how much re-innovating around $\Delta A_{t,i}$ innovator j can do.[5] In this context, λ can be considered as patent breadth. For example, if λ is close to zero then j cannot re-innovate around the innovation of innovator i. On the contrary, if λ is close to one then j can re-innovate around it, which suggests that j will end up with an innovation that is of equal size to that of the winner. Accounting for the above, the technology of innovator j is:

$$A_{t,j} = A_{t-1,j} + \max\{0, \Delta A_{t,j}, \lambda \Delta A_{t,i}\} \tag{1}$$

In equation (1) the zero is included (as it will become apparent in the following section) in case technology takes a wrong turn producing an innovation that is of inferior capacity, effectively a negative innovation. In this framework, one way of increasing tournament-based competition is to increase λ, making it easier for the followers to re-innovate around the leader's technology. This way, the followers will increase their technology getting closer to the leader. However, since $\lambda \neq 1$ and patent length is two periods long, *ceteris paribus* an increase in λ will not create a tournament where all innovators have identical technologies. Thus, the tournament is unlikely to become perfectly competitive. Henceforth, λ will be considered a policy instrument used by the central planner.[6]

The time-line of the model is the following. Competing innovators employ research workers and start their research while participating in a tournament. At the beginning of the tournament innovators make all the irreversible decisions regarding innovation, choosing what type of innovation path to follow. Production will take place immediately before the next tournament commences.

10.1.1 Technology

The purpose of this section is to study how technology is built. I will assume that any discovery is the combined result of four factors, prior art, luck, research workers and knowledge spill-overs. Prior art, in the form of the already made technological discovery $\Delta A_{t-1,i}$, is the building block on which research can be based. Without prior art one must start from scratch. In addition to prior art, research workers must be used because they are the ones who create the innovation. In the absence of the above inputs, the resulting innovation will be dependent on luck. Furthermore, as Segerstrom (1998) argues, the more advanced (complicated) technology is, the harder it is to innovate. Therefore, prior art can also affect innovation in a negative way. However, as Panagopoulos (2003) notes, an increase in knowledge spill-overs $s_{t,i}$ increases the innovator's ability to cope with complicated prior art, where in this framework knowledge spill-overs express the collective experience that all the tournament participants (absent i) generate by patenting their innovations. Subsequently, the greater the knowledge spill-overs that an innovator manages to attain, the less the difficulty that she will face during the innovation process.

In what follows, I will introduce a technology generation function, which describes how technological discoveries are created. Specifically, every innovator i uses the following technology generation function:

$$\Delta A_{t,i} = \Delta A_{t-1,i}^{\zeta} n_{t,i}^{\xi} - \frac{\Delta A_{t-1,i}}{s_{t-1,i}} + u_{t,i} \tag{2}$$

to develop a series of innovations $\Delta A_{t,\,i}$ that will allow her to create a technology and participate in the tournament. The initial condition for equation (2) is $\Delta A_0 \geq 0$. To avoid multiple winners in the first tournament, I will assume that only one innovator has the initial idea to generate the first innovation. In equation (2), $\Delta A_{t-1,i}^{\zeta} \, n_{t,i}^{\xi}$ expresses an innovation as the combined result of prior art and research workers. In addition, $\Delta A_{t-1,i}/s_{t-1,i}$ describes the increase in difficulty that an innovator faces when she tries to create increasingly larger innovations.

Lastly, $u_{t,i}$, which is distributed with a mean 0, is a random term that acts as a proxy for luck. Since it can attain negative values it is possible for the innovation to be less than zero. If this turns out to be true, it implies that research has followed the wrong path. In this case, the innovator will not make use of their innovation, having a technological increment of zero.[7]

In equation (2), $\Delta A_{t,i}$ is the result of the latest prior art $\Delta A_{t-1,i}$. True as it may be that such an assumption accords well with the way research is carried out in industries such as biotechnology and pharmaceuticals (because of the high obsolescence rate that they face), one can also provide an alternative/complementary intuition. Accordingly, bearing in mind that patents last for two periods, A_{t-2} must be common and well understood knowledge. Subsequently, considering that research workers are homogeneous, any research that uses A_{t-2} as a base for developing new knowledge should produce similar results among all innovators. Therefore, in addition to the innovation that is generated via $\Delta A_{t-1,i}$, through equation (2), one should expect innovators to create a common innovative step based on A_{t-2}. Accounting for the above, considering that the model will concentrate on the differences between the technologies created by the innovators, common terms will always cancel out allowing one to focus only on how the latest prior art effects the creation of an innovation.

In order for an innovator to win the tournament she must create a technology that is greater than the one created by all other innovators. Accordingly, I will endow each innovator i with an expected probability $p_{t,i}$ of winning the tournament. I will allow $p_{t,i}\left(EA_{t,i}, EA_{t,j}\right)\in[0, 1]$, $j \neq i$, $j \in [1, v_t - i]$ to be a function of the technology that i is expected to create, as well as of the technology that all other innovators $j \neq i$ are expected to create. In this context, one should expect that $\partial p_{t,i}/\partial EA_{t,i} > 0$, $\partial p_{t,i}/\partial EA_{t,j} < 0$. The latter inequalities imply that the greater one's expected technology is, the greater her chances of wining the tournament are. Moreover, the greater the expected technology of her competitors is, the lower her chances of winning the tournament are.[8]

10.1.2 The option value of investing

In this section, the innovators' motive to participate in the tournament is explored. Accordingly, I will try to determine which innovators find it profitable to enter the tournament (thus I will try to determine v). In order to find who enters, I will examine the value innovators assign to entering the current tournament. In doing so, I will treat the decision to innovate as an investment decision. In this case, the investment will have a limited horizon of one period and it must commence at the beginning of the tournament. Thereby, in a fashion similar to Dixit and Pindyck (1994), I will form the innovator's expected option value function to investing.

One should expect that only innovators who have a positive option value will decide to take part in the tournament. In this context, the expected option value of an innovator i is:

$$F_{t,i} = (1 - \varepsilon)p_{t,i}\,\pi_{t,i} - C \tag{3}$$

In equation (3), $F_{t,i}$ is the expected option value to the investment of innovator i (the option value of entering the tournament), C is the sunk cost of entry and $(1-\varepsilon)\pi_{t,i}$ are the profits that the winner gets from employing her technology in the production of a consumption good (thus $(1-\varepsilon)p_{t,i}\pi_{t,i}$ are the expected revenues from the innovation).

Only innovators who have a positive option value will take part in the tournament. Subsequently, since the greater $p_{t,i}$ is, the higher $(1-\varepsilon)p_{t,i}\pi_{t,i}$ is, innovators who have a higher probability of winning the tournament are more likely to participate in the tournament because, for these innovators, $(1-\varepsilon)p_{t,i}\pi_{t,i} > C$ and $F_{t,i} > 0$. The number v_t of the innovators who have a positive option value is of interest, since it determines the magnitude of the knowledge spill-overs; increases in the number of tournament participants increase the knowledge spill-overs available to the innovators, leading to a greater innovation.

10.2   Some comparative statistics based on patent breadth

In this section I will compare the effects that different types of tournaments can have on innovation. The main difference between tournaments will be on how close the innovators are positioned to each other. As I mentioned in Section 1, one can vary the distance between innovators by changing the patent breadth λ, allowing innovators to re-innovate more. Thereby, the question that this section poses is the following, what impact will an increase in λ have on innovation?

To this question the model indicates that patent breadth can affect innovation in two different ways. The first one indicates that an increase in tournament competition (caused by an increase in λ) can be detrimental for innovation. Hence, a tournament where only one (or a few) innovators can win is preferable to a tournament in which all innovators have equal chances. Specifically, as λ increases and innovators get closer (increasing $A_{t,j}$), the probability $p_{t,i}(EA_{t,i}, EA_{t,j})$ that innovator i has of winning the tournament is reduced, reducing the expected revenues from the innovation $(1-\varepsilon)p_{t,i}\pi_{t,i}$. Such a reduction in expected revenues should lead to less research workers and a drop in the magnitude of the innovation.

The above argument describes how the leading innovator will respond as λ increases. The second way that a change in λ can affect innovation reverses the above result, examining how the followers will respond. The rationale behind this rests on the increase in knowledge spill-overs that one should expect if more innovators participate in the tournament. Specifically, noting that the tournament never becomes perfectly competitive (since $\lambda \neq 1$ and patent length is two periods long), any increase in λ increases the technologies of the lagging innovators. Therefore, *ceteris paribus*, such an increase in technology should lead to an increase in the lagging innovators' probability of winning the tournament, making it profitable for more lagging innovators to enter the tournament, increasing knowledge spill-overs, leading to a greater innovation.

Specifically, Section 1.1 introduced for each innovator a probability of success. This probability depends on her $EA_{t,i}$, as well as on the $EA_{t,j}$ of all the other innovators. If an innovator has a greater $EA_{t,i}$ (compared to the other innovators), she increases her probability of winning the tournament, while decreasing that of the other innovators. However, a drop in the probability of winning the tournament (caused by a decrease in λ, which brings the innovators further apart) leads to a reduction in the innovators' option value, see Equation (3), forcing some innovators to abstain from entering the tournament, reducing ν_t and lowering knowledge spill-overs. Accounting for Equation (2), if spill-overs decrease, there should be a decrease in the magnitude of the innovation. Flipping the argument, any increase in competition that leads the followers to increase their expected technology, should *ceteris paribus* increase the followers' probability of winning the tournament, increasing their option value, which suggest that more innovators enter the tournament.

10.3 A growth framework

In this section I will introduce the main aspects of the growth model, which is broadly based on Aghion and Howitt (1992). Unless otherwise stated, all the assumptions included in the first part of the chapter continue to apply. Specifically, there are three classes of tradable objects. The first one is labour, the second one is a non-storable consumption good and the third one is an intermediate good. In addition, there is a continuum of infinitely-lived individuals, with identical intertemporal additive preferences, which are defined over lifetime consumption and a constant rate of time preference.

Assuming no disutility from supplying labour, there are three categories of labour. The first one is unskilled workers x. These workers are all equipped with one unit of labour and are used for producing an intermediate input, which will be employed in the production of the consumption good. Similar to Aghion and Howitt (1992), unskilled workers can also function as firms whose aim is to produce the consumption good. The second category is skilled workers in the form of research workers n. Both skilled and unskilled workers are homogeneous, operate in an environment of perfect labour mobility and can exchange roles. For simplicity, assuming no population growth, the total number of research workers n and production workers x is equal to $L > 1$, that is:

$$L + x_t + n_t \tag{4}$$

The third category of labour is innovators, the number of innovators who decide to take part in a tournament is ν_t. Contrary to production workers and research workers, innovators are heterogeneous. Innovators are assumed to be risk-neutral individuals and that their role is to form the idea that will become an innovation, where each innovation consists of the invention of a new intermediate good, whose use as an input allows more efficient methods to be used in producing the consumption good. Innovators employ research workers and create an innovation using Equation (2). However, as Jones (1998) notes, for this class of model growth stops being endogenous unless technology exhibits increasing returns to scale. Subsequently, in a fashion similar to Romer (1990), $\zeta + \xi > 1$.

Since no credit market is supposed to exist, all non-research workers consume their wage at each instant and research workers receive no payment unless they win the tournament, in which case they are paid a fixed percentage ε of the revenues from the innovation that they have created. The remaining revenues will be transferred to the innovator. If an innovator fails to win a tournament, since the research workers that she used will receive no salary, they have no option but to be employed in production.

Similar to the benchmark model, the consumption good is produced in a perfectly competitive market by a firm that licenses the patent from the innovator, using an intermediate good x_t with productivity ΔA_t, in the following fashion:

$$y_t = \Delta A_t^a x_t^b, \; \{a, b\} > 0 \tag{5}$$

In Equation (5), y_t represents the output produced using the innovation of the tournament's winner i. Since, no matter who wins the tournament, there is only one type of consumption good, I will abstain from attaching a subscript to y_t.

The time-line of the model is the following. Competitors employ research workers and start their research while participating in a tournament. At the beginning of the tournament innovators make all the irreversible decisions regarding innovation, choosing what type of innovation path to follow and how many research workers to employ. After the tournament they license their innovation to a production firm. Production will take place immediately before the next tournament commences. Solving the model in a fashion similar to Aghion and Howitt (1992), see the appendix, in the steady state the number of research workers is given by:

$$En = \left(\left(\frac{P\beta}{\xi} \right)^{1-\zeta} \left(1 + \frac{c}{s} \right)^{\zeta} \right)^{\frac{1}{\zeta + \xi - 1}} \tag{6}$$

where

$$P = p_{t,i} / p_{t-1,i}.$$

In what follows I will illustrate that the comparative statics of Section 2 still apply. In detail, the first way through which λ can affect innovation indicates that an increase in tournament competition (caused by an increase in λ) can be detrimental for innovation. Specifically, as λ increases and innovators get closer (increasing $A_{t,j}$), the probability that innovator i has of winning the tournament is reduced, reducing P. However, Equation (6) suggests that in the steady state: if $\zeta < 1$, any increase in λ, which decreases P, should lower n, negatively affecting innovation. Furthermore, the second way that a change in λ can affect innovation reverses the above result, examining how the followers will respond. This result is not based on the assumptions of the growth model. Thus, its intuition is identical to the one of Section 2.

10.4 A numerical experiment

Bearing in mind that the previous sections have indicated a possible non-monotonic relationship between patent breadth and innovation (production), this section examines if this non-monotonic relationship exists in the context of this model. Noting that I lack a data set that would allow me to calibrate the model, or even an exact function for knowledge spill-overs and $p_{t,i}$, it is best to view this section as a numerical exercise, run for educational purposes. Consequently, all the values/functions that I will be using during this experiment are ad hoc, even though they accord to what the literature has been using in similar cases. Nevertheless, when in doubt (such as with ε), I experimented with a whole range of values. Accordingly, in this section I will try and find the optimal patent breadth, the one that maximizes the economy's output growth rate. If such an optimal patent breadth exists, then there must be some form of concavity between output growth rate and patent breath.

With the above in mind, in order to account for the joint effects of λ on the economy's output growth rate I run a numerical experiment over a series of tournaments, gradually increasing the degree of technological competition by increasing the value of λ in each consecutive tournament. It should be noted that in order to avoid any unexpected effects caused by the randomness of u, each tournament consisted of 50 periods during which λ remained steady. It is the steady state solution of output growth from these 50 periods that I used as the output growth rate of each individual tournament.

Specifically, for each of the 50 periods (denoted by t) within a tournament, I numerically solved the maximization problem (described in detail in the Appendix) and run equations (2)–(4), (8)–(9) for 50 heterogeneous innovators. Throughout this numerical experiment, the technology of innovator j was equal to the ratio of $A_{t,j}/A_{t,i}$, where i is the winner of period t. Furthermore, I allowed the probability function to be equal to, $p_{t,i} = 1 - 0.5 \exp[(EA_{t,j} - EA_{t,i})/EA_{t,i}]$, which accords well to the assumptions made about p, where the 0.5 was included just in case the two innovators had identical technologies.

In the first period of each tournament a starting technology, randomly distributed (using a Normal distribution) in the interval $[1,\delta]$, was assigned to each innovator. This technology did not change between tournaments. Therefore, at the first period of each tournament all innovators had the same starting value as in the past one. This intuition implies that some innovators had a starting technology that was close to one and some close to δ. In the same fashion, each innovator had a different v, randomly distributed (using a Normal distribution) in the interval $[-\delta,\delta]$, which varied with each period.

With respect to spill-overs, I used the following functional form, $s_{t,i} = \sum_{j}^{w-i} \gamma_j \Delta A_{t,j}$, which treats knowledge spill-overs as a weighted sum of the innovations created by all innovators except i. In the latter equation, $\gamma_j \geq 0$ indicates the weight with which the technology of each innovator entered the spill-over's function, where, similar to Hall and colleagues (2000), not all innovations find equal use in generating knowledge spill-overs. Subsequently, similar to Panagopoulos (2003), I allowed the innovators who were close to the top of the quality ladder to generate more knowledge spill-overs compared to the ones that are further down. Following this type of reasoning, in this numerical experiment γ_j was equal to the inverse of innovator j's ranking. Thus, the fiftieth innovator had a $\gamma_j = 1/50$.

Bearing in mind that in this model the innovator and the research workers share the profits, I allowed the innovator to have an $\varepsilon = 40$ per cent share of the profits. Noting that the role of the innovator in this framework was very similar to the one in reality played by a venture capitalist, an $\varepsilon = 40$ per cents accords with the average percentage of firm stock that venture capitalists get by providing firms with capital and expertise. For b I used the share of labour in US production which is 0.33 and for α the share of capital, which is 0.7.[9] Since, production workers and research workers are homogeneous and employ similar production functions (the production function for the intermediate input uses ΔA and x in a fashion similar to the way Equation (2) employs ΔA and n) I used $\zeta = 0.7$ and $\xi = 0.33$. Finally, L was 100.

On par with Lerner (2004), who examines 150 years of patent protection, this numerical experiment was repeated for 150 tournaments. In these tournaments λ started from being zero in the first tournament, becoming one in the last tournament. Hence, each tournament becomes more competitive. The number of participants was derived from Equation (3), where C was arbitrarily chosen as 70 per cent of the winner's expected revenues from the innovation. Thus, in order for an innovator to find it profitable to participate in the tournament, her expected revenues must be equal to at least 70 percent of the winner's. If one is to increase C, then it becomes harder to take part in the tournament, while any decrease in C makes it easier. Bearing the above in mind, in the first tournaments, where innovators had starting technologies that were positioned far apart, only a few had an F that fulfilled this requirement, while as the tournament became more competitive, more innovators fulfilled Equation (3).

Running a numerical experiment for $\delta = 10$, which suggests that the 50 competitors were initially positioned far from each other, the humped-shaped relationship of Figure 10.1 was derived. Ad hoc as the above assumptions may be, this shape does not change drastically if one is to alter ε (in the range of 15–60 per cent, which is the usual share of profits a venture capitalist gets), δ (for values between 5 and 20, which allow for some observable heterogeneity among innovators), C (for values that do not make it either impossible or too easy to participate, that is, between 40 per cent and 90 per cent), or if one is to use the alternative probability function. What changes are the turning point and the steepness of the curve.

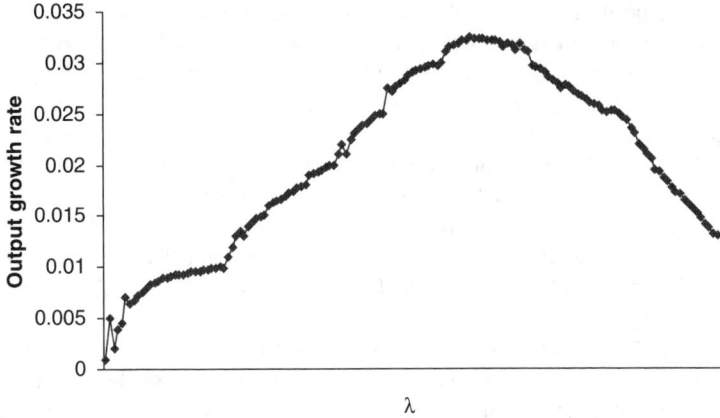

Figure 10.1 Results showing 50 competitors positioned far apart

10.5 Conclusions

Recent findings by Lerner (2004) point to a non-linear relationship between patent strength and innovation. The aim of this chapter is to offer a theoretical explanation for this non-linear relationship. The model is built upon a patent race in which many heterogeneous innovators participate. In this model, innovation is sequential. Hence, current innovation builds on past technology creating current technology. Therefore, the tournament's winner is in a better position to win the future tournament, since she has the more advanced technology. However, depending on the level of patent protection, the other innovators can re-innovate around the winner's patent and create an innovation of similar magnitude. Subsequently, if patent protection is weak the innovators who failed to win the tournament will manage to re-innovate around the winner's patent and position themselves close to the winner's technology. The closer they get, the more tournament competition increases, because all innovators start the tournament from similar starting points. As the model shows, an increase in patent protection increases the incentives to innovate, but also leads to less knowledge spill-overs.

Simulating the model, the above are combined in an inverted U relationship between patent protection and growth. For future research, one could run a more detailed simulation calibrated using US-EU data. This would be interesting on account of the considerable increase in US patent protection in the 1980s and the current EU debate on following the US example. As the model suggests, it is important to know on what side of the curve the economy is before increasing (or decreasing) patent protection.

The notion of patent protection used refers to patent breadth, where patent breadth will be defined as the re-innovation that is allowed to take place within the boundaries of legal protection. In addition, patent breadth will be a choice variable for the central planner, who is supposed to act on behalf of the courts and the PTO, and whose objective is to maximize output growth. This definition differs from the ones used in the literature. Overall, in broad terms, one can interpret patent breadth as either the number of patent claims the PTO allows for, or on the strength of the courts' attitude towards infringement. Hence, the model will not be discussing the time dimension of patents. This is due to the already extended discussion that this issue has received during the 1990s, albeit in the context of models whose objective was to minimize the deadweight loss that is associated with patents; see Gallini (2002) for a literature review.

This work is not the only one examining patent breadth in the context of a tournament.[10] Tournaments have also been studied by Denicolò (2000 and 1996); however, the emphasis here is on the patent breadth that maximizes output growth. Therefore, the model distances itself from Denicolò (2000), Chang (1995) and Nordhaus (1969) who concentrate on social welfare. In addition, this is not the only chapter that finds a non-linear relationship between patent protection and innovation/output.[11] The argument that they present is that an increase in patent length leads to larger, but less frequent, innovations. The model is not without its drawbacks. For example, in order to clarify the analysis, I have laboured under the assumption that there is no cross-licensing, and I have limited any strategic interaction between the innovators.

Appendix

In this appendix I will solve the model. Specifically, the research workers $n_{t,i}$ that innovator i employs receive a payment $w_{t,i}$ that is equal to an ε percentage of the expected revenues from the innovation that they expect to create. If they fail to win they will receive no payment. Therefore, the wage that research workers receive can be found from the following relationship:

$$w_{t,i} = p_{t,i} \frac{\varepsilon \pi_{t,i}}{n_{t,i}} \tag{7}$$

Since the consumption good is sold in a perfectly competitive market, similar to Aghion and Howitt (1992), the profits from the sale of the consumption good $\pi_{t,i}$ are:

$$\pi_{t,i} = b \Delta A_{t,i}^a x_{t,i}^b - w_{t,i} x_{t,i} \tag{8}$$

where $w_{t,i} x_{t,i}$ expresses the wage that the production workers will receive. Substituting equation (8) in equation (7) one can derive the expected wage as:

$$Ew_{t,i} = \frac{b\Delta A_{t,i}^{a} x_{t,i}^{b}}{\dfrac{n_{t,i}}{\varepsilon p_{t,i}} + x_{t,i}} \tag{9}$$

The innovator maximizes its expected revenues with respect to the research workers that she intends to use, accounting for Equation (2). The maximization problem that each innovator solves is:

$$\max_{n_{t,i}} \sum_{t=1}^{\infty} \beta^{t} (1 - \varepsilon) E\pi_{t,i}$$

$$\text{s.t.} \ \ E\Delta A_{t,i} = \Delta A_{t-1,i}^{\zeta} n_{t,i}^{\xi} - \frac{c\Delta A_{t-1,i}}{s_{t-1,i}} \tag{10}$$

$$\Delta A_{0} = 0$$

where ΔA is used as a state variable and β is the rate of time preference. In Equation (10), the time horizon is between t and ∞ because the innovator may win more than one tournament. Throughout the above problem the innovator maximizes her expected profits, accounting explicitly for all the re-innovation that will take place at time t. This is because $p_{t,i}$ accounts for the technologies of all the other $j \neq i$ innovators, including the technologies that they develop by re-innovating. Furthermore, she also implicitly accounts for all future innovations that will be based (due to re-innovation) on her technology. This line of thinking suggests that innovators account for both lagging and leading breadth.

In the steady state all innovators are expected to develop innovations of non-changing magnitude ΔA. Thereby, the distance between innovators is not expected to fluctuate. Subsequently, if λ does not change, the ratio $P = p_{t,i} / p_{t-1,i}$ should be equal to one. In total, the expected n is given by the following FOC, $En = [(P\beta/\xi)^{1-\zeta}(1 + c/s)^{\xi}]^{1/(\zeta+\xi-1)}$.

Notes

1   A.panagopoulos@lancaster.ac.uk
2   In the absence of trade secrets the innovator must patent her ideas even when she fails to win the tournament. Otherwise, she will allow other innovators to free ride on her technology, making it harder for her to win future tournaments, because she will have to compete with many other innovators who have the same technology.

3   There is a considerable literature which explores the time technology generation process in situations where the R&D investment of the firm endogenously shapes technology. For a review see Baldwin and Scott (1987).

4   This assumption implies that the tournament will not be a memory-less race, unlike the tournament models in Reinganum (1984).

5   λ cannot be one because in reality there exists tacit knowledge, which does not allow full re-innovation to take place. In addition, it is practically impossible to allow no re-innovation to take place. Therefore, $\lambda > 0$.

6   In reality, even though (in the US) patent breadth is decided by the PTO, the courts and Congress, it is up to the firm to seek litigation if it finds out that rivals have used its technology.

7   An example of a technology that did not generate the expected results would be the High Definition TV (HDTV). In 1991 the European Commission, in an initiative that was backed up by various satellite interests, proposed an expensive plan, which was worth 850 million euro, to support the HDTV standard plan. There was considerable debate in the Council about the budget, but finally the issue was dropped, with the justification being that a more advanced technology was already available in the US. For a detailed discussion of the HDTV project, see Braithwaite and Drahos (2000).

8   Intuitive as $p_{t,i}$ may be, it is always preferable to provide some mathematical intuition and an exact mathematical function that backs such an assumption. This can be done by working in continuous time, viewing Equation (2) as an Ito's stochastic differential equation. This being the case, using Kolmogorov's backward equation one can derive the probability that i has of creating a technology that is greater than j's. The main drawback of this approach, even though it leads to similar results as the rest of the chapter, is its increased mathematical difficulty, and its reliance on graphical interpretations.

9   These numbers are taken from Mankiw et al. (1992).

10 For a review of tournament models see Reinganum (1989).

11 See Gallini (2002) for a survey.

References

Aghion, P., and Howitt, P. (1992), 'A model of growth through creative destruction', *Econometrica*, Vol. 60, pp. 323–5.

Baldwin, W., and Scott, J. (1987), 'Market structure and technological change', in *Fundamentals of Pure and Applied Economics*, Vol. 17, Harwood Academic Publishers, New York.

Braithwaite, J., and Drahos, P. (2000), *Global Business Regulation*, Cambridge University Press, Cambridge.

Cohen, W., Nelson, R., and Walsh, J. (2000), 'Protecting their intellectual assets: Appropriability conditions and why US manufacturing firms patent or not?', NBER Working Paper 7552.

Dixit, K., and Pindyck, R. (1994), 'Investment under uncertainty', Princeton University Press, Princeton, NJ.

Gallini, N. (2002), 'The economics of patents: Lessons from recent US patent reform', *Journal of Economic Perspectives*, Vol. 16, No. 2, Spring, pp. 131–54.

Hall, B., Jaffe, A., and Trajtenberg, M. (2000), 'Market value and patent citation: A first look', NBER Working Paper, No. 7741.

Hall, B., and Ziedonis, R. (2001), 'The patent paradox revisited: An empirical study of patenting in the US semiconductor industry, 1979–1995', *RAND Journal of Economics*, Vol. 32, No. 1, pp. 101–28.

Jones C. (1998), 'Growth with or without scale effects?', Working Paper, Stanford University, CA.

Jones, C. (2001), 'Was the industrial revolution inevitable? Economic growth over the very long run', *Advances in Macroeconomics*, Vol. 1, No. 2, Article 1.

Lerner, J., (1995), 'The importance of trade secrecy: Evidence from civil litigation', Working Paper, Harvard University, NJ.

Lerner, J. (2004), '150 years of patent protection', *American Economic Review Papers and Proceedings*, Vol. 92, pp. 221–5.

Loury, G. (1979), 'Market structure and innovation', *Quarterly Journal of Economics*, XCIII, August, pp. 395–410.

Malliaris, A., Brock, W. (1987), *Stochastic Methods in Economics and Finance*, Advanced Textbooks in Economics, Vol. 17, North Holland, Amsterdam.

Mankiw, G., Romer, D., Weil, D. (1992), 'A contribution to the empirics of economic growth', *The Quarterly Journal of Economics*, Vol. 107, No. 2, May, pp. 407–37.

Nordhaus, W. (1969), *Invention Growth and Welfare: A Theoretical Treatment of Technological Change*, MIT Press, Cambridge, MA.

Panagopoulos, A., (2003), 'Understanding when universities and firms form RJVs: The importance of intellectual property protection', *International Journal of Industrial Organization*, Vol. 21, No. 9, pp. 1411–33.

Reinganum, J. (1984), 'Practical implications of game theoretical models of R&D', *American Economic Review, Papers and Proceedings*, Vol. 74, pp. 61–6.

Reinganum, J. (1989), 'The timing of innovation: Research development and diffusion', in Schmalensee, R. and Willig, R. (eds), *Handbook of Industrial Organization*, Vol. 1, North-Holland, New York .

Romer, P. (1990), 'Endogenous technological change', *Journal of Political Economy*, Vol. 98, No. 5, October, pp. S71–S202.

Segerstrom , P. (1998), 'Endogenous growth without scale effects', Michigan State University, Working Paper.

11

Consumer Learning Roadmap: New Buzzword or Necessary Tool?

Seppo Hänninen and Birgitta Sandberg
Helsinki University of Technology, Lahti Centre, Finland

In order to cope with the increasing competition, high-tech firms need to continuously launch new products. However, adoption of the new products may require substantive cognitive efforts from consumers. Therefore, firms should be able to monitor and influence their consumer's knowledge base. The aim of this chapter is to evaluate the usability of a consumer learning roadmap for high-tech marketing. A tentative framework is built based on the previous literature on innovation adoption and consumers' knowledge development. The usability of this framework is then evaluated on the basis of case studies. The study indicates that in the case innovations, firms were actively triggering, monitoring and guiding consumer's knowledge base in order to promote the adoption of successive product generations. This supports the idea that a consumer learning roadmap is a relevant and indeed successful concept for high-tech marketing. The fact that a consumer learning roadmap has so far been used only marginally means that the most prominent high-technology marketers are likely, little by little, to dominate their market.

Introduction

Being the first to introduce a new feature into an existing product is an effective competitive tool, provided that the feature is needed and valued by the consumers. However, the need to bring new products on to the market quickly may lead to the addition of features that are not really needed or that may even confuse the consumer. In fact, fewer and fewer of the new features appear to be adding real value or helping consumers' lives. When concern with the supplying of new features exceeds the understanding of how people actually consume, there may be troubles ahead (Szmigin, 2003). Particularly in high-technology products, the addition of novel features tends to require substantive cognitive efforts from consumers and, hence, may actually reduce their willingness to adopt the product (Mukherjee and Hoyer, 2001). The adoption may be further discouraged by the marketing's eagerness to emphasize the new more advanced features.

Furthermore, diversification related to new attributes in high-tech products is problematic, since the diversification may be unintentional and lead to difficulties with the current target group. Burns and Stalker (1961) describe how a firm ruined its knowledge base when redirecting to a new target group. Bower and Christensen (1995) stress how new firms can be the first to adopt new technologies which change the market. Both reports assume that established firms are not able to revolutionize the current market. Kim and Mauborgne (1997) show that firms try to change the dominant market logic with new products. For example, Sony Walkman created a new context for music consumption. The risk of failing in diversification is highly significant, and development to a profitable level is mostly slow.

Despite the accentuated need to understand the consumers, new product developers often fail to do so. The present chapter emphasizes that co-operation with consumers and facilitation of their learning can build a bridge between new product features and consumers. One solution to promote co-operation with consumers in the long run may be to roadmap consumer learning. The basic assumption in this concept is that providing opportunities to learn some skills lowers the resistance typical of high-tech product adoption situations.

Traditionally, roadmaps have been used to guide R&D strategy, and these roadmaps have been defined in technical terms that in turn define the facets of the technology to be worked in order to achieve certain planned performance characteristics in future (Jolly, 1997). This research transfers the roadmap concept into field marketing strategy. *The aim of the study is to evaluate the usability of a consumer learning roadmap (CLR) for high-tech marketing.* First, we build up an a priori framework based on the previous literature on innovation adoption and consumers' knowledge development. The usability of this framework is then evaluated on the basis of case studies.

11.1   Theoretical background

11.1.1   Characteristics of the new product that influence buying and using behaviour

The advent of the new generation of an already existing product provides buyers with an opportunity to switch from earlier generations to the newer one (Norton and Bass, 1992). New product generations tend to include more advanced features. The ease with which consumers are able to transform their existing knowledge to accommodate the discrepant information presented by new product features largely determines how continuous they perceive the new product to be (Moreau et al., 2001a).

Even though consumers buy and use the product, they may not use all its features. These over-served consumers often feel that they do not need the features. However, certain factors inherent in the new product seem to encourage the consumer both to buy the new product and to use all its new features. First, the product in general and the new feature in particular has to be superior to other products and features with which it competes, that is, it should provide relative advantage. Relative advantage is the advantage perceived by consumers, and thus is not necessarily the same as objective advantage. Second, the new product and its features should be compatible with existing ways of doing things. Compatibility stems from prior experience. New products that require changes in consumers' routines tend to face resistance. Third, the complexity ought to be low, that is, consumers should be able to understand and use the new product in general and the new feature in particular without difficulties. Especially in high-technology products, added product features tend to increase the complexity. Fourth, the product and its features should be trialable, to be experimented with on a limited basis. Fifth, features which are apparent to observation tend to foster consumer adoption (Robertson, 1971; Rogers, 1983; Castelluccio, 2003; Szmigin, 2003). Sixth, certain products tend to benefit from network externalities, as a consumer's evaluation of a product rises when other consumers have compatible products (Mahler and Rogers, 1999). Seventh, other products and services may also support the use of the new product and its features (Porter, 1980). However, besides product-related factors, the consumers' existing knowledge base also affects their abilities to adopt a new product generation.

11.1.2   Increasing the consumer's knowledge base

In this study, the consumer's knowledge base is seen to encompass the amount of accurate information held in memory about the product (objective knowledge), and their self-perceptions of this knowledge (subjective knowledge) (Brucks, 1985; Raju et al., 1995). Consumer knowledge is composed of both familiarity and expertise. Familiarity means the number of product-related experiences the consumer has had, and expertise is the ability to perform product-related tasks successfully (Alba and Hutchinson, 1987). The knowledge base influences the entire consumer decision process, from the decision to purchase to the perceived decision outcomes (Raju et al., 1995). Particularly in high-technology products, consumers often need to combine their knowledge from various information domains in order to understand the new product (Saaksjarvi, 2003).

The knowledge base is accumulative; prior product knowledge facilitates the acquisition and use of new knowledge (Park and Lessig, 1981). Use of the product further increases the consumer's knowledge base by bringing in 'experience knowledge' (Kolb, 1984; Raju et al., 1995; Szmigin, 2003). Use is a very important source of knowledge since consumers tend to regard it as more trustworthy than information obtained from other sources (Smith and Swinyard, 1982). Many new product features share properties with existing product features. Through analogical learning, consumers may also be able to make use of their existing knowledge to learn about product features that are completely new for them. Analogical learning means that knowledge is transferred from a familiar base to a new base as a function of structural correspondence between the two (Gregan-Paxton et al., 2002; Moreau et al., 2001a).

Hence, the consumer's knowledge base develops in conjunction with buying the new product and learning to utilize its functions. Consumers' learning is an important factor in persuading them to continuously buy new, more sophisticated products. Besides, learning tends to increase loyalty towards a firm's successive similar products, since the more the consumers learn to utilize certain types of product, the less likely they will be to switch to competitors' products, which would require additional learning efforts (Moreau et al., 2001a).

However, consumer's learning may also be facilitated by the firm's active involvement in the learning process. Through a consumer learning roadmap, a firm may be an active shaper of the consumer's knowledge base. The roadmap consists of three distinct and parallel behaviours. First, a firm may *trigger* the knowledge base by informing them about the new innovation. Information focusing on the relative advantage and compatibility of the new innovation seems to have the biggest direct influence on trial and adoption. Positioning the benefits against those of other products is also likely to improve understanding of the relative advantages (Guiltinan, 1999; Easingwood and Koustelos, 2000). Nevertheless, getting consumers to understand how an innovation works or giving them information on as yet unobservable benefits does not make the innovation less complex or its benefits more observable. Therefore, the more radical the technological capability inherent in the innovation, the greater is the need for market education (Beard and Easingwood, 1996; Song and Montoya-Weiss, 1998; cf. Easingwood and Koustelos, 2000).

Second, in order to order to target education and advertising based on the amount of consumer's prior knowledge, a constant *monitoring* of the knowledge base is needed. Moreau, Lehmann, and Markman (2001a) argue that knowledge may be used as an effective tool of segmentation. Expert consumers should be provided with more complex information, whereas novice consumers need simpler information (Baker et al., 2002). Monitoring also helps in deciding when to launch a new modified product and what kinds of features to include in it. When consumers do not use or do not know how to use existing features, there is no justification for introducing a new product with similar new features. In this case, it would be more beneficial to explore whether these kind of features are not and are unlikely to be needed by consumers, or whether the consumers merely need guidance in order to utilize and benefit from all of the product's features.

Guiding consumers' learning, for example, by providing product training courses or educational newsletters to those that have already bought the product, can help in turning novice consumers into experts. Experts are more likely to buy new more advanced product modifications and, since they have already invested in learning to utilize the firm's product, they are less likely to switch to competitors' offers. Moreau, Markman, and Lehmann (2001b) stress that marketers launching new products ought to get consumers to benefit from their existing knowledge when learning. Since consumers with limited knowledge of a new feature depend strongly on knowledge in a comparable base when forming their judgements, the marketer may foster analogical learning of consumers through highlighting commonalities between a new feature and old features (Gregan-Paxton et al., 2002).

Figure 11.1 illustrates the firm's efforts in contributing to the increase of the consumer's knowledge base. The framework in the figure is based on the existing literature. Since there was no clear theoretical guidance for studying consumer learning roadmaps, and the theoretical background had to be built up from diverse streams, the study has *exploratory* elements. In the next section the framework is further modified in response to the case study results.

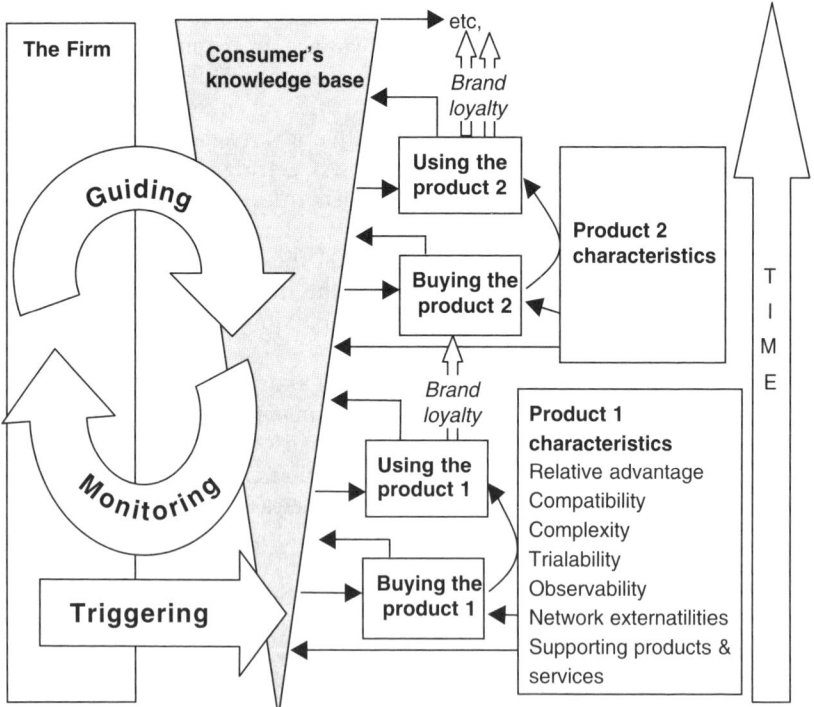

Figure 11.1 Framework for getting the consumer to absorb successive product generations

11.2 Methodology

In order to evaluate the viability of the preliminary framework presented in the previous section, an explorative case study was conducted. The framework was compared with two instrumental cases (cf. Stake, 1995): Suunto Diving computers and Microsoft Explorer. These cases were selected through literal replication logic, that is, on the prediction that they would support the a priori framework (cf. Yin, 1989). The selected cases represent behaviour where the introduction of successive product generations has been successful. Data for the case studies was collected in the Suunto case mainly through interviews. However, the data for Microsoft Explorer case was collected via secondary sources, since these were plentifully available.

11.3 Cases

11.3.1 Case: Suunto Spyder

In Suunto is a Finnish compass manufacturer focused currently on information management equipment for specialized sports. The mission of the firm is to replace luck with control equipment. It launched the world's first wrist-top diving computer, Spyder, in 1998, and since then has successively introduced various modified wrist-top diving computers. Suunto has actively tried to *trigger* consumers' knowledge base by giving them simulated experiences of the computer use through product demos. Suunto, in fact, created the world's first interactive demo for diving computers. These demos have been distributed on CD-rom, and have also been available on the firm's Internet pages:

> So the fact that you can just simulate with it what the product does in different diving situations or on the surface, we've had that from a very early stage. That's the concept our competitors have started to copy as well.
>
> (Director: Dive, Specialty and Military)

Simulation was important since it gave the diver practical experience of the computer display in dry conditions, hence he or she could practise reading it before diving. It also encouraged the buyer to enjoy the full benefit of the device by teaching him or her to utilize all its functions. In particular, it was acknowledged that customers often do not understand the full potential of the device when they purchase a wristop computer, and they tend to discover its various functions and capabilities later on as they use it.

Internet also plays an important role in *monitoring* the consumers' knowledge base. Because the target groups of the products, that is, diving enthusiasts around the world, are relatively small and very dispersed, traditional word of mouth is not possible. To activate users' communication, Suunto has created an Internet site for discussion about the product and its use. It also actively follows discussions on other Internet discussion forums, where the firm observes the discussion, but does not participate, that is, defend its products.

> And you've got several for divers! When you follow them you can see directly what people think about your product, and competitors' products, for example improvement suggestions…They're extremely valuable as information sources, especially for smaller companies.
>
> (Director: Dive, Specialty and Military)

These discussion groups were significant word-of-mouth communication channels through which divers around the world could discuss their experiences. When word-of-mouth communication is conducted on the Internet instead of on the streets, the firm feels that it has at least some chance to turn negative experiences into positive ones:

> It's been better not to interfere with it so that you stay invisible. In some cases if someone's had really bad experiences then you can approach the person directly and say, 'If you've had some problems, then get in touch or send the product back to us.'
>
> (Director: Dive, Specialty and Military)

Based on the feedback gathered from Spyder's customers, a new model, Stinger, was developed. It included new software and new graphics and was launched in 2000. Mosquito and D3 followed later, and the company began to diversify from wristop diving computers into the outdoor wristop-computer market in general: Special wristops have been developed for golf, marine, alpine-skiing and snowboarding enthusiasts. Regardless of the sport for which they are designed, all these computers provide the same level of information and the same kind of usability, and reflect the same basic philosophy of supporting performance.

Guiding consumers' learning is difficult when the consumers are dispersed. The Internet site, however, allows users to learn about each other's experiences. The Internet is the third dimension of the manufacturer–consumer relationship. It also enables launching new components for the set. Users' discussion strengthens group feeling and extends the consumers' knowledge base. Hence, the Suunto case incorporates the Internet community as another stakeholder in the CLR. Consumers' learning has also been facilitated through product-related factors: layouts and user-interfaces on successive products are built to resemble each other.

Table 11.1   Summary of findings

	Suunto Spyder	Microsoft Explorer
Triggering	Simulated experiences	Free software with Microsoft Windows
Monitoring	Internet site for consumer discussion	'Explorer vs Netscape' discussions
Guiding	Users learning about each other's experiences through Internet site	Composing the features on the free software

11.3.2   Case: Microsoft Explorer

The Microsoft Explorer case started in 1996. Netscape had been the standard for Internet software until Microsoft became interested in the industry. As a *trigger*, the first version of Microsoft Explorer was bundled as free software with the Microsoft Windows operating system. Consumers who used Microsoft Windows were thus all given the opportunity to learn the skills needed to use the software before buying the large version of Microsoft Explorer. Triggering thus took place through the product, instead of through promotion or other market communications.

Monitoring through internet discussion groups seems to have been rather natural choice since 'Explorer vs. Netscape' has been one of the favourite discussion topics in several online forums. By using Microsoft Windows as a marketing platform, the promoters of Explorer were able to establish the consumers' knowledge base on the new software. Consequently, the idea of buying the next product upgrade could be introduced in the current product. However, giving free products was not enough. A visual icon led users to open the package and test out the software's capabilities. Composing the features on the free software was thus important in *guiding* consumer learning. The tasks set to the consumer were simple: to learn to click the Microsoft Explorer icon, test the capabilities of the software and explore the Net. Table 11.1 summarizes findings of the cases.

11.4   Modified framework

The modified framework below shows the findings from these case studies. It seems that at least these two companies have actively tried to utilize a consumer learning roadmap in increasing their consumers' knowledge base. Case studies increased our understanding of the specific tools utilized in triggering, monitoring and guiding. Microsoft Explorer case revealed that in order to *trigger* consumers to become familiarized with a completely new kind of a product, it may be necessary to give them the first product for free. In both cases the internet discussion groups seem to have played a key role in *monitoring* the knowledge base. They provide an easy and

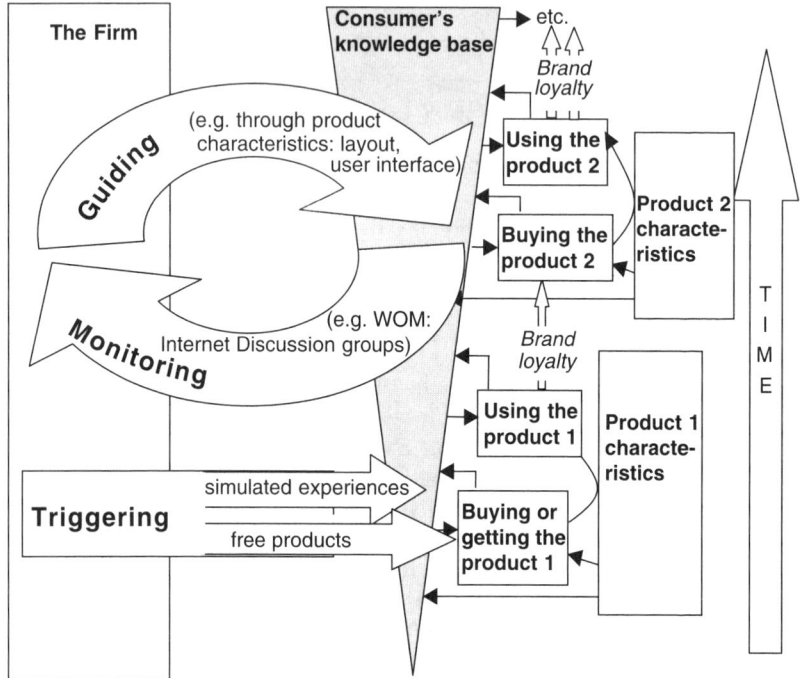

Figure 11.2   Modified framework based on case studies

cost-effective way to follow the communication between consumers. However, they may also give a distorted picture of the whole market since it is likely that the technology enthusiasts are keen to comment on the product and participate very actively in those discussions, whereas the mainstream customers may not be willing to use their time in online discussions (Moore, 1999). It is thus important not to be blind-sided by the enthusiasm and ease with which the former might use the product. The *guiding* in both cases rested heavily on product features instead of consumer education. It may work fine with the technology enthusiasts, but it may not be sufficient for mainstream customers (see Figure 11.2).

11.5   Contribution and implications for further research

We have developed what we believe to be a unique framework for a consumer learning roadmap. The framework is consistent with, and builds upon, well-known work on innovation adoption and consumers' knowledge development, and acknowledges the firm's role as proactive shaper of the consumer's knowledge base.

The findings indicate that in these study cases, the innovating firms were active in triggering, monitoring and guiding their consumers' knowledge base in order to promote the adoption of successive product generations. This supports the idea that a consumer learning roadmap is a relevant ,and indeed successful, concept for high-tech marketing. The fact that a consumer learning roadmap has so far been used only marginally means that the most prominent high-technology marketers are likely, little by little, to dominate their market.

It was also interesting to notice that in the studied cases, the characteristics of the product, such as layout and user interface, played an important role in guiding the consumer's knowledge base. This finding highlights the importance of continuous co-operation between R&D and marketing.

However, the limitations of the consumer learning roadmap are also obvious. Its usability is high when the product can be customized and involves participation. For high-tech products that are designed to be used more passively, it may prove very difficult to utilize a consumer learning roadmap.

We have assumed that the use of a consumer learning roadmap is related to brand loyalty to a high-technology company. Even though Intel has created brand equity with the slogan 'Intel inside', consumers have by and large accepted the personal computer processor as a black box. Similar passive acceptance with a software product is not possible, because consumers have to learn to use it. We assume that creating brand loyalty on high-tech products may depend on consumers' ability to learn new skills and on their experiencing the new features offered by the innovation as valuable.

In this study, the a priori framework was pre-tested and modified on the basis of only two case studies. Since at this stage the results are exploratory, there is clearly a need to test the framework further with other cases. A constructive case study approach could be particularly suitable since it allows the testing of the framework in a concurrent real-life business situation (cf. Kasanen et al., 1993). Eventually, it would be useful to test the framework through a large quantitative survey.

References

Alba, J. W. and Hutchinson, J. W. (1987), 'Dimensions of consumer expertise', *Journal of Consumer Research*, Vol. 13, No. 1, pp. 411–54.

Baker, T. L., Hunt, J. B. and Scribner, L. L. (2002), 'The effect of introducing a new brand on consumer perceptions of current brand similarity: The roles of product knowledge and involvement', *Journal of Marketing Theory and Practice*, Vol. 10, No. 4, pp. 45–57.

Beard, C. and Easingwood, C. (1996), 'New product launch: Marketing action and launch tactics for high-technology products', *Industrial Marketing Management*, Vol. 25, No. 2, pp. 87–103.

Bower, J. L. and Christensen, C. M. (1995), 'Disruptive technologies: Catching the wave', *Harvard Business Review*, Vol. 73, No. 1, pp. 43–53.

Brucks, M. (1985), 'The effects of product class knowledge on information search behavior,' *Journal of Consumer Research*, Vol. 12, No. 1, pp. 1–16.

Burns, T. and Stalker, G. M. (1961), *The Management of Innovation,* Tavistock Publications, London.

Castelluccio, M. (2003), 'Escaping the catch,' *Strategic Finance*, Vol. 84, No. 12, pp. 59–60.

Easingwood, C. and Koustelos, A. (2000), 'Marketing high technology: Preparation, targeting, positioning, execution', *Business Horizons*, Vol. 43, No. 3, pp. 27–34.

Gregan-Paxton, J., Hibbard, J. D., Brunel, F. F. and Azar, P. (2002), ' "So that's what that is": Examining the impact of analogy on consumers' knowledge development for really new products', *Psychology & Marketing*, Vol. 19, No. 6, pp. 533–50.

Guiltinan, J. P. (1999), 'Launch strategy, launch tactics, and demand outcomes', *Journal of Product Innovation Management*, Vol. 16, No. 6, pp. 509–29.

Jolly, V. K. (1997), *Commercializing New Technologies: Getting from Mind to Market*, Harvard Business School Press, Boston, MA.

Kasanen, E., Lukka, K. and Siitonen, A. (1993), 'The constructive approach in management accounting research', *Journal of Management Accounting Research*, Vol. 5, Fall, pp. 243–64.

Kim, W. C. and Mauborgne, R. (1997), 'Value innovation: The strategic logic of high growth', *Harvard Business Review*, Vol. 75, No. 1, pp. 103–12.

Kolb, D. A. (1984), *Experiential Learning: Experience as the Source of Learning and Development*, Prentice Hall, Englewood Cliffs, NJ.

Mahler, A. and Rogers, E. M. (1999), 'The diffusion of interactive communication innovations and the critical mass: the adoption of telecommunications services by German banks', *Telecommunications Policy*, Vol. 23, No. 10/11, pp. 719–40.

Moore, G. A. (1999), *Crossing the Chasm*, 2nd edn, Capstone, Oxford.

Moreau, C. P., Lehmann, D. R. and Markman, A. B. (2001a), 'Entrenched knowledge structures and consumer response to new products', *Journal of Marketing Research*, Vol. 38, No. 1, pp. 14–29.

Moreau, C. P., Markman, A. B. and Lehmann, D. R. (2001b), ' "What is it?" Categorization flexibility and consumers' responses to really new products', *Journal of Consumer Research*, Vol. 27, No. 4, pp. 489–98.

Mukherjee, A. and Hoyer, W. D. (2001), 'The effect of novel attributes on product evaluation', *Journal of Consumer Research*, Vol. 28, No. 3, pp. 462–72.

Norton, J. A. and Bass, F. M. (1992), 'Evolution of technological generations: The law of capture', *Sloan Management Review*, Vol. 33, No. 2, pp. 66–77.

Park, C. W. and Lessig, V. P. (1981), 'Familiarity and its impact on consumer decision biases and heuristics', *Journal of Consumer Research*, Vol. 8, No. 2, pp. 223–30.

Porter, M. E. (1980), *Competitive Strategy*, Free Press, New York.

Raju, P. S., Lonial, S. C. and Mangold, W. G. (1995), 'Differential effects of subjective knowledge, objective knowledge, and usage experience on decision making: An exploratory investigation', *Journal of Consumer Psychology*, Vol. 4, No. 2, pp. 153–80.

Robertson, T. S. (1971), *Innovative Behavior and Communication*, Holt, Rinehart & Winston, New York.

Rogers, E. M. (1983), *Diffusion of Innovations*, 3rd edn (1st edn in 1962), The Free Press, New York .

Saaksjarvi, M. (2003), 'Consumer adoption of technological innovations', *European Journal of Innovation Management*, Vol. 6, No. 2, pp. 90–100.

Smith, R. E. and Swinyard, W. R. (1982), 'Information response models: An integrated approach', *Journal of Marketing*, Vol. 46, No. 1, pp. 81–93.

Song, X. M. and Montoya-Weiss, M. M. (1998), 'Critical development activities for really new versus incremental products', *Journal of Product Innovation Management*, Vol. 15, No. 2, pp. 124–35.

Stake, R. E. (1995), *The Art of Case Study Research*, Sage Publications, Thousand Oaks, California.

Szmigin, I. (2003), *Understanding the Consumer*, Sage Publications, London.

Yin, R. K. (1989), *Case Study Research. Design and Methods*, 1st edn in 1984, Sage Publications, Newbury Park.

12
Knowledge Economy: New Trends in Economy in the Twenty-First Century

Wu Jisong
Beijing University of Aeronautics and Astronautics, and Environment
School of Hehai University, China

This chapter explores the origin, connotation and characteristics of the knowledge economy in against the background of China. The author, first, introduces the economic growth of China in recent years and the four momentums laying behind to this drive this to growth. Each one is based on the contribution made by the relevant knowledge power. Second, the author presents a retrospectives of the history of knowledge economy; the relationship between knowledge and economy; the three stages of the laborlabour economy, resource economy and knowledge economy, and thus summings up the features of knowledge economy; and, finally, a primary indicator to view this difference among the three is proposed. Third, concepts concerned about high-tech are discussed since high-tech industrialization is the primary pillar in knowledge economy. After looking into the prospect of knowledge economy, a general picture for the development of China's Science Parks, which are the forcing bed for developing knowledge economy, has been provided, with Zhongguancun Science Park, Beijing, as a case. At present, after the industrial revolution, the entire world is in a new era, which is also the post-industrialization era for developed countries and the new and high-tech industrialization era for developing countries. Since the reform and opening of China at the end of the 1970s, the per year growth rate has been over 8 per cent, and the total economic output of China has doubled. China is now the fifth largest economy and the third largest exporter of goods worldwide. GDP in China accounts for 4 per cent of the world, and the contribution to world economic growth is as high as 17 per cent. Over the past two decades, China has made enormous achievements and received tremendous accolades from international economists. How has this been realized? It is necessary for us to go deep into the reasons.

12.1 Analysis of economic achievements in China

How could China achieve such a miracle? The reasons can be drawn as follows.

12.1.1 The reform: the unprecedented liberation of labour in large quantities and at low wages

Since the late 1970s, millions of individuals who had been restricted for 2000 years become available for cheap labour; this has propelled the unparalleled force of the Chinese miracle.

How China can maintain the past century's rate of progress and continue this prosperity into the future, are two of the most pressing questions warranting research by Chinese academics.

12.1.2 The opening: the sufficient use of two types of resources and markets

Under the trend of integration into a world economy, China has not only utilized its abundant natural resources and large national market sufficiently, but it has also employed the resources and product markets of the world. The scale of production and of resources has exceeded that of industrialization in both England and America. The use of these resources and markets are the strong basis for the rapid development in China.

At the same time, how to continue the past century's successful utilization of the two resources and markets into a sustainable future is a key question facing the economy of China. The recycling of resources and the improvement of technology are the most important contents for the problem.

12.1.3 Large investment from both domestic and international sources

The continuing investment from Chinese and foreigners has been an important capital force for rapid growth in China The quantity exceeds that of foreign investment in England and America at the time of their industrial revolution.

How to continuously attract investment, improve its fundamental structure, and form a positive cycle is a key aspect in the research and innovation of China's economy.

12.1.4 The socialistic market economic policy to 'explore one's way carefully'

The base policy to 'explore one's way carefully' was established through the abandonment of the so-called planned economics of the Soviet Union and through broad utilization of different schools of Western economic thinking. The policy acts to settle the successful socialistic economic policy and lead to the sustainable and rapid growth of China's economy in a free economy.

12.1.5   The contribution of knowledge to economy

We can above see clearly the reasons that lead to a miracle of the economy. Further, there is a spirit that goes though all the measures taken by the government, it is that of knowledge, which has been paid a great deal of attention by the Chinese government when drawing the development plan. The close relationship between economy and knowledge can be reflected in the spectacular forcing of the high-tech industry's fast development to that of the whole economy in China.

According to the statistics of the Ministry of Commerce of the People's Republic of China, the gross value of China's foreign trade was over 1150 billion dollars, with China listed in third place in global trade, and high-tech products accounting for 28.5 per cent. Since the strategy of developing trade by relying on science and education was taken into practice, high-tech has played a very important role in improving foreign trade and optimizing the structure of export and so on, and it is expected that the proportion of the vale of high-tech in the whole of foreign trade would be up to 30 per cent, 400 billion dollars. Nowadays, there are more than 14,000 high-tech companies in China, among them are 53 state-level high-tech industry areas. The number of people who are engaged in the high-tech industry is about 6 million, and the gross value has climbed to 2720 billion dollars. The third largest high-tech industry, just next to that of America and Japan, has been reached by China.

The huge impact of knowledge on the economy can be seen above, and it is the knowledge economy that represents the trend of economic development. Therefore, on the question of economic development in China, it is very crucial to understand comprehensively both the concept and the meaning of knowledge economy.

12.2   Origin of the knowledge (intelligence) economy

Since the 1970s, the progress of science and technology has been the vital factor in economic development. The statement, 'Science and technology constitute a primary productive force' has become true. At present, the competition among different countries has focused on comprehensive national power, which is based on the economy, and led by science and technology, especially high-tech. Actually, in 1997 the production value of information in the high-tech industry exceeded the whole US GDP by 10 per cent, and the gross export value of knowledge-intensive services, mainly based on information technology, accounted for 40 per cent of the whole export value. Nearly 50 per cent of the GDP of the main members of the OECD comes from the knowledge-based industries.

Since the early 1970s, there have been many views about the forthcoming economy, first among these was the 'electron technology era' faced by all of us, which was brought up by Z. K.Brzezinski, ex-assistant of US state security, in the article 'Between Two Eras – the Commission of the U.S. in the Electron Ear'. Then, in 1973, Daneil Bell, the American sociologist, called it 'post-industry society'. After that, another socialist in America, A.Toffler, once a journalist, made a great effort to publicize the 'post-industry society' in the book *The Third Wave* in 1980. He described it as a 'super-industrial society', saying a new economy, different from the industrial economy, had come into being. Two years later, J. Naisbitt, US economist and futurologist, put forward 'information economy' in the book *Big Trend*, in which he identified it with the main pillar industries of the new economy. In 1986, Englishman, Forest, advanced 'High-tech economy' in the book *High-Tech Society*, where he identified it precisely with the pillar industries' cluster in this new type economy. In 1990, the research institute of the UN brought forward the concept of 'knowledge economy', which fixed on the character of this new type of economy. In 1992, the author released a paper mentioning the concept of 'intelligence economy' that is supported by the natural science, technology and social economies in a UNESCO magazine published in English, French and Spanish (*International Social Science Journal*, No. 132). Afterwards, I demonstration this again in many publications in Chinese. In 1996, the OECD clearly defined the concept 'knowledge-based economy', and for the first time, it associated it with the indicator system and an estimation of the new type of economy. On 30 December 1996, US *Business Weekly* issued a series of papers, putting forward 'new economy' and stating that the new economy had come into being. In February, 1997, Clinton, former US President adopted the concept of 'knowledge economy' put forward by the research institute of the UN. A year later, the World Bank publication, *World Development Report 1998* was subtitled as 'Knowledge for Development'.

These confusing words were in actuality gradually building a concept, that is, 'humanity is stepping into an economy age, in which the most important factor is the possession and distribution of intelligence sources and the production, distribution and use (consumption) of knowledge.' In other words, it is an age in which 'science and technology constitute a primary productive force'. We can see the development from the start of the forming process of this concept: first, the sensitivity of politicians; then the exploration of scholars and the research of scientists; and finally, the adoption of the government and international organization, which went though over 30 years. We can see it as a scientific concept. In the view of economic history, economy can be classified into three types in light of industrial structure: they are agricultural economy, industrial economy and the high-tech economy. While, according to the allocation of resources, it can be separated into label economy, (natural) resource economy and intelligence economy, which has been agreed by many experts. Although 'knowledge economy' seems not to be in line with the previous division, it indeed is the same meaning. What is called 'knowledge economy' means a new economy which is different from the former economy with traditional industries as the pillar and based on rare resources. In this new economy, the high-tech industry is the vital pillar and it is based on the intelligence economy, so it is a sustainable economy.

12.3   History of the relationship between knowledge and economy

The ultimate difference between humans and other animals lies in the human ability of innovation, and the original force to innovation comes from knowledge. Consequently, any human activities go with knowledge, and the human economy in the history of man can't function without knowledge. People accumulate and conclude knowledge to a system, which is science. The two offspring of science research, knowledge and technology, are what is called scientific knowledge and scientific technology, which are close to each other and familiar to us. We can say that the relation between them is 'knowledge economy' and it is necessary for us to track its history.

12.3.1   The history track of the classification

Ancient research was so simple that the fundamental research and development of a product were not separate from each other. Ancient Greek Archimedes, 'Father of Physics' (287–212 BC) did his research both in the field of physics and in making tools based on the physical principles. In the fifteenth century, Leonardo da Vinci, the omnipotent genius of Italy in Renaissance Europe (1452–1519), was a physical scientist and an engineering expert as well as a painter. He at one and the same time composed the profound physical papers and was engaged in the design of precise machines.

The separation of research and technology began in the seventeenth century. Physical scientists, represented by Newton (1642–1727), started the research of academicism, considering less the engineering application of the research. The main reason lies in two aspects: one is the separation of some kinds of knowledge with the establishment of the natural science system, and the research goes deep to such an extent that one person cannot do well in both theory study and engineering. In the meantime, the application of engineering technology became more and more difficult with the development of research. The other reason is the academicism in the European scientific community that led to the disjointing of theory and practice, which had lasted for about two centuries. Until the early twentieth century, the engineering application of theory had not taken a spectacular step (Table 12.1).

Before the twentieth century, it would take 30 years for a discovery to transform to invention, while it would take ten years in the first half of the twentieth century. When it came to the latter half of the same century, it reduced to five years. And then discovery and invention went into a beneficial cycle. As a result, in the early days those who achieved some fruit in

Table 12.1 Comparisons between scientific discoveries and technological inventions

Scientific discovery	Year	Technological inventions	Year	Gestation (years)
Photography theory	1782	Camera	1838	56
Electronic theory	1831	Electronical machine	1872	41
Internal-combustion theory	1862	Gas engine	1883	21
The theory of communication with electromagnetic wave	1895	The first public broadcast station	1921	26
Turbojet theory	1906	Turbojet engine	1935	29
Discovery of bacteriophage	1910	Production of bacteriophage	1940	30
Radar theory	1925	Radar	1935	10
Uranium nuclear fission	1938	Making out Automatic bomb	1945	7
Discovery of semiconductor	1948	Producing the semiconductor radio	1954	6
Coming up with the concept of integrated circle	1952	Producing the first monolithic integrated circuit	1959	7
The theory of fibre optics communication	1966	Optical fibre and cable	1970	4
The idea of mobile communication without cable	1974	Mobile telephone	1978	4
Multimedia plan	1987	Multimedia computer	1991	4

science discovery, perhaps aged about 40, would 30 years later be considered an old man at 70 and it was hard to reach anything in the field of technological invention. However, if the cycle shortens to 5–10 years, it would be possible for one person to complete both discovery and invention, which could make the invention grow up more quickly.

The history of science and technology has proved that the relation between the discoveries of fundamental research, the probes of application study and the technological inventions of development study becomes more and more close, and the transmission cycle shortens day by day, and finally, they could be unified.

12.3.2 Thinking about the borderline between three studies

Before the twentieth century, it would take about 30 years for science discovery, the fruit of fundamental research, to transforms to technological invention, from the production of development study through to the application study. In this time, the three strands of the development pattern, fundamental research, the application study and the development study, can be seen clearly, and basically, they can't be achieved by only one person or one group.

However, when it came to the latter half of the twentieth century, especially the 1970s, the cycle could complete within some five years. Those scientist who had been afraid of, or had a soul above, technological study, saw with their own eyes that their research had been transformed into product and brought a huge benefit. And then, they came up with such an idea: why didn't they go further, to both discovery and invention, by themselves?

Meanwhile, some high-tech has realized that the factor of knowledge is far over the material factor. Take the short-term biological project, for example, it costs less money from research to product and is easily completed by one person or one group.

Besides, some studies, usually of knowledge, such as computer software, can skip over the application research to market to gain economic benefit.

These new phenomena make the concept and the idea of fundamental research change greatly:

- The present fundamental research doesn't have an exact aim, but with the development of the study, some useful things could be found out, so that even the exploitation study contributes to transforming to application. Study on thermonuclear fusion is a case in point.
- The fundamental researches could bypass the phase of application study and go directly into that of exploitation, such as in the study on light-guide fibre.
- Fundamental research could be found to be useful for business and directly become product and go into the market. We can take study on computer software as an example.

The great changes happening to fundamental research make it necessary to connect knowledge and market with some mechanism of organization. Consequently, some new things, including the science park, emerged as the times required, and the knowledge economy moved from the research of theory to practice.

12.4   The concept of knowledge economy

According to all kinds of ideas over the last 30 years, the more exact concept of 'knowledge economy' refers to 'economy in which the production, distribution, and usage (consumption) of knowledge is the crucial factor, which is based on the occupation and collocation of intelligence, with science and technology as the leading guidance'. In other words, it is the economy put forward by Deng Xiaoping, ex-leader of China, 'science and technology constitute a primary productive force'.

12.4.1 Resources allocation of the knowledge economy

In knowledge economy, intelligence resources and invisible capital are the most important elements. It depends on knowledge and intelligence allocating the natural resources reasonably, comprehensively and intensively, not basing it on the collocation of rare natural resources such as land, petrol and so on. On this point, Dong Xiaoping made a clear statement, 'the complete resolution of the agriculture problem lies in the top technology, the gene engineering.' Meanwhile, in the knowledge economy, the intelligence resources will be used to exploit rich natural resources to create new fortune, instead of those which are the vital elements in industrial economy, but have been scarce. For example, in information high-tech the chip in the computer comes from stone, while controlled thermonuclear fusion materials in the new energy sources and renewable energy high-tech stem from the hydrogen in water.

Therefore, it is more important for the placing of intelligence resources, such as patents and knowledge, to be in the knowledge economy than it is for rare natural resources, such as land and petrol, in the industrial economy. In other words, countries that depend on the control of natural resources, such as in the Middle East, could be hit easily in the knowledge ages if it fails to invest in intelligence resources, which is what caused the financial and economic crisis in Southeast Asian countries.

12.4.2 The industrial pillar in knowledge economy

The high-tech industry, which is mainly based on high-tech that is different from the simple innovations of traditional industry technology, is the pillar in knowledge economy. According to the classification of the UN, high-tech includes science and technology in the field of information, life, new energy sources and renewable energy, new material, space, ocean and some technology beneficial to environment and management (also called soft science and technology). The concept of high-tech is dynamic in that there will always be new technology coming along. But one point needing to be mentioned is that some traditional technologies would still not be high-tech even after being injected with some high-tech elements, we can see auto technology in America as an example, it always remains the traditional technology, even when some new things are poured in. Only when the proportion of high-tech is more than some 70 per cent can the traditional technology be considered as high-tech, according to the criterion of the international science and technology industrial park. Also, takeing auto technology as n example, if it uses the new energy fuel battery instead of an engine, thus cutting pollution to the environment, and if it adopts an electronic control system, which can greatly improve the safety of operation, then it can become comprehensively high-tech. Of course, just like the industrial economy, including agriculture, in knowledge economy there are also agriculture and industry, and not all the traditional technology will be transformed into the high-tech.

12.4.3   Social consumption in knowledge economy

The high-tech products and new knowledge brought by information will be the main products of consumption (usage). Material fortune, which is obtained by using knowledge and intelligence to exploit abundant natural resources, will dramatically exceed material fortune gained through using rare natural resources in traditional technology. For example, in the field of food, the gene food is more than that of traditional food, and in the field of energy, the proportion of solar energy and controlled thermonuclear energy is more than that of coal and petrol, and in the field of the information network, the usage of terminal multimedia exceed that of train, auto, plane and telephone.

12.4.4   Usage (consumption) of knowledge and 'knowledge-driving'

It is more reliable to consider 'consumption' as the 'usage' of knowledge, since it is different from the characteristic of goods in that it will not disappear, transform or depreciate after it is used. Besides, the other differences can be as follows:

- *The number of public goods is increasing greatly.*   Compared with the traditional goods, the part of public goods in the knowledge economy is climbing dramatically, and increasingly globalized. For example, people can get all kinds of knowledge from the Internet without cost, or for just a little.
- *Semi-public goods are mounting up at a large scale.*   The usage of semi-public goods, which is more specialized and determined by the domain of knowledge, industry and the knowledge area, is rising greatly. At present, it can be used only under licence; however, the cost of usage is definitely less than production costs. Just take a look at many special sites on the Internet; we can obtain information through paying fees which are not very high. We call it semi-product.
- *Stricter protection of intelligence property rights.*   Intelligence property right will be protected more seriously and effectively in the knowledge economy, since it is the protection intelligence property right that can guarantee both power to the innovation and the development of intelligence resources. Although knowledge won't be depreciated when used, it can be behind the times with the innovation of knowledge, so we can see that the innovation system of knowledge of a nation (including law, institutions and talents) is the guarantee for sustainable intelligence resources.

Like the consumption of goods, the usage of knowledge doesn't mean you needn't do anything. As to knowledge itself, everyone must study and further digest it, Only once this process is completed can it be something belonging to you, which is a far cry from the immediate using of traditional goods. In addition, in order to use it easily, like goods, it relies on the ability of everyone for turning knowledge into skill. Therefore, there is no 'free' knowledge. How much knowledge can be obtained (distributed) by anyone depends on study and ability of transformation, and then the 'richer' one in the knowledge economy becomes the one with the highest level of knowledge.

In contrast with the 'benefit-driving' of industrial economy, it is 'knowledge-driving' in knowledge economy. The main source of innovation is aiming to obtain the property right of knowledge, which is in relation to money-driving, but not exactly equal to it. 'Knowledge-driving' in the knowledge economy is about obtaining new knowledge (even if there are no intelligence property rights or profits), in addition, it is also aiming to get public recognition and social status, which may be acquired by mover-driving; however, the original motivation and measures can be different from that of the former. Therefore, 'knowledge-driving' is multi-driving, which is more reasonable and at a higher level. 'Knowledge-driving' will contribute spectacularly to some important issues facing humanity, such as population, resources, environment, science and technology, education, the gap between rich and poor, the economic and political systems of the world and so on, which will be more effective than that of the benefit-driving of the traditional economy.

12.4.5   What is knowledge

As to this question, the OECD cites the concept of '4 Ws' which has come into being since the 1960s in the West in its report on, 'economy based on knowledge'. They are 'know-what', 'know-why', 'know-how' and 'know-who'. In the author's opinion, 'know-when' and 'know-where' should be added to make it perfect, a point agreed by many experts in the UN. If we miss the latter two, behaviour based on knowing the '4 Ws' well, could be proved wrong as to both time and place. Therefore, the '6 Ws' is a nicer concept of knowledge. Maybe someone might say, 'know-when' and 'know-where' have been involved in 'know-what'; however, history has demonstrated that it is the wrong time or place that contributes to a failure, no matter whether in the past or at present, no matter whether Chinese or anyone else, no matter whether a big event in relation to the whole nation or a small one in the person's daily life. Given such a fact, it is necessary to add the '2 Ws' to make knowledge be equal to '6 Ws'. Different from Western countries, China has been paying less attention to the quantity of a concept, so, a 'Q'(quantity) can be added to 'know-what', meaning 'know-quantity'. And then we get '6 Ws' and '1 Q'.

12.4.6   Labour economy, (nature) resource economy and intelligence economy

In 1992 when the author was the high-tech and environmental consultant in UNESCO, I proposed the concept of 'intelligence economy' so as to guide the development of the International Association of Science and Technology Parks and the industrialization of world high-tech. My colleagues told me the concept of 'knowledge economy' had already been proposed before; it was published in 1990. My feeling is that, according to taxonomy, it's still better to use the classification: agricultural economy, industrial economy and intelligence economy; according to resource allocation, it can also be classified as labour economy, resource economy and intelligence economy. The concept of knowledge economy accounts for the same meaning as that of intelligence economy, so there was no necessity to deny either. Many experts had approved this classification. So in order to show the original research process, here the author still uses the term of 'intelligence economy' in the following section.

From the new technology revolution's springing up in the 1950s, leap development has been accomplished within half a century. The establishment and fast development of electronic information technology, life technology, new and renewable energy technologies, eco-sound high-tech, new materials technology, space technology, marine scientific technology and soft technology (highly synthetic science) has combined closely with science and technology. Not only has science and technology become the productive force, but it is a also primary force. Therefore, this development is bound to change the former economic structure and the economic essential, which will drive the industrial economy developing to knowledge (intelligence) economy.

12.4.6.1   Three stages of economic development

According to technology progress and productive force development, there are three stages: labour economy, resource economy and intelligence economy.

- *Labour economy stage.*   In this stage the economic development was mainly dependant on the possession and allocation of the labour force. As science and technology was undeveloped, the ability of mankind to explore natural resources was low. For most everyday resources, shortage was not a problem. So labour was the currency, trading slaves in history demonstrates this point.

  Labour economy started from the beginning of human civilization, and lasted for thousands of years. During this period, though science and technology developed, and instruments of production kept being improved, this situation did not change until the industrial revolution in the nineteenth century. At that time productivity mainly depended on the physical strength of labour.

  In the labour economy stage, the distribution of production was through possession of labour resources or of labour resources gained by possessing the land.

In the labour economy stage, life is hard. Human beings cannot resist the economic crises caused by natural disasters; education was notwidespread, talents could not be exchanged and suffered effects.

- *(Natural) Resources economy stage.* Economic development in this period mainly depended on the possessing and distribution of natural resources.

With the development of science and technology, the ability of human beings to utilize natural resources kept growing. The main target of the wars of the nineteenth century was the scrabble or search for resources. And from that time, the Western countries had successively finished their industrial revolutions, tractors and lathes took the place of the handicrafts; cars, trains and airplanes replaced the old transport means. Productivity has risen greatly but it still cannot be decisive. The iron stone, coal and oil which are main energy sources for machines had become rare resources and began to confine economic development.

In the resource economy stage, distribution was mainly by possessing natural resources (including the means of production formed by labouring). Therefore, although productivity rose, and material fortune increased greatly, the lack of a rise in standards of living was for most people disproportionate in comparison. Most Western countries took more than 150 years moving from starvation to becoming wealthy. During this period, secondary education was popularized generally, talents began to flow freely, and intelligence resources were explored.

- *Intelligence economy stage.* Economic development in this stage depends on thepossession and distribution of intelligence resources, and science and technology became the primary productive force.

With fast developing of science and technology, the time for transfer of scientific and technological achievements is greatly reduced and the ability to exploit rich resources to replace rare ones has been greatly enhanced. For example, controlled thermonuclear fusion can change the 'seawater' into oil, and the large-scale integrated circuit can change 'silicon' into a computer. Therefore, science and technology become the decisive factors for economic development while natural resources fall back to the secondary place. The development and industrialization of high-tech will bring forth a new economic revolution.

The acquisition of a knowledge resource cannot be realized by means of war. With the development of an intelligence economy, the possibility of avoiding world war is increasing. 'Peace, development and environment' will become the matter of primary importance.

Science and technology constitute a primary productive force. For industrial structure, current classification of the first, second and third industries cannot define new high-tech industry. For example, some life technologies belong to the first industry, but they are essentially different from traditional agriculture. And many information technologies are acombination of the second and the third industries. Due to these facts, high-tech industry can be called 'the fourth industry', in which the intelligence economy plays a leading role. For the market itself, the traditional concept of the market starts to change. Firstly, macro-orientation should be enforced. Otherwise, the orderless market state will prevent the intelligence economy from developing.In addition, the old market concepts as to expanding the share of a market, or expanding the market only by the output of production and so on will change accordingly. The value of a high-tech product may be thousands of times of the traditional economic product which consumed the same material.

A more important reason to propose is that: current problems in the world cannot be solved only by the resource economy though it has developed to a high level. Take the problem of poverty as an example, from the 1970s to the 1990s, the resource economy developed highly, and there was no worldwide war. Many developed countries and almost all the international organizations had made plans to aid those undeveloped countries. However, the bad situation in those countries did not change, and even more, the gap is widening. This accounts for the fact that poverty cannot be solved in a resources-based economy but may be in a knowledge-based economy.

During the development of the knowledge economy, there may also be some potential problems, like unemployment. Currently in the developed countries, highly developed technology has not brought the large increase in job opportunities the industrial revolution did. Disparity between the high requirements in knowledge and education of workers and the current quality of workers cannot be overcome in the shortterm.

12.4.6.2   *Transition from the resource economy to the knowledge economy*

* The highly developed resource economy is the prerequisite for transiting to the knowledge economy. The basic characteristics for a highly developed resource economy are that:
  * agriculture, industry and the third industry are highly developed
  * infrastructure facilities are complete
  * a mature market economy
  * new technology is highly developed

  All these are indispensable requirement for the transition. Without a high quality of people's lives, without a popularization and improvement of education, without fostering special talents and long-term practice, it is not possible to develop the high and new technology which is the base for the knowledge economy. All the above require a highly developed resource economy.

- *The choice of economic model in the transition period.* When looked at in retrospect, in the transition from the labour economy to the resource economy, most countries in the world adopted a market economy or a planned economy. The planned economic model is suitable for developing infrastructure such as heavy industry, transportation and national defence. Most undeveloped countries adopted this model, and had gained an effective result.

However, because the development of management science had fallen badly behind that of production technology, plans cannot be made correctly and on time. Planned economy is a kind of shortage economy. Only competition could realize the rational distribution of natural resources, while mandatory planning prevented the establishment of a competitive mechanism and could not satisfy the multifold demands of the masses. Therefore, it has been proved thatfree information transfer and a self-regulation of the market economy could realize a better distribution of natural resources. The market economy could establish a good competitive mechanism by giving full scope to the initiative of the enterprises.In addition, it could better reflect the changing demands of the masses. Especially after adjustment of the market economy, added at the macro control level, the market economy has showed its superiority.

Key to the market mechanism is the independent legal person state of the enterprise. The main reasons that the market economy can realize the effective allocation of natural resources lies in the fact that it can explore the intelligence resources in a larger scope, and it will stimulate their initiatives and creativity. However, it still has to be pointed out that the current market mainly allocates natural resources and labour resources, but not intelligence resources.

There will be the following tendencies, according to the current development of knowledge economy:

- The future market will not be like a relatively stable traditional market, but will be dynamic. Therefore, to focus on its changing process is more important than just occupying it.
- Constructing and fostering the market will be superior than marketing. The market structure should be favourable to establishing a closer connection between the producers and the consumers, and be favourable to promoting the progress of technology.
- A market of good quality will be more import than one just of considerable quantity, and this should be paid special emphasis in the high-tech product market.

Obviously, compared with the traditional market, in the competition of the knowledge economy, better planning ability is needed.

12.5   Characteristics of the knowledge economy

The knowledge economy is developed in a fully educated society.

12.5.1   Sustainability of economic development

The knowledge economy is a kind of economy which can promote the harmonious and sustainable developing of mankind and nature. The guideline to invention in traditional industrial technology is to utilize natural resources to the greatest extent, aimed solely at profit maximization, in spite of harm to the environment, ecosystem and society. The premise of the guideline is based on a notion of infinite resources and a tremendous environmental carrying capacity; this includes obtaining resources by stealing from nature, which is a tragedy. When multiple resources are used up, and the environmental crisis is increasingly severe, the call for high-tech uniting science and technology into one appears, reflecting the scientific and overall recognition of nature. So the guideline of high-tech is to use resources comprehensively and efficiently in a scientific and rational way, while at the same time exploring the rich renewable resources instead of the rare resources.

12.5.2   Intangibility of the assets input

The input of intangible assets accounts for a major part of the knowledge economy. Industrial technology, where tangible assets play a crucial role, needs a great deal of capital and equipment. While in the high-tech industry, intangible assets such as knowledge, intelligence and so on play a significant role,. Certainly, high-tech assets also need capital as well as more information, knowledge and intelligence. Presently, the intangible assets of many high-tech enterprises have exceeded 60 per cent of their total assets.

12.5.3   The integration of the world economy

The knowledge economy is born under the circumstance of the integration of the world economy. Since the 1990s, the American economy has been growing stably, based on little growth of resource consumption, and owing in large part to the vast world market, and, as stated above, high-tech has a very wide range. In information technology, for example, a single country cannot lead in all fields, such as computer technology, micro-electronics, photoelectrons, CMOS chip manufacture, large-scale integration, optical fibres, multimedia, networks, software and emerging high technologies, and the like. Nonetheless, any country can make full use of their own intelligence resources to develop technologies for a large share in the global market, and in this manner become an indispensable part in the integration course of the global economy.

12.5.4 Knowledge-oriented decision-making

Decision making and management in the knowledge economy should be knowledge-oriented. Scientific macro-control efforts play a more and more important role in the knowledge economy. We can see as an example that after the Clinton government came into power America, a series of policies concerned with the high tech economy, like 'the information high way' were carried out, which made a significant contribution to continuous economic growth.

12.5.5 New value orientation

The value of the agricultural economy lies in the possession of labour and land, and that of industrial economy lies in the possession of resources and capital, while the value of the knowledge economy is in possession of intellect and knowledge. By taking reform of the social and economic system so as to promote the realization of 'respect knowledge, respect talent' and to guide the changes of the social value orientation, is thus to ensure knowledge becomes the primary element of distribution in a new law and organization system,. Future education should focus on talents for high-tech industrialization.

12.5.6 New market concept

The knowledge economy was generated and developed in market economic circumstance, but it will influence the market economy and provoke reform of the traditional market economy. This reform will deepen along with the development of knowledge economy. There have been a few of obvious features: firstly, the 'network economy' has been the new features of the market; the electric trade forms a revolution of the traditional market economy. Secondly, macro-control becomes more important, for example, the EU has come to an agreement forbidding the cloning of humans by law. Thirdly, competition among multinational corporations performs differently from that in the traditional market. Co-operation and competition exist at the same time among them. In addition, new laws of the market economic cycle may emerge, in which case new countermeasures would have to be taken under this new situation.

12.5.7 New form of social organization

The science park, or so-called high-tech industrial zone in China, which centralizes the intelligence resource, information, knowledge and high-tech, can resolve problems concerning capital, technology, market and risk by standardization, networking, internationalization and industrialization, and thus creates high productivity dozens of times higher than traditional industry. Just as factories attracted investors and farmers without land,

Table 12.2   Main traits of four kinds of economy

	Agriculture economy	Industrial economy	Knowledge economy
Significance of scientific research	Slight	Much	Most
The cost of scientific research accounting for GDP	0.3%<	1%~2%	>3%
Contribution of science and technology to economical growth	<10%	20%>	80%>
Significance of education	A little	Much	Most
The cost of education as a percent of GDP	<1%	1%~2%	6%~8%
Average educational level of civilization	high level of illiteracy \\	elementary school	technical secondary school
Agriculture	>50%	20%~30%	10%<
Industry	15%~20%	>50%	20%<
The third industry		20%~30%	>20%
High-tech industry			>50%
Informational high-tech industry		3%~5%	~15%
Life high-tech industry		2%	~10%
New and renewable energy high-tech industry		2%	~10%
Sea high-tech industry		2%	~10%
High-tech industry benefiting environment		1%	~5%
New material high-tech industry		1%	~5%
Spatial high-tech industry			~5%
Soft high-tech industry			~5%
Life span	36 years	>50 years	>70 years
Leisure time in life	6 years	8 years	18 years
Growth rate of population	high	higher	lower
Level of civilization	25%	>50%	decreasing
The effect of media	slight	much	most
Level of social organizing	simple	complicated	most complicated
Integration of the global economy	low	high	highest

science parks attract researchers from universities and institutions, and provide services such as information, technology, capital and market, and so on, and a special government organization has been established to manage them. Science parks help the high-tech to industrialize, which can drive China's shift from an extensive economy to an intensive economy.

12.5.8 Creativity is the soul of the knowledge economy

The former Chinese President, Jiang Zemin, always pointed out that 'Creativity is the soul of a nation and an inexhaustible source of a country's prosperity.' Creativity is also the soul of the knowledge economy. The economist, Schumpeter (1883–1950) promoted the concept of 'innovation' in the *Theory of Economic Development* (1912). He didn't regard all technical inventors as 'innovators', but only those who could take risks and introduce these new inventions into the economy could be called 'innovators'. In the high-tech industry, the one who starts the high-tech business is called the 'innovator'. This concept came from Schumpeter's idea. He also thought there was a difference between an entrepreneur and the common organization manager, only those who advocate and do creative business can be 'entrepreneurs', otherwise, they are only 'bosses'.

12.6 Primary studies on the indicator system of knowledge economy

Since the knowledge economy is just starting to take shape, it's still too early to establish a scientific and complete indicator system. The OECD has already set up a primary indicator system, and estimated that the proportion of knowledge-based economy in some OECD countries has been up 50 per cent. Though some foreign experts, and the author, think this number is a bit too high, it has provided us with an indicator system so that we could have a better understanding of the knowledge economy. Table 12.2 shows some characteristics of the knowledge economy.

12.7 High-tech industrialization is the primary pillar in the knowledge economy

12.7.1 New Technologies, High Science – Technology, and High-tech

After World War II, some technologies which had a huge impact on humans came into being, such as nuclear fission reactor art, semiconductor engineering and the new computer technology and so on, which are called 'the new technology', followed by 'new technology revolution'. Basically, these technologies were separated from science, except in semiconductor technology, among others, in which field the amalgamation of science and technology had started. Until the 1960s, 'science' and 'technology' had been two different concepts. 'Science' was the exploration, and nature, which was systematic and could be summarized into a certain model, and run by a researcher in an 'ivory tower'. The two offspring of 'science' are 'knowledge' and 'technology', and the innovation of knowledge is called 'discovery', while that of technology is 'invention'.

In the 1970s, there were some other new technologies coming out, bridging the gap between science and technology. When it came to the 1980s, these technologies gained a name, being called 'high technology' as the proper noun in English. Because of the amalgamation of science and technology in them, it could be also call 'high-tech'. According to the UN's classification, high-tech includes science and technology in the field of information, life, new energy sources and renewable energy, new materials, space, ocean and some technology beneficial to environment and management (also called soft science and technology). The high-tech differs from traditional 'science' in the following aspects:

1. Different from those sciences such as mathematics, physics, chemistry, astronomy, geography and biology and so on, the classification of high-tech is no longer based on the exploration of systematic knowledge, but with the standard of efficiency. Take information science for example, it aims to enlarge and speed the storage, transaction and transmission of information, and the optoelectronics and large-scale integrated circuits all serve this goal. The new materials science is to obtain new materials, and we can see that the biomembrane art is far beyond the traditional material concept of chemistry and physics. Ocean science is a comprehensive science targeting the whole ocean, including some high-tech projects like generating electricity by tidal wave, holobios and deep prospecting and so forth.

2. Different from in former science, the period from science to technology has been cut down dramatically. We can see from Table 12.1 above, it took 41 years for the discovery of generator theory in 1831 to transform into the working generator of 1872, spreading over two generations and impossible for any one person to achieve. While it took only four years for the theory of mobile communication, released in 1974, to become the mobile phone, which is possible for one to fulfil. Nowadays, the extensive use of mobile phone in developing countries like China has come about within about 20 years. Therefore, the worldwide industrialization of science and technology has been realized in a very short time.

3. Due to the characteristics, the knowledge-extensive and highly integrated, high-tech disciplineis above all very different from traditional science which is done in the 'ivory tower'. It penetrated to every field including economy, polity, culture and military directly and promptly, with an inestimable and fateful impact on people's ideas, their lives and

the social structure. Those who underestimate this influence will fall behind the times. At present, the concept of 'high-tech' has been standardized in the whole world to its particular meaning. High-tech doesn't mean some science and technology higher than that of before, or something that's highest in the countryside.

These changes should bring some transformation to our education and research; for example, developed countries have redivided the 'ologies' in high school, and multi-disciplinary studies including social science has become the modern style for research.

12.7.2 The industrialization of high-tech and new and high-tech: four trends of industry

High-tech will bring forward the most important means of the revolution, industrialization. At present, the industrialization of high-tech has become a tendency of the times. In 1988, Deng Xiaoping, leader of China had put forward in advance the statement, 'develop high-tech and realize the industrialization' from the view of the 'plan' of high-tech study.

From the history, we can see that industrialization has always been the lifeline connected to the future of one country. As discussed before, 300 years ago, Kang Xi, Emperor of the Qing dynasty, was not interested in the industrialization of that time, but 150 years later, in 1840, the sharp weapon, the product of industrialization of the Western economy, beat the broadsword and pike of China which was in the farm economy. In fact, until 1860, the gross output of industry of China and India take the first and second lowest place. So we can see the great historical significance of the innovation of knowledge, especially that of leader, and the technology innovation, especially that of epoch-making, which is just as in the statement of Jiang Zeming, former Secretary-General of China, 'innovation is the soul of the nation's advancement and sustainable power of prosperity.'

To realize the industrialization of high-tech, first of all, we should know the essence of it, which is also been demonstrated in the eight kinds of high-tech:

1. The guidance for the traditional technological invention of industry is single, it is using the natural resources as much as possible to gain the benefit as much as possible, failing to think about the environmental benefit, the ecosystem benefit and the social benefit. Besides, it is based on such an idea that the natural resources and the environmental capacity could be unlimited, what's more, it aims to plunder from nature, which is a tragedy because of the separation of science and technology. While high-tech came at such a time that many kind of natural resources were almost exhausted and the environmental crisis was worse and worse. It brings science and technology together, and shows the reasonable and comprehensive understanding of humans about nature and

social society. Therefore, the guidance of high-tech is to use the present resources properly and efficiently, meanwhile exploring new and abundant natural resources to take the place of the failing rare resources. For example, the software of the information sciences and the gene engineering of life sciences are very different from traditional technology. We can conclude that an industry run on the latter thinking is either definitely high-tech, or it is not. One point is that high-tech is decided not only by the number of the large-scale integrated circuits.

2. There is a great deal of capital and equipment in traditional industrial technology, among which visible capital plays a leading role. However, it is knowledge, intelligence and invisible capital that play a leading role – high-tech needs capital, even venture capital, but it is the amount of information, knowledge and intelligence that can list a company as high-tech. At present, the invisible capital of US high-tech enterprises accounts for over 60 per cent of general capital.

3. Compared with traditional industry such as steel, machine and spin, the distinctive characteristic of high-tech is that its industrial technology field is very broad. Taking just information high-tech, for example, there is no country that can top every high-tech area, including computer technology , micro-electronics, chips, large scale integrated circuits, photoelectronics, fibre optics, multimedia, network, software and other new applications, but every country can use its own intelligence resources to perform an innovation, choosing some fields, but not all of them, and take its place in high-tech industry, which is also the economic basis of the multipole structure of the world after World War II.

The distinction between high-tech industry and traditional industry actually brings us a new industry. Since the 1950s, industry has been divided into three parts, the first is agriculture, the second is industry, and the third is serving industry. Today, it is necessary to reconsider the classification due to the obvious identity of high-tech, maybe we can call it the fourth industry which has been the crucial field of competition in a multipole world.

In China, the developing base of high-tech was called the 'developing zone of high-tech industry'. In fact, some new technologies rising in the 1950s and 1960s were not exactly high-tech, and only some of their performance could be termed innovative in today's view. Therefore, the 'developing zone of high-tech industry' should continue its high-tech developing and industrializing. In the meantime, it has the responsibility to reconstruct traditional industry, and then traditional technology can be called high-tech after the reconstruction. Today, we can see the real meaning of the name 'developing zone of high tech industry'. What needs to be paid more attention is the fact that not all traditional technology can be transformed into high-tech with the input of some new thing, but it is the high-tech content of that can drive a decision. With such a standard, we can call the

Chinese machine industry's CIMS a high-tech industry, which has been agreed worldwide. Only when it brings high added value, makes a great deal of profit on a large scale, and produces sound economic benefit can it be called high-tech industry.

12.8 The future of knowledge economy

12.8.1 The knowledge economy is coming

Just as the agricultural economy moved to industrial economy 300 years ago, nowadays, the knowledge economy has just started to take shape. Even America, leading in this area, has not formed a knowledge economy on the whole. Today in America, the pillar industries are still the traditional ones like car, steel, construction and so on. The information industry is the only one which occupies a similarly large proportion. The traditional industries have benefited a lot from high-tech. However, in the most effective car industry, there is no essential change, the engine of a car is still basically the same as it was at the beginning of twentieth century.

Meanwhile, we cannot ignore that:

- Many knowledge economy laws have already taken effect. Sustainable development has gained a consensus throughout the world; intangible assets have been given great emphasis; high-tech industry is developing faster and faster; the position of high technology in traditional industry becomes increasingly important.
- The emergence of the knowledge economy has been viewed totally differently from that of the industrial economy 300 years ago. At that time, Europe, which brought new industry to the Americans and supported the industrial economy, was the exception; Asia, Africa, and Latin America paid little attention to it, which made them fall behind 150 years later. However, nowadays, Asia, Latin America, and even Africa, all value the emerging knowledge economy highly and are beginning to catch up with America and Europe in all aspects.
- Like factories before them, emerging in the transitional period of the agricultural economy to industrial economy, science parks appear from 1980s all over the world. The cells of the knowledge economy have come out and begun to grow fast. Therefore, the time of the knowledge economy is not far away.

Transition to the knowledge economy will greatly raise productivity and solve the increasing crises of resources and environment. Meanwhile, it should be recognized that the transition will also be a tough period, for it will bring some unconventional concepts and thinking, thus many people will have to learn new things. Some people may lose their vested interest, and in the short term, as the industry adjusts, some people may lose their jobs.

In the process of global economy integration, all the countries may benefit. However, the higher the proportion of high-tech industry is, the more benefit the country will get, and the ratio of benefit will increase gradually. The continuing growth of the American economy from 1991 can account for this point. While the lower the proportion of high-tech industry is, the less benefit the country will have, and the ratio of benefit will reduce. Once there is light unrest, it could lead to great crisis. The Asian financial crisis was just such a case. As the frightening situation of resource shortage and environmental deterioration deepens, the economy of a country in which the high-tech industry ratio is low will be unsafe.

12.8.2   When will the knowledge economy take shape?

Some economists estimate that in 2010, the output value of the software industries of the information science, life industry, new and renewable energy industry, eco-sound high-tech industry, new material industry and marine scientific industry will all go beyond the traditional industries. Whereas I think the UN estimation in December 1996 is more scientific. In that estimation, it kept the view that over high-tech industrialization will be realized in 2030 or so. The formation of the knowledge economy will be much shorter than that of the industrial economy which is about a century's time.

Certainly, no one could ignore the tough transitional period of this half a century. There is no doubt that at the beginning of the knowledge economy times, there will be some negative influence, such as changes of social value, re-constitution of the social organization and readjustment of social distribution and so on. In addition, with the development of social economy, some matters like macro-control of the market, the law of the economic cycle and so on should be reconsidered.

12.8.3   Perspectives on the knowledge economy

What will the future the knowledge economy brings us look like that?

The value of information lies in its spreading. In an economic stage where the information is highly developed, the application of information should be socialized. That is, it should be owned by everyone but not be monopolized. The current Internet shows this trend. It is believed that knowledge will be shared by mankind like water and air.

Material fortune can be private or public, but one thing can only be used by a limited amount of people – the more persons use it, the less its value is. The wealth of knowledge can also be private or public, but on the contrary, the more people use it, the larger the value it has. Engels had even said at Marx's tomb that in Marx's view, science would be a momentum of revolution in history. When gross knowledge wealth greatly exceeds material wealth, it may be independent of man's will that the gulf between the rich and the poor will be eliminated, and the necessary conditions for realizing socialism will have been provided.

For China, the knowledge economy is both an opportunity and a challenge. It is better to enforce research and explore the law of knowledge economy. A national-level government organization should be set up to readjust the national knowledge and technology innovation system. Industrialization of high-tech should thus be supported to make science and technology become the primary productive force and to realize sustainable development of China in the twenty-first century.

12.9 General picture of China's science parks and the case of Zhongguancun Science Park in Beijing

The greatest change from agriculture to industry in the eighteenth century was the building of 'factories', while in the twenty-first century it is to build a new factory – the science park. The science park is been regarded as 'the most important innovation in the field of commercialization of scientific and technological results within this century.' In this way, the combination of industrial development and scientific and technological activities have successfully solved the tough problems of separating scientific and technological activities from economic development, which has facilitated the smooth and rapid transfer of the discoveries and inventions of mankind to the industrial arena to achieve its economic and social benefits.

Since the first state-level development area for new and high-tech industries Zhongguancun Science Park was established in 1988, a batch of science parks have been approved for establishment from the 1990s in China. During more than ten years, China's science parks have grown from have-not to have, from small to large, and have already become bases for developing the high and new industry. Furthermore, they have been pushing forward regional economic development: by the end of 2004, there were 38,000 enterprises within 53 science parks, achieving a total revenue of more that RMB2.7 trillion. The GDP generated by the science parks reached RMB717.5 billion, accounting for 5.3 per cent of the national GDP. In the past ten years, the science parks have gained rapid growth with a more than 100-fold increase of the major economic indexes over the year 1991, when the State initiated the construction of science parks. The annual growth rate of the science parks has been more than 40 per cent. The construction of science parks will have the positive effects of exploring, demonstrating, influencing and driving the development of technological industrialization.

A successful science park should embrace the following conditions and have the following characteristics:

- well-known universities and research institutions in the neighbourhood with top talents

- excellent environment for both human habitat and industrial development
- excellent business incubating system and infrastructure to support technological innovation and the undertaking of a high technology project.
- a central administrative organization planning and managing the political, economic, cultural and social affairs of the park
- world-famous enterprises and distinct industrial clusters characterized as having high-tech content and high added value in the region, making visible contributions to the economic growth of the region
- being world-wide technological innovation centres in certain fields
- a market economy system and investment environment in line
- international practice
- unique cultural environment that promotes innovation and entrepreneurship as well as internationally famous brands

The Zhongguancun Science Park, the first high-tech one at the state level and established in 1988, is so far the most perfect, innovative and internationally famous science park in China.

Zhongguancun Science Park is China's biggest science park with a high concentration of scientific and technological institutions and intelligence resources. Located in this area are 39 institutions of higher learning represented by Beijing University and Tsinghua University. There are 213 research institutions as exemplified by the institutions of the Chinese Academy of Sciences (CAS) and the Chinese Academy of Engineering (CAE).

- Each year, thousands of sophisticated research discoveries emerge in this area and pour out to all places throughout China. Many state-level laboratories and important engineering and technology centres are concentrated in this area too. Zhongguancun Science Park is the largest software development and production centre in China.
- The Administrative Committee of Zhongguancun Science Park, as a branch organ of Beijing municipal government, guides and manages the affairs of the park. In recent years, the committee put more emphasis on planning and investment work. Some special bases like Zhongguancun Software Park and Zhongguancun Life Science Park have been established inside the central Zhongguancun Park, which provides space for the rapid development of these high-tech enterprises.
- Incubators in different areas inside Zhongguancun Science Park have been the cradle for the transfer of technological inventions and the development of high enterprises. Currently, there are 39 special incubators inside Zhongguancun Park.
- Zhongguancun Science Park has attracted international talents and innovative teams, many having overseas study experience. Many top scientific achievements and fruits are generated by them with the number

growing of enterprises set up by those talents who came back from foreign study up to 2500.

Zhongguancun Science Park is composed of the Haidian Development Area, Fengtai Development Area, Changping Development Area, Electronics Town Science and Technology Development Area, and Yizhuang Science and Technology Development Area. It is currently home to 8000 enterprises armed with new technology. There are 180 enterprises whose income on technological transfer and trade each surpasses 100 million yuan; over 1600 foreign-funded enterprises, 43 out of the Top 500 in the world; R&D institutions run by Microsoft, IBM, Motorola and 20 other multinational corporations; and about 1200 enterprises launched by more than 3600 fellows who studied abroad. Lenovo (Legend), Founder and some other enterprises, which represent the image of hi-tech enterprises in modern China, have also set up businesses in Zhongguancun Science Park.

In terms of the income from technological trade, added value, tax payments to the State and export value, Zhongguancun Science Park's ranking among the 53 high-tech Development Areas in China raises with each passing year. Its contribution to Beijing's industrial economic growth stayed at over 60 per cent for many years running. In 2004, the total revenue of Zhongguancun Park was as high as 360 billion yuan, up by 25 per cent year on year; tax payments to the State were 13.3 billion yuan, up by 11 per cent. Furthermore, it generated GDP 76 billion yuan, which accounted for 18 per cent of the total GDP of Beijing. Zhongguancun Science Park has become a vital source of Beijing's economic growth. Batches of new high-tech enterprises emerge from this area, thus they have become important bases for the development of high-tech industry in Beijing.

The twenty-first century is a time in which knowledge capital will play a significant role. With rich intelligence resources, standard market operations and effective regulations by government, science parks will become the new factory model of the twenty-first century and promote the development of the knowledge economy under the circumstance of the integration of the global economy.

Conclusion

We can see it is knowledge that is playing a leading role in the development of the modern world, turning the traditional economy into a newer and more dynamic economy – knowledge economy.

Knowledge economy is a economy which is going on in a world full of rationality, innovation and honesty. In this light, our nation has a clear consciousness of a great deal of advantages; meanwhile, we need significant bravery to face the disadvantages. Based on the resources, including visible and invisible resources, we can transform the advances in thinking into reality by continuously practice. Most important, we are eager to share with the whole world the precious experience gained in the process of building a knowledge economy with those who are interested in it and to make the planet more beautiful.

References

Clarke, R. (1985), *Science and Technology in the Developed World*, Oxford Paperbacks.

Richadson, J. G. (1988), *Windows on Creativity and Invention*, Lomond, Scotland.

OECD (1997), *Industrial Competitiveness in the Knowledge-Based Economy*, OECD, New York.

World Bank (1998), *Knowledge for Development – World Development Report 1998* Annotated Outling, World Bank, Geneva.

Wu Jisong (1986), *Comparing Expertise for Decision-Making and Management of R&D between Developing and Developed Countries*, IFIAS, UNESCO, Geneva.

Wu Jisong (1992), 'The role of natural science, techonology and social sciences in policy-making in China' (English, French and Spanish versions), *International Social Science Journal*, Vol. 132.

Wu Jisong (1999), *Knowledge Economics – Theory, Practice and Application*, Science and Technology Press, Beijing.

Wu Jisong (2000), '1984–2000: my research on knowledge economy and its management – from Paris to Beijing', Science and Technology Press, Beijing.

Wu Jisong (2001), *New Trends of 21st Century Society Knowledge Economy*, Science and Technology Press, Beijing.

Wu Jisong (2002), *Modern Water Resources Management Methodology*, Tsinghua University Press, Tsinghua.

Wu Jisong (2005), *New Recycle Economics*, Tsinghua University Press, Tsinghua.

Index